cool, hip & sober

cool, hip & sober

88 WAYS TO BEAT BOOZE & DRUGS

BILL MANVILLE

INTRODUCTION BY DR. DAVE MOORE,
Scripps McDonald Center for Alcoholism
and Drug Addiction Treatment

 A TOM DOHERTY ASSOCIATES BOOK
NEW YORK

COOL, HIP & SOBER: 88 WAYS TO BEAT BOOZE & DRUGS

Copyright © 2003 by Bill Manville
Introduction copyright © 2003 by Dr. Dave Moore
Afterword copyright © 2003 by Doug Tieman

This book is printed on acid-free paper.

Book design by Michael Collica

A Forge Book
Published by Tom Doherty Associates, LLC
175 Fifth Avenue
New York, NY 10010

www.tor.com

Forge® is a registered trademark of Tom Doherty Associates, LLC.

Library of Congress Cataloging-in-Publication Data

Manville, William H. (William Henry), 1930–
    Cool, hip, and sober : 88 ways to beat booze and drugs / Bill Manville.
        p. cm.
    ISBN 0-765-30314-0
        1. Substance abuse—Prevention. 2. Alcoholics—Rehabilitation. 3. Addicts—Rehabilitation. 4. Recovering alcoholics—Life skills guides. 5. Recovering addicts—Life skills guides. 6. Self-help techniques. I. Title: Beat booze and drugs. II. Title.

HV4998.M36 2003
362.29—dc22

                                                            2003049231

First Edition: December 2003

Printed in the United States of America

0 9 8 7 6 5 4 3 2 1

For Beverly

"Live as if you were living a second time, and as though you had acted wrongly the first time," wrote Viktor Frankl after coming out of Auschwitz. Someone said it to me the day I came out of rehab. I quote it again here as an amend: to remind myself a central mistake in my first life was to let Bev Bartlett sail out of it without me. I'd like to dedicate this second life, and this book, to her.

Bill Manville

Contents

Contents

Contents

Contents

Contents

Contents

Contents

An Introduction to Recovery

In my twenty-one years in the field of recovery from alcohol and drug addiction, many books on the subject have crossed my desk—factual and up-to-date but difficult for the troubled layman to act on. If knowledge and common sense could end chemical dependency, "Cut it out!" would do the job. But common sense is the aspect of intelligence that tells you the world is flat. Addiction is more complicated than that. What these books lack is emotion and motivation.

In *Cool, Hip & Sober,* Bill too is medically and technically accurate but goes further—bringing to the printed page the same engaging and straight-ahead personality I have enjoyed as a guest on his radio show . . . a point of identification that gets the reader "into" the book.

"The road of excess," I've heard Bill quote William Blake, "leads to the palace of wisdom." Illustrating the siren songs and perils of addiction with stories from his own life and answering questions from listeners, Bill gives us a sure-footed guide to the road to recovery. A reader-friendly guide that will be useful not only to counselors in the field but even more so to addicts and those who love them.

As a psychologist and chemical dependency professional myself, I find it of great value to be able to provide my university students with this accurate portrayal of addiction—a unique portrayal that engages the human dimension of why they are in the health care professions. As a member of the growing community of recovery, I am grateful for a text that creates a bridge from that professional perspective to the world of families who have known the personal truth of the journey so richly described in Bill's remarkable text.

—Dave Moore, Ph.D.
Associate Director for Safe and
Drug-Free Schools and Communities,
University of Washington; former Director,
The McDonald Center for Alcoholism and
Drug Addiction Treatment,
Scripps Health, San Diego, California

cool, hip & sober

How to Use This Book

This is neither textbook nor Ph.D. thesis by an academic who has a glass of sherry once in a while. You may choose to read straight through as if this were a novel or murder mystery, but that was not my design. These pages sum up what I've learned in over forty years of research—twenty as a drunken dope fiend, over twenty in recovery.

If you've ever been to a good 12 Step meeting, you'll recognize the tone of *Addictions & Answers*, the weekly radio show I do on KVML in Sonora, California. The conversational voice, some medical and psychological expertise, anecdotal and grim personal reminiscences, and my three and one half jokes—life and death discussed with high spirits and a laugh, maybe some drunk-tested rules of thumb, someone's dark wisdom mixed with pratfalls and a bit of hope.

Many questions in these pages grew out of the radio program. Some combine three or four conversations with people to whom I spoke off the air. (Names and identifiable details have been changed.) And if a subject was new to me, it became the topic for the next show.

Over the years, I've had a broad spectrum of guests. They were my teachers: rehab counselors, psychiatrists, psychologists, family therapists, clinicians, licensed booze & alcohol people, MDs, academics, and a ton of plain and fancy drunks and dopers—people who have been kind enough to let me draw on their time, experience, and knowledge. Occasionally, our talks turned on my own past addictive conduct—rejected thoughts, resentments, and denials I still did not want to face. I did not always thank them for their insights at the time. I hope I have not forgotten, nor distorted, nor left out too much of what they said.

The answers in these pages, then, are the result of more time for research and reflection than the hurly-burly of live broadcasting would ordinarily allow. That also explains their greater length and why they're numbered: The answer to one will often cross-refer to another asked by someone else.

Some questions came in about the caller's own bedevilment; many from people worried about a spouse or child, lover, or friend. I've tried to make my answers useful either way, often allowing myself poetic license—writing as if conducting the conversation on the air.

I've heard a puritan defined as someone afraid that someone else, somewhere else is having a good time. "If you're drinking and doping pretty good," I like to say to my audience, "and your life is still all green lights, GO—good luck to you. You need no advice from me. But, if like me, you went for a ride on the tiger, and the tiger ended up riding you, stay tuned. This show is for you."

I understand addiction to be behavior that may have begun as fun or enjoyment but now adversely affects your health and finances, your job, marriage and family, your social life. An alien will colonizing your heart and brain, a monster within you who is not you. The pleasure is long gone; you hate it but can't stop. If this sounds like you or someone you know, I've been there too; this book can help.

Go through the four sections and Afterword in the Contents. Decide which section describes where you are right now in your use of pills/booze/speed/name your dope. When you find the question that sounds as if you wrote it yourself . . .

Bingo.

Later in time you may want to read the rest. That's about you too. And if all else fails and you're in trouble right now, see Q. #88.

—Bill Manville

PS. I say this at various places in the text, but for emphasis, let me put it here right up front: In the early days of AA, lushes somehow thought themselves morally and socially superior to "drug addicts," and did not want them at their meetings. No less a personage than Bill W. himself—one of the founders of AA—went along with the idea (see Q. #58), though I believe he somewhat fudged his reasons.

Out of this historical bit of snobbery comes the convention we find even today, distinguishing between alcoholics and drug addicts. For instance, the rehab at Scripps Memorial Hospital in San Diego (where I was a volunteer for two years) calls itself the McDonald Center for Alcoholism *and* Drug Addiction Treatment. (My italics.)

Just as it's boring always to be writing "himself/herself," so is it always to be writing "alcoholics and drug addicts." My feeling is that alcohol is a drug, and alcoholics are drug addicts—the terms are interchangeable. Some people use the all-inclusive term, "chemical dependency." Since my own drug of first choice was gin, the words "alcohol" and "alcoholic" flow most easily onto the page. But it's a kind of shorthand, always to be understood to include people addicted to drugs other than, or in addition to, alcohol.

—BM

"Me, Stop Drinking?
And Do What for Fun?"

The problem begins with pictures: I read this morning that the big distillers just bought $60 million commercial time on NBC. A TV first for the hard stuff. It reminded me of my early advertising career.

My boss stood with his back to the windows facing Park Avenue, smiling at what he was about to say. "We need to sell the consumer what the poor, lonely schnook already suspects," he said. "There's a great world rushing by out there, glittering and perfumed—life's a big party going on without him. Bill, find the right words and music, especially the right pictures—convince him he buys our product, that's his ticket of admission to life's big blast."

And what better symbol for someone having a good time? You see it in all the TV commercials. Someone with a glass in the hand. Greed can be romanticized with pictures of big houses and fast cars, alcohol with moonlight cocktails on sixty-foot yachts. But some of my most abiding pleasures come from getting a sentence right on a page . . . watching Bev play shoestrings with Sally, our cat . . . waking each day sober. How illustrate such exaltations of the spirit? Picture of a guy in a chair, wearing memory's goofy half smile? Would that make you want to buy that product?

I drank my way into two hospitals in ten days and still thought the end of drinking meant the end of fun. Today I know that merely showed what a narrow idea I had of what fun meant. Can you sell that to a drunk? This section gives it a try.

THE FIRST QUESTION:

#1.

"Nobody Worse than a Reformed Drunk Who Wants to Kill Everyone Else's Good Time. Bill, What the Hell Qualifies You to Offer Advice?"

Q. My name is Marie. In our marriage, my husband had one stretch of three years sober, three periods of two years sober, and there were six times when he was off it a year. Plus he always gave it up for Lent. In between, he was always drunk.

I stayed with him for the sake of our children. Now our youngest is off to college, and divorce is not far from my thoughts. I love Fred, and would be happy to live with him for the rest of my life but not this way.

On your program you often say the subject is hope. But Fred says with his lousy job, having a drink with some interesting friends is one of his few pleasures in life. To him, you're just some radio know-it-all, not a doctor, not a psychologist, not even a licensed alcohol and drug counselor—no degrees in the subject. Is he right? He says there's nobody worse than a reformed drunk who wants to kill everyone else's fun. What qualifies you to offer any realistic hope that alcoholism and addiction can be overcome? Bill, why should we believe you?

A. The first page of the first book I ever published began like this:

> *There was a fountain in the center of the room of a bar I used to make*
> *when I first came to the Village. I remember a brass merman perpetually*
> *sounded a sea trumpet there, forever calling surrounding mermaids to a*
> *wilder dance. No cold water flowed from that fountain—something bet-*
> *ter: The great basin offered all the bottled wines of the world. It all*
> *seemed an image of the way I wanted to live—generous, naked, over-*
> *abundant, and noisy.*

That was how my drinking career began. What follows is how it
ended, a picture of myself walking around London, someone left back
home, crying.

Wearing a black raincoat, I have a pint of gin in each pocket. At
every little red telephone kiosk, I stop and take a bottle out. I hope I
don't drink it, I say to myself, and drink it. I hope I don't buy another,
I say to myself and buy two.

My (then) wife may have thought I'd slammed out to buy a newspaper, or have a drink and get over our most recent quarrel. I don't know
today where I got the money, how I got the ticket, why I was carrying
a passport—I flew the Atlantic in a blackout and woke fully dressed on
the floor of a little apartment we kept in New York.

I did not ask how I got there, what had happened, was anyone worried about me. I looked around. I was alone. I was an alcoholic. I knew
what to do. I got on the phone and ordered a case of gin.

There were some pills in the medicine cabinet—left behind by who
knows who. I washed them down with the first martini, drinking my
way into two hospitals in the next ten days.

That was over twenty years ago. I went to a twenty-eight-day rehab
in Pennsylvania—then carrying (for historic reasons) the slightly
comic name, Chit Chat, now the very eminent Caron Foundation. On
New Year's Eve six months later, overconfidence (*hubris*, the Greeks
called it) led to my one relapse. It lasted two weeks—perhaps the
worst of my life. I haven't had a drink since.

The way liquor worked for me, it speeded me on the way I was
already going. If I were gloomy or sad, it made me feel worse (not bad

enough, of course, to stop). If I felt good, it lifted me higher. But ultimately, in some existentialist sense, I don't know why I began drinking,
I don't know why I stopped. I don't know why so many of the people I
used to drink and dope with . . . people smarter than me, more talented and many more useful to the world—I don't know why they
chose not to stop, why they died. I am not sure questions like these
have an answer.

What is important is that I did stop.

A few years ago, I trained as a volunteer facilitator at the famous
rehab run by Scripps Memorial Hospital in San Diego. I did that work
at the McDonald Center for Alcoholism and Drug Addiction Treatment for two years. One of my jobs was to give an orientation lecture
to new patients. Occasionally, an M.D., new to the place and wishing
to get familiar with all aspects of treatment, would speak first. He'd
give a very knowledgeable talk, then ask for questions.

Trembling, hung over, suffering withdrawal, sick in mind, body, and
soul, a patient would get up.

"Doc, you ever been addicted yourself?"

No, the doctor would say. But I've trained for fourteen years in the
field, and written extensively on the effect of intoxication on the cells
of the brain, published fifty-two papers . . . et cetera.

Eyes would glaze over.

"Medical knowledge is important to recovery, but addicts don't care
how much you know—they want to know how much you care. There's
a vast literature on how addicts will trust another recovered addict
when they will not trust a doctor, no matter how experienced."

So says Larry Bouchard, a friend of mine upon whose broad range
of knowledge I have come to depend. He's a clinician with the mental
health providers in the county where I live, and perhaps the most frequent guest on my show.

"When addicts hit bottom, and denial no longer works," says Larry,
"when they realize they DO have a problem, and better seek treatment, they very often have the feeling no one else can understand
what they've been through. Doctors and trained counselors are very
important in treatment, but nobody ever got sober listening to lectures
on brain chemistry. What people seek at first point of contact is reas-
surance—that they are not alone, that whoever is talking is nonjudg-

mental, has been through addiction too, and come out the other side okay. Most important, that the speaker has reached recovery him/herself . . . that the promise being made, the hope being offered, that addiction can be overcome, is firsthand, personal, and real."

Larry goes on: "In working with addicts for over twenty years I've come to think recovery is not an exact science. It's 80 percent art, 10 percent science, and the rest, guts and hope."

I believe that's true in my own recovery and for most people I've met in AA. I know the pleasures and joys of intoxication, I know the despair to which they can lead. In the more than twenty years since I left rehab, I've gone to more meetings than I can count, talked to and listened to thousands of drunks and dopers—firsthand experience in seeing what works, what does not. I'm sober today.

One of my favorite writers, Elmore Leonard, once described a conversation, one guy asking another how he went through ten million dollars so fast. The man says he spent maybe five million on horses, women, and booze, "and the rest I wasted." It was my favorite joke, I understood that joke, at moments of utmost gin and crystal clarity, *I knew it was no joke.*

Like my caller, a reader too may ask who am I to offer hope that alcoholism and addiction can be overcome. That's where this book is unique. Sobriety is in the title, sobriety is the way I've run my life for more than twenty years. My qualification is I've been through it myself. This is my second life. I represent no bullshit hope.

PS. A final word to Marie: Fred's notion that having a drink is one of his few pleasures in life turns reality upside down. He has so few pleasures *because* he drinks. And if he keeps asking what's so hot about sobriety, or thinks the only way to meet interesting people is in a bar, those are valid questions; they come next in Qs. #2, #3, and #4.

#2.

"I Never Met Anyone Interesting in My Life Who Doesn't Drink"

Q. Bill, you have your experience, I have mine. Call me Ray, twenty-nine and single. Maybe it's not PC, but let me be honest: What I like to do after work, there's a pretty good bar where I know good-looking girls hang out. I drink, my friends drink, every woman I ever met drank too, probably because I met them in one bar or another. We're all employed, and enjoying our lives.

I sometimes hear you say on your show, that just because you no longer drink, that doesn't mean you're a blue-nose puritan, afraid somebody, somewhere was having a good time. *Well, good for you.* But the way my friends and I feel, you're not a pretty good drinker, we don't want to know you. Tell the truth, Bill—the "sermons and soda water" people in AA aren't the most interesting you've known in your life, right?

A. I met her at a cocktail party not long after I moved to Key West. Someone was playing the piano; couples were flirting on the veranda; slowly turning overhead fans. I was living alone, separated from my wife. "Got some Fly-Me-to-the-Moon Black Jamaica Rum," the bartender said. "Giggle you up with some of that?"

"Just soda and ice, please. Thanks."

The woman standing beside me turned. Tall, slim, cool, expensively understated clothes.

"Not a bad party," I said to her.

She said most people were born a drink or two behind. "A little booze, they're more fun to be around."

Like mine, the glass in her hand held soda.

"Burned the candle at both ends yourself, have you?"

"I usually broke it in half," she said, "and burned all four. An Englishman once told me the dry martini was the one American invention perfect as a sonnet. I thought if one or two could make me the life of the party, ten would win me Love Everlasting."

I said, "That takes fifteen."

We walked outside, and down to the Pier House for a sandwich and some iced tea. Beginning of a friendship of some dozen years. Dinner or an AA meeting . . . picnics at the beach. Once we acted as surrogate parents, giving a young AA friend away in marriage. We almost went partners on a two-apartment house, but I got sandbagged in a long-drawn-out divorce and couldn't afford it. Our friendship was never a romance. It was more important than that.

Polly S.

She'd been in the fashion business when young, and even in her fifties (when we met) was still very jazzy and good-looking, always smartly dressed. I was out of town a lot. I used to phone from New York. I remember one call well.

"I ever tell you," she said, "cancer runs in my family?"

"You been to the doctor?"

"Today. The divorce not going well?"

"My lawyer's on cocaine."

Three months later, back in Florida, I called again.

"Bill," she said, "I keep losing weight."

"Let's have breakfast," I said, and drove to pick her up.

She looked thin and frail but still dressed in wonderful shades of cream, ivory, beige, and tan. She took my arm. "I've come to the time of life," she said, "when my clothes are braver than me." She suffered dizziness, and had begun to fall. She pulled up a sleeve. Purple splotches on both arms. "My legs and thighs too," she said. "Black and blue. The bruises won't heal."

She smiled. "Don't worry," she said. "I won't lift my skirt."

We drove to one of our favorite waterfront cafés; we'd had dozens of meals here together over the years. Pink, purple, and gold; the sun floated up over green water. Palm trees rustled. "Polly," I said, "we're all alone here."

The unspoken half of the sentence was we both knew she was soon going to die.

I asked a question important for people like us. "You're all alone in the world," I said to her. "Widowed a long time, children grown, immersed in their own lives and living far away. Even I'm almost never here. And now pain and cancer. Ever think of taking a drink?"

" 'All neurosis stems from man's attempts to escape life's legitimate sufferings,' " Polly said, a quotation from Jung—one we both knew. "Bill, I cannot escape this one. I have only one thing left. That's my dignity. I'm not going to die drunk." Five weeks later, I got an envelope in the mail. It was her bronze AA medallion. It said XXXIII—sober thirty-three years. Polly was dead.

I wear her medallion on my key chain. I think of Polly every time I start my car, every time I open my door. She left me something I will never forget. Sober thirty-three years. "One day the divorce will be over," she said. "Meantime you don't take that first drink," the last words she ever said to me, "even if your ass falls off." I've dedicated this book to Beverly Bartlett. I'd like to put Polly's name on it too. I never saw her take a drink, she never saw me. If we both hadn't been in AA and sober, we would never have met.

#3.

Let's Try It Again—What's So Hot About Sobriety?

Q. You can call me Frequent Flyer—an ad executive, recently divorced. I'll e-mail this because I've left the West Coast. Let me give you a picture of what drinking is in my life, a moment from a few days ago when I flew into SFO. "United Airlines regrets headwinds made us a little late," said the pretty flight attendant who'd just arrived herself, "but welcome to the Bay Area. Watch your step." She'd changed, put on heels, eyeliner, and perfume—the shine of her eyes was her own.

The world of the twenty-eight-year-old woman.

You get dressed first, tell her you'll be waiting in the hotel bar downstairs. Nantucket, New Orleans, maybe Paris, San Francisco, or Aruba. A tinkle of ice and the first martini sits before you. She arrives with the second, radiant and ready for the evening ahead. You have a third together. World of the twenty-eight-year-old woman. Bill, I'm going to be fifty next birthday. I will never live in that world again.

What can you say to convince me I'd rather be sober?

A. Ah, Mr. Frequent, if only we could be thirty again. Weren't those the days—

Young Ernie had his mop out and was beginning to stack bar chairs on the tables when Frannie came in with Handsome Jack Bailey— they'd been married at City Hall only the day before. Ira Slomon murmured, "Already?" and Bev said, "Frannie better run see her psychiatrist and get all her money back." Danny Eastman was with them and the model Cathy Ayres. "Marriage pays for the honeymoon," said Ira, put on his coat and left.

I had a martini in my hand, another waiting on the bar, Bev beside me, black pointed toe shoes, poison green lizard heels, smoking a Chesterfield and waiting for me to finish and take her home. "Get out of here everybody," Jimmy Hamilton called from behind the wood, flicking the lights on and off. "Last call, don't you people live any- where? Last call, time to go home." I finished the one martini, drank the second, and looked up from telling Ollie Turner and Helen Lawrenson about a new English writer I'd just found, finishing Bev's half-empty glass and ordering another last one for us both.

Someone put a final quarter in the jukebox, the drinks came, the gin so cold it smoked off the ice, Ella Fitzgerald sang "The Party's Over"; the barroom whirled around my head, cigarette smoke thick as dreams veiled Bev's face and in that moment—that moment in the White Horse was more than thirty years ago, but I can still remember the way Bev looked when she raised her arms to knot a white silk scarf at the nape of her neck and I knew we would never grow old. I finished my drink. We were in love and were never going to die.

What's so hot about being sober, asks Frequent Flyer, skewing the question to equate getting sober with growing old—an example of what the Big Book means when it says alcohol is cunning, baffling, and powerful. Put like that, I agree—who wouldn't want to remain eternally young, drunk, and in love? Who wouldn't rather live forever and know one day you'd write like Anthony Powell? Ruminating on the chaos and confusion sex had brought into his life, the dying Philip the Pious of Spain is said to have murmured to his Cardinal

Confessor that if God had consulted him in the matter, he might have suggested a more graceful procedure. And ruminating myself these days on the vicissitudes that time brings us all, it occurs to me that if asked, I too might have a few words to say to the Almighty on *that* subject.

When we were little, we longed for an adult to tell us, There, there, everything will be all right. But part of learning to be the grown-ups now ourselves is to accept that the end Will Not Be All Right. And if so, how can it not be tempting to turn to coke, pot, gin, crank, heroin, and speed—the seductive Saints of Disrepair whose lie it is that tomorrow never comes? But now, for more than twenty years, I have not heard their siren song.

—and, I am grateful to say, not yet so far today.

Booze almost killed me, two hospitals in ten days—and yet I am not sure, given the choice, that I would not rather forever remain back in that Faustian moment in the White Horse Tavern. But the horses of night are not obliging. You must grow old. You need not grow wise. You can keep on drinking, yes, but Time does not have a stop. The seduction of addiction, Mr. Frequent, is to tell you it does.

"I'll think about (the rent, your marriage, children, health, job, or time itself) later. Right now I need a drink."

The years go by.

My own drinking career left me in a kind of arrested development, the Fourth and Fifth Steps mirrored someone devoting too many of his allotted days thinking too much about money and facile approval— naïve about love, operatically stupid about women. A second chance to figure out who I wanted to be the rest of my life was sobriety's first great gift. Time to understand Viktor Frankl was another.

An Auschwitz survivor, the Viennese psychiatrist said one lost everything in the death camps except "the last of the human freedoms, to choose one's attitude in any given set of circumstances." To allow yourself to fall into What's-the-use despair was to surrender heart and soul to the Nazis. Even in Auschwitz, said Frankl, prisoners had a moral choice: from finding value in something so slight as loving memories to persuading a fellow inmate not to commit suicide.

Addiction is not Auschwitz, but I believe it too is a matter of morale. Reading Frankl showed me that return to my old flip cynicism was a sure swooning glide back to the bottle, and if I wanted to stay sober I would order my new life along more "spiritual" lines.

Don't stop reading, the quotation marks are to alert you I have difficulties with the word myself. If sobriety is a spiritual journey, my own halting path had nothing to do with karma, dharma, New Age crystals, Billy Graham, Billy Sunday, TM, alien abduction, nor living on yogurt-and-brown rice. But since I now feel the spiritual is perhaps the most important and least understood component in recovery, I don't want too easily to kiss it off. I will leave the consolations of formal religion to a professor of theology (Q. #42); you'll find my own dissenting views in Q. #41.

To illustrate what I've so far learned, let's sidestep to what is perhaps a less emotional subject: food addiction. Calling American obesity a "public health nightmare," the *San Francisco Chronicle* recently editorialized:

"Servings have grown exponentially in recent years; 7-oz muffins, for example, are equal to 7 slices of bread. . . . At the movies, viewers typically consume huge, 64-ounce soft drinks (500 to 900 calories) with half-gallon buckets of buttered popcorn." And on and on.

What this tells me is: If you try to fill a hole in your life, or the hole in your stomach with the wrong stuff: food, money (ah, there, Enron and Arthur Andersen), gin, TV, dope, sex, work, religion, shopping, gambling, cars, entertainment, applause, fame, or roller coaster rides—you can never get enough.

"All neurosis stems from man's attempts," Polly S. used to say, one of the slogans of our friendship, "to escape life's legitimate sufferings." Substitute "addiction" for "neurosis," and you have the theme of this book. Time and sobriety taught me to understand the friendship of people like Polly. "It was never a romance," I say about the two of us somewhere else. "It was more important than that."

And so while I hope I've stopped trying to escape life's legitimate sufferings, I cannot yet say I have surrendered to time gladly. What I try, Mr. Frequent, with whatever grace I may muster, is to live by something Polly once said: Time-fighters are never happy. Stop wasting the time you have left regretting the passing of time that's gone by.

Here are some of the other consolations of sobriety. To start: If I hadn't stopped, I'd be dead. Half my old drinking friends died young, two with wet brains. Sobriety got me out of a marriage once "blue, green, and gold," later gone wrong through too much money/not enough money and dying of afternoon infidelity, glib presentation of the self, and competitively understated restaurant selection. Sobriety got me though a Bleak House divorce and while I never did learn to write like Anthony Powell, I did publish some things of which I am proud, this book for one, and *Goodbye*—the first book I wrote sober.

None of this is meant to say I consider myself an ethereal soul above the considerations of mere money. The economics of publishing force writers (their editors too) to ride a two-headed horse, trying to yoke commercial goals with hopes of doing something not devoid of literary interest. (Would Proust get a contract today?) Using Jane Austen as model, the sainted Miss Agnes Hay, my fifth-grade English teacher, taught me discussion of the literary merits of one's work is best left to others, so I will note here only that the writing of these sober years bought me a house in Key West.

But on the other hand: AA taught me there were nifty things to do if you did not ask how much it paid. The twelfth Step counsels carrying the message to others still addicted and so I did facilitation at the Scripps McDonald rehab in San Diego for two years without pay. I hope I helped some patients stay sober. I know it helped me.

And when I lived in England, the BBC was example of what radio talk shows could be. I'd never worked in the field, but in sobriety asked myself, Why not? and began *Addictions & Answers* on KVML AM 1450 in Sonora, California—out of which these pages grew.

When I sold him the idea for the show, the station's general manager asked how much doing it meant to me. "You have no experience," he said. "We'll put you on the air if you'll do it without pay. In six months, we'll see what your ratings are, and talk again." That was three years ago. For the past two years running, Eastien Resources has rated my show a 15 share—number one in my time slot, in my market, almost outpulling the next two stations combined.

I once lived in a multimillion-dollar two-story penthouse on Central Park West, and told myself I was happy. My brain may have been physiologically sober—mind and heart were not: I was living on other people's envy, the picture of happiness, not the thing in itself. Halcyon days up on that beautiful roof were rare: I used to think up long, pointless errands all over the city; I hated to be home. Long after I'd left New York, Freud told me why.

"Happiness is the deferred fulfillment of a childhood wish," he wrote. "That is why wealth brings so little happiness; money is not an infantile wish." My denial ran so deep I did not see Chekhov's famous remark—*if you fear loneliness, don't get married*—applied to me. I wanted not mahogany-columned dining rooms and stained-glass ceilings but someone to love who would also love me. Imagine that—all that old-timey stuff your mother talked to you about when you were a kid turns out to be true.

And so when my Key West phone rang after thirty years and Beverly Bartlett (as I think of her still) was on the other end, inviting me to come to California for a visit—I got in my car and drove three thousand miles, never to leave her again, and did I mention that sobriety brings the gift of time? Without nursing myself through blinding hangovers every morning nor having to clock into a bar every night— my life is made up of spacious vistas of time stretching off into what feels like serene thirty-six-hour days. Not one hangover in more than twenty years. Who could have imagined that?

"When I get up in the morning," says Jim Antonowitsch, who runs the Oasis Treatment Center, Anaheim, California, "I know sober I can handle anything the Lord chooses to send me that day. Sobriety delivers the great gift that alcohol falsely promised: freedom from anxiety."

> Learn to live well, or fairly make your will;
> You've play'd, and loved and eat, and drunk your fill:
> Walk sober off; before a sprightlier age
> Comes tittering on, and shoves you from the stage.
>
> *Imitations of Horace*
> Alexander Pope

#4.

Really the Bottom Line: Dollars & Cents, What's Sobriety Worth?

Q. Bill, that story you told last week about your friend Polly was fine, but what's missing in my life is more than a friend or two. Drinking cost me a six-figure career and there went my house, husband, and family too. Everybody knows everybody in the corner of finance in which I specialized, and today I can't get a job. Drinking helps me bear it that my life is over.

Maybe money doesn't buy happiness; one thing for sure is no money means no happiness. I get your radio show on the Internet, and when I listen to you, sometimes you make me feel better. But Smirnoff does it more reliably and whenever I want, not just once a week. My mirror tells me vodka is affecting my looks, but when I think of never drinking again, it feels like death, and I drink even more. Don't tell me about AA. Is AA going to get me a job? Bring my husband back? Bottom Line: Sober or drunk, I'm never going to make six figures again. Call me No Exit. Why shouldn't I drink? (E-mail message)

A. The movie opens with the white stretch limo pulling up beneath the wing of the private Lear Jet. As the credits roll, the chauffeur opens the door, the tall, handsome hero steps out. The second pilot (she is young and beautiful) brings him a drink and over the director's credit, the plane, carrying just the one passenger, rises majestically into the power and glory of a Technicolor sunset.

Later in the story we learn he is flying from one city where his embittered wife, resentful of his workaholic habits, is having an affair with his best friend; it barely registers that an indictment for criminal stock manipulation awaits him in the city in which he lands. Perhaps inner unhappiness is shown in the bitter way he crushes out a cigarette, but what is that? Those are mere feelings. That first, visceral image is the one we remember: the power of money.

Lucky guy!

We envy him: Imagine, a fifty-million-dollar plane to himself, a pretty blonde bringing him hot and cold drinks. The visual has turned emotional reality on its ear. Addiction does the same thing. No Exit, I know how you feel. I've felt it myself.

Driving across the country recently I read Cal Thomas in the *North Platte Telegraph*—"the most widely syndicated columnist in the nation," the Nebraska paper called him. Talking about the reigning ethos of our time, Thomas writes (quoting someone else), "Greed is the universal motive, sincerity is a pose, honesty is for chumps, altruism is selfishness with a neurotic twist, and morality is for kids and fools."

At the end of my own drinking career, fueled by a naïveté so fatuous it called itself cynical, I too believed the pursuit of happiness and the pursuit of a buck were the same (Q. #3). And in my time—I was a Madison Avenue copy group head at thirty-three—I made my share. What I did not understand—why, then, was I drinking all the more?

After more than twenty years of hanging out with recovering lushes and dope fiends I've come up with my own answer, a little signature phrase that sums up the theme of this book: If you try to fill the hole in your life or the hole in your stomach with the wrong stuff—money, booze, food, whatever—you can never get enough.

No Exit, the dollars-and-cents terms in which you put your question, the airy way you shrug off friendship, dismissing the emotional life as fluff—a six-figure income is what matters—all that is moral bankruptcy. The question alcohol poses the addict is not, How do I go back to my old life but without the glass in my hand? To get sober, you have to find value not in your bank account but in yourself. I do not expect you to believe this yet.

Here's the trap you've set yourself: You will never make six figures again, says Mr. Smirnoff, stick with me, I am your only friend.

Odds are, keep your brain sodden and Mr. Smirnoff is right.

In the long-ago days when I first stopped drinking, it was mostly men who made this assumption, that money was the yardstick of happiness. But as more and more women buy into the business ethic of unending greed, it's become an equal-opportunity malaise. Isn't one million dollars better than one thousand, isn't one hundred million better than one million, etc.—*At what price?* is never asked.

Reality once again turned on its ear.

I would say this to No Exit: It is drinking itself that's causing you the unhappiness money will never allay (see Freud's remarks, Q. #3). Cunning, baffling, and powerful, alcohol has closed all doors except the one that says the only way out is to drink even more.

No Exit indeed.

I believe the least understood principle, the last to be grasped, and perhaps most important in any 12 Step program, entails spiritual growth (Q. #41, or if you prefer, #42). It calls for an exaltation of the spirit that booze and dope counterfeit, thus arresting development. So, No Exit, at this early stage in your attempt to get sober—because no matter how despairing, that is what your e-message to me really is—let's go at your question in your own terms.

Bottom Line: Dollars and cents, what is sobriety worth?

Let me tell you a story of Dominick Dunne, back from alcoholic unemployment and now one of the most acclaimed writers of our time.

After I stopped my own boozing back in the seventies, I wrote a piece about rehabs—in those days, still a new idea. Nick Dunne, then a big-time Hollywood producer, became interested, and we did a little waltz about doing it together as a movie. Nothing came of it, one of the reasons being, I have since learned, because of his drinking.

If you were to name the Top Best Jobs in the World, high on the list would be Hollywood Producer. No Exit is in despair because she no longer earns six figures. What if you were Nick Dunne, to whom it came he would never again produce another movie? To answer that, I got in touch with Nick, and asked him to describe the moment he decided booze was not the answer to his problems, but their cause:

"*Bill,*" he wrote, "*I actually don't specifically remember my last drink, although I do remember my last hangover and vividly remember the occasion that led up to it. I had come home from a rather splendid party at which I had been a last-minute replacement, when someone had unexpectedly backed out. The party was at a house where I had once been a welcome guest but was no longer, because my drinking had made me an undesirable addition to any social occasion. I was just someone to fill up an empty gold chair between two women I knew who barely spoke to me. I realized that night what should have been apparent a long time earlier, that my life in the Hollywood community, both business and social, was over, irretrievably over. Home,*" *afterwards, I sat alone and drank into the night. I woke up in the same chair some hours later—smelly, filled with self-hate, vomit-sick, and with a head that ached so badly I wanted to die. I knew then that I couldn't go on any longer. The next morning, I got into the crappy Ford that had replaced my convertible Mercedes and drove to the Cascade Mountains in Oregon, where I rented a one-room cabin without a telephone or television in a hamlet called Camp Sherman and stayed there for six months, mostly in silence. It was there, in sylvan glade, twenty years ago, that I stopped drinking and began my second career as a writer."*

"Live as if you were living a second time, and as though you had acted wrongly the first time," wrote Viktor Frankl after coming out of Auschwitz. It's a line I quoted in the dedication to this book. Let me write it here again. Some people end their addiction and begin a second life by going to a rehab, others work their passage via NA or AA. Nick did it by spending six months in silence. I have my own ideas about how to maximize the odds in your favor (Q. #26), but each of us must find his/her own way. Alcohol tells you there is no hope outside the glass in your hand. Nick's second life, like that of millions of others in recovery, is evidence this is a lie. Addiction glamorizes self-pity, making it a prison we do not want to leave. No Exit, it is up to you to open the door.

#5.

"When I Think of the Awful Men I Woke Up With, Still Drunk . . . Ugh!"

Q. Bill, remember saloon closing time? The 3 A.M. panic and despair, the fear of dying if you went home alone? I'm Ellen B. I used to order doubles to blot out the memory but recently spoke of it when I took a chip at a women's AA meeting; two or three people rolled their eyes in recognition. Pretty soon, we all began to laugh, and I felt healed. I'm grateful for my five years in recovery, grateful that will never happen to me again. You have any embarrassing memories like that?

A. I've had my share of closing time turmoils, Ellen, but while you've taken the sting out of yours by talking about them, one memory still makes me cringe. An AA rule of thumb is your secrets will get you drunk, so here goes one of mine. My first published writing was "Saloon Society"—a weekly, theoretically humorous column for the *Village Voice.* It enjoyed a certain éclat, and three New York publishers asked to bring it out in hard cover. I signed with Duell, Sloan & Pearce. One day, after a boisterous four- or five-martini editorial session with Cap Pearce, I went to a big party in a painter's loft on Spring Street, feeling in my secret heart I was at the beginning of a notable literary career. Buoyed by that idea, I drank even more.

Kenneth Tynan, the vastly learned and eminent English critic/playwright, had just been brought across the Atlantic by the *New Yorker* to do their book reviews. He soon became a figure of some presence in Manhattan himself—known for his caustic wit and I believe he popularized the year-round white ice cream suit for men long before Tom Wolfe made it his trademark.

Anyway, the painter Annie Truxell gave me a drink and said that Tynan was there. "He especially asked to meet you," she said. " 'Saloon Society' is one of his favorite bits of American writing." Cameras were popping behind Annie and indeed here came Tynan himself, creamy white shoes, blindingly white Savile Row suit, Turnbull & Asser white shirt, pink-and-white silk tie knitted by the Empress of Japan.

"My dear Bill Manville," he said, right hand outstretched, "I have so wanted to—" Blinding white flash and Freddie McDarrah, the ubiquitous photographic chronicler of arty Village life in those days, has a picture in his files of me throwing up into the palm of Kenneth Tynan's outstretched hand, all over his shoes, shirt, and beautiful white suit; and there went my literary career.

Ellen, when people say sobriety is merely a negative idea—the absence of booze—I tell them of my positive relief that like you, I know episodes like that, at least, will never happen again.

Are You Addicted? Getting Past Denial

Is this you? Drinking and doping are still mostly fun, but you've begun to worry. Too many mornings of aspirin and regret, too many nights ending in tears and fights. Maybe one or two DUIs and they're giving you funny looks at the office when you call in one Monday too often with one more "sudden dental emergency."

Are you merely an occasionally heavy drinker/user—as you claim—still able to take it or leave it alone? Or have you crossed that mysterious line? Half of you secretly worried that you are addicted even though the other half says you're not? If you have to stop drinking and/or using, is that the end of fun? This section is about getting past denial. Yours or someone you care about.

THE MOST OFTEN ASKED QUESTION:

#6.

Am I an Alcoholic/Addict? ("I'm Not a Joiner, So Don't Talk to Me About AA")

Q. My name is Freda, and I've been listening to your radio show for a couple of months now but never phoned in before because this is a small town, and someone might recognize my voice. But listening to you, I've begun to worry.

I understand that when you talk about alcoholism, the same rules apply to drug addiction. I like beer, and smoke some pot almost every day, sometimes go for a little crystal or cocaine. I never have tried any of the opiates, never will, and I give up smoking dope every year for a couple of weeks just to prove I can, and go on the wagon just to give my system a rest.

When you talk about addicts, do you mean me? And PS, I'm not a joiner, so don't talk to me about 12 Step programs.

A. When I used to give the orientation lecture to new rehab patients at Scripps McDonald, I'd tell them maybe you're in a hospital, but you don't have a disease where the doctor cuts you open, takes out your diseased gall bladder or appendix, and cures you. In this one, you're the doctor and you cure yourself.

Freda, it's not for me to tell you whether you are an alcoholic or not. Let's see if I can help you diagnose yourself.

The essence of addiction is: *It speeds up.* That's why it's called progressive. It runs faster and faster on a predictable course.

The first stage for most of us is experimentation, usually in some social situation. You and your friends try beer, booze, or pot, maybe cocaine, whatever. It cuts down boredom and/or pain, breeds confidence, it feels good, you like it. You *progress* from doing it only at parties or with someone else and now occasionally have a drink and light up when you are alone.

Use becomes customary: maybe a drink or two before dinner, TGIF, Saturday night becomes party night . . . New Year's Eve's a big blowout . . . maybe so is Thanksgiving . . . Christmas . . . the occasional stroll on the other side of the moon in between times . . . and so it goes . . .

I've just described 80 to 90 percent of the population.

After a while, the consequences of drinking/using ensue. Hangovers, DUIs, fights with loved ones, getting fired . . . We get older, a little less adventurous. Nonaddicts will say, I've been overdoing this. *And they are able to stop, or cut down.*

The remaining ten to 20 percent of us do not.

For instance, our cure for a hangover is a beer first thing on getting out of bed, maybe a hit off the stub of last night's roach, or a good big jolt of Jack Black. We begin drinking and drugging earlier than we used to—and later too.

Booze and pot and maybe a little crystal meth, it begins to hurt our health, job, and family, but the first question we ask about anyplace we are invited is, What will there be to drink or smoke? And if the answer is nothing, we won't go: indication that we're speeding up, "crossing the line," as they put it in AA. Our drinking is verging on the pathological. Medically, we've entered a diseased condition.

That notion of a "line" is difficult to the alcoholic, but very obvious to friends and family around him. And it's like ringing a bell. It can never be un-rung. As a Key West friend of mine used to say (Hello, Marion), "They don't call it alcoholwasm, do they?"

In my experience, no one has ever been able to go back across that line and drink or dope socially again. No exceptions. I haven't had a drink for more than twenty years, but as sure as the law of gravity says one step off a roof and you will fall, I know one drink and I will fall right back into addiction again.

So the question for you, Freda, is: Are you drinking more today, using more, than you did last year? It used to be you never had a drink before 6 P.M. Now you have two at lunch, the cocktail hour starts at 5, you've gotten to like a brandy or a joint at night to mellow you out for sleep, and maybe a little crystal to get you going in the morning . . . In a word, are you speeding up?

"Am I an Addict/Alcoholic?" is the most often asked question in the booze and dope industry, but I am not naïve enough to believe just this one Q&A from me will convince anyone who's truly addicted. The National Council on Alcoholism and Drug Dependence (800 622-2255) has a very good, free 22-question self-diagnostic, and there will be others in these pages as we go along.

But Freda, if you're anything like I was in my drinking days, you've already decided it's too much trouble to call that 800 number, maybe you'll do it tomorrow. Which we both know means never. So here's a hip little quiz to take right now, right on this page. (I got it from John T. O'Neill, Editor of *Findings/Sci-Mat*, a newsletter published by the Betty Ford Center.)

1. Do you consistently break promises to yourself about drinking and/or using?
2. Do others have a different version of your drinking/drug use than you do?
3. Are you paying an emotional price for your alcohol/drug use?
4. Do you do things under the influence that violate your own values?

And here comes the crunch:

5. Freda, did you lie to yourself when you answered the first four questions?

The official answer is even one yes means you better get "professional assessment." But aren't we past that? Like the young, philandering St. Augustine who used to pray, Dear God, make me better "but not yet," your very question reveals you know you should go to a 12 Step meeting. You're just hoping I will say not yet.

When the old-timers thought up the phrase, *the Demon Rum*, I've come to believe they were onto something. Addiction is a form of demonic possession, an alien presence living within your heart, body, brain, and soul, and which, in your sober moments (for instance, I hope, right now, while reading this) *you know is not you.*

When you tell me not to advise you to go to a 12 Step meeting, that's your addiction talking, saying it does not want to die. Do yourself a favor. Save your life. Get yourself to a 12 Step meeting tonight. My bet is you'll find they're singing your song.

#7.

Hitting Bottom (Booze and/or Dope)

Q. My name is Martie. I got fired from my job because of too many martinis and lines of cocaine, and my wife walked out because of it too. That did not make me stop. I felt sorry for myself, an excuse, I can see now, to drink and dope even more.

One day, I was driving my daughter and her friend to the movies. I was a little high on some Nicaragua Red but thought I was okay. I stopped for a red light, and was not even moving when another car—the guy was drunk—took a wide turn around the corner and clipped us as he went by.

The sound of that crash, the realization my daughter was in the car, all that stays with me still. Nobody was hurt, but it suddenly came to me, I might have been driving that other car, I might have killed my daughter. That was my bottom.

It focused my mind that my drinking and smoking dope had gone far past having fun and had become dangerous. I went to an AA meeting that night, haven't touched a drop, nor smoked any weed ever since. That was eleven months ago. But when I tell my story, how terrible I felt, old-time AAs laugh and say I got off lucky—that I'd come in on a high bottom.

This may sound trivial, but their laughter makes me angry. So I shut up. But I've been to too many meetings by now not to know that silence and rankling resentment are dangerous for people like me. For the record, please tell me what's a high bottom, what's a low, and what difference does it make. Do I have to hit a low bottom—jail, cirrhosis, mental wards, bankruptcy, and suicide attempts—before I can feel safe about my decision never to drink again?

A. One summer years ago, Dennis D. and I rented a summer house on Fire Island. My own drinking had not yet turned pathological and so I may have thought how odd that Dennis never had breakfast, just a glass of orange juice he carried around all day long. He never mumbled or slurred, gave no hint that the constantly replenished juice glass was half vodka. The years passed, and Dennis and I lost touch. Until his wife phoned in tears.

"Dennis is in the hospital," she said. "He's blown his liver. He asked to see you."

Dennis was the youngest son of a movie star family, and the Dennis D. I remembered looked like a movie star himself: tall, slender, dark, and handsome, but lying there in that hospital bed, he looked so gross and yellow, so swollen he didn't even have gender. He asked his wife and the nurse to step out of the room.

"Bill," he said when we were alone, "if you ever had a moment's friendship for me, smuggle in a bottle of gin." I didn't. It did not matter. Dennis had made his choice. He died the next day.

Did I learn anything from his death?

No.

Like a lot of addicts, I had to see a lot of other people die, had to crash more than once myself before I came to believe this wasn't kidding around, that all my big talk about next time I would be more careful to drink less—all that must end. "High bottom, low bottom, who cares?" says Scott Munson, Executive Director, Sundown M. Ranch, Yakima, Washington. "It is whatever it takes to bring you to the willingness to do something about your addiction."

"Each time your addiction brings you smack up against trouble or grief," says Brian Halstead, a program director at the Caron Foundation, "you are being presented with a choice. Do you want this to be your bottom, or do you want to be hit harder?"

One way to tell if you have hit your final bottom: Has whatever happened brought you past denial, and convinced you to change? "High bottom or low is a personal evaluation," says Sharon Hartman,

MSW, LSW, twenty years' experience and a certified relapse prevention specialist at Caron. "It takes what it takes. How often do you hear people at 12 Step meetings get up and say they were 'slow learners'? It took years of ruin, job loss, broken marriages, and lost children for them to wake up to the deadly pattern of their chemical dependency. If I were talking to Martie, I'd tell him no need for resentment: I admire him for recognizing the dangers in his drinking and doing something about it sooner than most people ever do."

In my drinking days, I had a secret friend, one who never let me down. No matter what dire event was going on, all I had to do was wait until whoever was yapping at me would shut up. Then I could go around the corner and find my secret friend—a pint of gin. One long gulp and I would be all right again.

After my transatlantic flight to oblivion, when I woke out of my second blackout in ten days, this time in Roosevelt Hospital, and realized my secret friend had put me there—that moment was one of the saddest of my life. It was like a death. The painful realization that my secret friend was not a friend but an enemy who wanted to kill me.

When I told this story to Sharon Hartman, she laughed. "Despite your poetic language, Bill," she said, "that moment was not 'like a death.' Getting past your own denial was your first step toward life."

#8.

What Was Marilyn Monroe's Secret Sorrow?

Q. I'm Frailler, forty-four, a lawyer here in Sonora. I heard a police report this morning—the Phoenix Suns multimillion-dollar star, Stephon Marbury, arrested for speeding, almost double the legal blood alcohol limit. A month or so ago, Ben Affleck, the movie star of *Pearl Harbor*, came out of rehab, while Robert Downey, Jr.'s dope habit keeps him in jail. Elvis died sitting on the toilet with a needle in his arm, and what was Marilyn Monroe's secret sorrow—she died of pills and booze too. President Bush's daughters and niece are in the news about the stuff, where's Darryl Strawberry, and every time you wonder where some rock star has disappeared to, the answer is drugs.

When I was a kid in law school back east, I worked as chauffeur one summer for an oil sheik being treated for cancer at Mass General. He could pay for any treatment they named, bought the whole hospital if that's what it took. He was so rich he couldn't understand why he had to die.

Bill, it's easy to say so many celebrities become addicted because they're young and think they're bulletproof, above the usual rules. But isn't there a deeper reason? With everything to live for, why does it happen to them so often?

A. I met Frailler at the coffee bar during intermission at one of our local playhouses. He'd recognized my voice and turned for a talk. "You know the story about Betty Ford? Agents check their starlets in for a smart career move. So many powerful Hollywood people there all the time, the client comes out not only sober but with a three-picture movie deal too." His anecdote about the sheik brought to mind two memories of my own.

In the years I lived in London, I got to know Alan Pakula, director of *To Kill a Mockingbird, Klute,* and (later) *All the President's Men.* When my novel *Goodbye* was published, Alan wanted to discuss buying movie rights. I was then living back in New York, he flew in from California. I picked him up at his hotel. Our talk continued during a meandering walk in Central Park and on to the Plaza.

"How about lunch," Alan said, "the Oak Room okay?"

There is a genial bit of folklore—it may even occasionally be true— that says old New York money is quiet and understated. Nobody stares and it is never flaunted. If you ask a New Yorker to name a hotel to fit that description s/he will say the Plaza—a string quartet plays Mozart for tea in the Palm Court below while the King of Spain has breakfast somewhere above (and everybody politely pretends to believe he is merely the Count of Aragon).

Certain private clubs may live up to that Platonic ideal but the Plaza's Oak Room is its perfect public expression. How surprising then, that though Alan himself is one of the most soft-spoken of men, when we walked in it was like the parting of the Red Sea waters.

Someone murmured his name and someone else said *Jane Fonda* (who had starred in his last picture). Heads turned, people stood aside to let us pass, and one dowager got up on a chair to see us better. We had no reservation, but the maître d' nodded, Alan and I followed and when our little procession stopped walking there was a quiet table for two waiting.

"You come here often?"

"They do a very nice iceberg lettuce salad."

With a nod and a smile, he waved off a bottle of champagne two Miss Atlantic City contest winners (ten years past prime perhaps but obviously very sumptuously married) wanted to send us. And over the top of his menu, a faint rueful smile for me. "You have to keep reminding yourself," he said, "you can't walk on water."

The second story dates from the same time of my life—a year or so out of rehab. I was walking along Park Avenue when I saw Sterling Hayden for the second time in two days. The first had been in a movie the night before, in which he played—starred—was it as a writer?—someone who went around carrying a six-foot wooden staff. And here he was again, dressed as in the movie, including the six-foot staff. The light turned red. We stood side by side watching the traffic.

I said, "I liked you very much in the movie."

"Let's have a drink."

The light turned green. The Statler Murray Hill was across the street. There was a quiet little bar off the lobby. He ordered scotch. I told the guy make mine soda.

"You don't drink?"

"I've had my share."

"Come upstairs," he said. "You're too interesting to waste time talking to in a bar."

He was drunk of course, had been drinking for a week. He was registered at the hotel, and there was a bar in the living room of his suite. He poured himself a couple. "I've got a wife I love, a contract for a book I want to write, a sixty-foot yawl I dream about. I don't want to die before I get on my boat with my typewriter and my wife and sail around the world. Except I can't stop drinking. You think your rehab would work for me?"

"They always have a waiting list."

"You know anyone there?"

"They might remember me."

"There's the phone."

I can't recall the exact details. Schedules were rearranged, suddenly there was a bed. My phone rang long before his twenty-eight days were up. He'd had his chauffeur come get him.

"They don't understand people like me."

Never heard from him again—I'd been dismissed, just one of those faceless ciphers, another among how many hundreds in his movie star life who'd gone out of their way to oblige him? "We cut corners for VIPs," says Dr. Joseph Pursch, a specialist in addiction who treated Betty Ford herself and the astronaut Buzz Aldrin. "The minute you give a VIP a weekend pass, you invite a relapse."

Nothing came of Pakula's interest in my novel, nor does anything said here mean he needed help staying sober—he was a very abstemious man. I include his story to illustrate what extraordinary treatment celebrities get, and to show some do have the sweet modesty to withstand it. The Sterling Hayden story is different and my role in it small, but it was of the destructive order mentioned by Dr. Pursch.

"You meet a perfect stranger on the street," said a friend of mine, the therapist Lynn Telford-Sahl, "and because he's a celebrity, immediately let him talk you into going into a bar. At that early stage in your sobriety, Bill, a very foolhardy move. Next, you get involved rescuing him, moving right into his movie star fantasies there will always be a lawyer, a wife, an agent, *someone* to clean up his mess." Her reproof brought back memories, long-ago readings—was it in Freud?

"Infantile omnipotence" is the name psychologists give an early stage in development. Is Baby cold? Almost before the thought is formed, a blanket magically appears. Hungry? Here's food. This is Eden . . . a never entirely forgotten dream of earthly bliss.

Weaning the little emperor from all this is hard. Who wants to bear frustration, to accept that life does not always furnish the big sweet milky tit the moment we scream? Expulsion from paradise. We go reluctantly and the dream of return never ends: Mom to her two- or three-year-old: You want to go out? No. You want to stay in? No. Why are you crying, what do you want? I want to be a blue pony.

What "growing up" means is accepting the frustration that not every wish is immediately fulfilled, the sad realization that not everything is possible. But movie stars? Their money and fame, the never-ending adoration of the press and cameras, the army of gofers around them saying just name it and its yours—all, all work to reawaken the old seductions of infantile omnipotence. Megan Megastar does not know what she wants but she wants it *right now!*—and a joint, a drink, a line of blow will barely get her through the anger of realizing when she has it, she didn't want it in the first place.

And so while the stars seem to have everything, their hunger for satisfaction grows, their ability to stand frustration diminishes. "Ironically," says Lynn, "they live with this nagging sense of frustration—one foot back in the Garden, but one foot out . . . and booze and dope seem to reopen the gate, their ticket for a return to omnipotence—a feeling they chase over and over again." As Carrie Fisher, a movie star herself, once put it: "Immediate gratification isn't fast enough."

Final note: When I spoke to Dr. Keith Humphreys, Assistant Professor of Psychiatry at Stanford University, he felt my notions about infantile omnipotence sounded right but added a gloss of his own:

"Many movie stars," he said, "never get out of that infantile stage to begin with—indeed, that incredible narcissistic self-regard may have helped them endure all the disappointments and criticisms that accompany a career in the arts. So they may not be regressing to a previous stage, just living the stage they never got out of but in grander style." All of which reminds me of an old joke about Moss Hart.

At the height of his Broadway success, he bought a big, rambling but neglected Bucks County estate and laid in fruit trees, an artificial lake, huge fireplaces, tennis courts, garages, stables. . . . "It shows," said Oscar Levant, "what God could have done if He'd had the money."

#9.

The Two Faces of Robert Downey, Jr.

Q. My name is Lynette, and I heard your program about why so many movie and rock stars get messed up with alcohol and drugs. I've been a Robert Downey, Jr., fan ever since *Chaplin*. I understand that if you're a hot property in Hollywood, they assign you a kind of bodyguard—I guess you might call it a sponsor—some other actor, maybe a bit older, who's gone the drug route himself, and is now clean.

Bob Downey's got it all. Why does he need dope too? In your experience, Bill, how much chance do you give him for ever getting and staying clean and sober?

A. My superb English teacher, the aforementioned Miss Agnes Hay (Q. #3), liked to say one of literature's great moments comes when Huck Finn is faced with the problem of the runaway slave, Jim. Everything Huck has been taught is *right*—the path of truth, justice, light—"his finer self, the morality of the angels," is how she put it—all tell him to turn Jim in. It is important we not bring our twenty-first-century values to this story, that like some movie tough guy we don't merely say, That's a no brainer, of course he doesn't rat Jim out. Huck has internalized the values of the nineteenth-century rural society in which he was raised, *in his own heart and soul he feels that his only hope of heaven is to turn Jim in.* But in the end, he decides he doesn't care if he goes to hell. He gives in to what he feels is his weak, sinful, debased self. The decision tears him in half, but Jim is his friend; he won't do it.

To thine own self be true, said Polonius. "I've gotta be me," sang Sammy Davis, Jr. What if the me you have to be is not acceptable even to yourself? *There's a man inside who does not like me*, says the protagonist in one of Graham Greene's early novels.

When the young Robert Downey, Jr.—Hollywood's favorite Fallen Idol—won the Golden Globes best-supporting-actor award for his work on *Ally McBeal*, fellow actors roared their approval. "More for his defiant way of life," an actor friend who'd been in attendance said to me, "than for his work. Many of them, maybe most of them, are users too. Julia Roberts, not a user herself, nevertheless, topped it all off by pinching his ass to show her love."

In a speech afterwards, the often rehabbed (and three times jailed) star said it meant everything to him to know so many people were rooting for him, and after his most recent dope bust, his on-line fan site registered a 300 percent rise in hits.

Lynette, which Downey were they cheering?

I'm not in the fortune-telling business but your question about Downey's chances brings to mind a nineties documentary in which he talks about a war between what he names his Good Boy side, and the other, which he calls Goat Boy. (That he calls himself a "boy" in both avatars is a reminder of how chemical dependency leads to arrested development [Q. #53]). I asked my old friend, clinician Larry Bouchard, how addiction ties in with this notion of a split or double self.

"Someone ever fall in love with you for the wrong reasons?" he asked, coming at me, as usual, from an unexpected angle. "Remember how uncomfortable it made you feel?"

"I do remember falling extravagantly in love in high school. She was flattered at first, but in the end said it felt coercive. Living up to my exalted picture of her made her feel like a fraud. 'I can't be your Lily Maid of Astolat,' she said. 'Edmund sees me the way I am.' "

"You were messing with her sense of identity," said Larry, "making her feel, in John Bradshaw's sense, *inauthentic*. So she dumped you. But how many times have you heard an actor say he feels at home in the world only when he is playing someone else? *Public adoration vs. private annihilation*—the idea is common enough in Hollywood. I've often thought movie star can be a dangerous profession.

"The actor sits in makeup and watches the face he knows best disappear beneath foundation creams, eye shadow, toner, maybe a toupee—what emerges in the mirror is someone who is not himself—not only better looking, but more beloved, more popular too. And then he goes on camera and speaks terrific lines he did not think up. How easy to feel that other self is more acceptable than the unmade-up, maybe inarticulate schlubb he feels deep down he really is. I've never talked to Downey," Larry went on, "but I know clients with the same problem—the false ego versus the real self: authenticity."

I told Larry about the opening line of a poem by April Bernard on what she calls her "divided soul":

"Stupid as a movie star, I was someone else's idea . . ."

"Exactly," said Larry. "The more Downey's Hollywood friends and fans cheer him, the more he thinks all they want to see is the Good Boy (who is a cosmetic artifact anyway) . . . but deep down he feels that the bestial Goat is really who he is. So all that mindless, so-called support is really killing him, separating him from finding his real self. Unless he can integrate the two selves—get past his own façade—my bet is he'll go on using dope to numb the pain of losing his authentic self."

#10.

Maintenance Drinking

Q. You can call me Johnny Walker (which I understand was Winston Churchill's favorite scotch, as it is mine). I heard you say last week that he was a maintenance drunk. What evidence do you have? You're like all the puritanic ex-lushes and ex-smokers I ever met, miserable. You can't stand it that someone else can drink (even if you can't), and have a good time. Sure, Churchill liked his cigars, champagne, and brandy, but nobody who was a drunk could have led Great Britain so ably through the dark days of World War II.

I've also heard you say on the radio that the mark of alcoholism is progression—that it speeds up. If Churchill was a maintenance drunk, how come his drinking didn't speed up?

A. If I may, Johnny, let me ask you to put down your eponymous glass long enough to listen a bit more closely. I never said Churchill was a maintenance drunk. I said he was a *maintenance drinker*, which I believe is something else.

Was Churchill an alcoholic? No-nonsense fellow that you are,

Johnny, you want evidence, black or white. And yet if there's a con-
tinuum, people who don't drink at one end, the alcoholic at the
other, and in the middle, people who hit the bottle to various
degrees but are not, and may never be, addicted—"hardheaded" yes
or no answers naïvely miss the point. Nor would they tell us much
about you—an instructive subject to which we will return.

In *The Last Lion*, William Manchester's magisterial biography of the
great prime minister, the second volume begins with a day in the life. It
is 1932, Churchill is fifty-eight and just getting up.

Arriving with the breakfast tray is "a weak [three-ounce] scotch and
soda . . . which Winston will sip over the next four hours. . . . There is
always some alcohol in his bloodstream, and it reaches its peak late in
the evening after he has had two or three scotches, several glasses of
champagne, at least two brandies, and a highball, but his family has
never seen him the worse for drink. . . ."

I can just hear my caller beginning to fume.

Well, was he an alcoholic or not?

Manchester once again, with some very concrete facts:

Between 1931 and 1939, not only did Churchill continue his very
public political career but he largely had to support his family by writing, "publish[ing], eleven volumes and over four hundred [magazine
and newspaper] articles . . . and deliver[ing] 368 speeches." More than
a book a year for eight years, and topped off with something like a
speech or article every three or four days!

More evidence: How well I know from my own alcoholic days as a
husband how sadly, devastatingly, booze incapacitates the lush for
marriage. How did Churchill's drinking affect his? Winston and his
wife were often geographically separated in their lifelong union, but
conducted a voluminous correspondence. In *Churchill: A Study in Great-
ness*, historian Geoffrey Best surveys this (and other) evidence, contrasting it with the private lives of Churchill's great contemporaries.
Best calls Winston and Clementine Hozier's fifty-six-year (!) marriage
a great success, "one of the most remarkable . . . of any great man in
twentieth-century political life." And the astute Lord Ismay weighs in
too: "The most ideal marriage there ever has been."

If the term *alcoholic* is used not as some mere pejorative but to reflect
events in the real world, I would not apply the term to Churchill. If he

had indeed been addicted, his booze consumption would have speeded up, his marriage would never have continued so well, and he would never have lived to his nineties, getting more work done than any two writers I have ever met. Nor is there any evidence that he came to that defining point (as I did myself), where you hate the glass in your hand, pray to God not to drink it, and lift it to your lips and gulp it down anyway.

The definition I find most useful says addiction is behavior that may have begun as fun but continues long after the fun is gone. It adversely affects your health, your marriage and family, your finances and social life—you hate it but keep it up anyway. By this definition, then, was Churchill a drunk? Not by my standard, and more important, not by any standard he set himself. " 'All I can say,' " Manchester quotes the man himself, " 'is that I have taken more out of alcohol than alcohol has taken out of me.' "

Easy enough to say this is denial and the man undoubtedly alcoholic. To me, the question is moot: No one I ever knew stopped drinking because someone else defined him as alcoholic.

Am I saying Churchill was merely a social drinker? No, he was far beyond that. There is evidence the man was a depressive, and used alcohol to medicate himself. A maintenance drinker? This is where we began, Mr. Walker, and circles us back to you.

I suspect your vehement (and unnecessary) defense of Churchill, like the high dudgeon you vent at me, are both stalking horses for anxiety about yourself, you classy old Johnny Walker drinker, you. But none of this can justify you to yourself. You tell us you drink Churchill's own brand, but not how much. If you're afraid you may well have crossed the line and have arrived, a full-blown alcoholic yourself, I know some tests that will help you decide. For a starter, try Q. #6.

PS. If you decide not to take it, that's a clue too.

#11.

I'm Not an Alcoholic, Merely a Heavy Drinker

Q. What's a heavy drinker? What's an alcoholic? My wife and I have a couple of martinis before dinner every night, some wine with and brandy after. And Gloria says smoking a joint before making love makes it all the sweeter. We often get a little tight, and maybe a little drunk on New Year's Eve and times like that, but we never drive a car when we're drinking or do anything dumb like that. When I went for my annual checkup last week, my blood pressure was maybe marginal. My doctor asked right out, 'Lou, how much do you drink?' When I told him, he told me we better run more tests. Bill, just like it's the easiest thing in the world for a lawyer to tell you don't do it, it's easy for a doctor to play it overly safe and tell you to stop drinking. Sure, but it's not him who's going to be deprived of the pleasure that booze brings into my life and Gloria's.

A. In my answer to the Churchill question immediately preceding, I gave my opinion that not all heavy drinkers are alcoholics. As I understand the notion of a heavy drinker, it's someone whose admittedly high consumption brings no adverse effects into their lives . . . it does not threaten their health, their jobs, their families, jobs, or finances. Doubtless they'd be better off taking less on board, but that's their business. Unless their doctor or loved ones beg them to stop or they begin collecting drunk driving tickets, etc., and they still keep on, even speeding up . . . I would not say they are addicted to alcohol.

The way I hear you, Lou: You talk as if your heavy drinking is merely like a mole on your face. An ugly fact perhaps, but not life threatening . . . until/unless, one day, the mole begins to grow, or change color. That would be warning it may have become cancerous, and something has to be done about it. But as long as you don't, for instance, drive a car drunk, you seem to be saying, that time is not yet.

I would suggest that your high blood pressure—which you glide right by as if it were not important—might be such a sign. And the new tests your doc is going to run may well furnish others.

The defensive note I hear in your voice sounds like denial. Are you getting ready to ignore your doctor's medical advice? I suspect you're lying to your doc, yourself, and me about how much you're drinking.

If the heavy drinker does not stop when his habit begins to threaten his life, well—he's a heavy drinker no more. If you keep on drinking now that your doctor feels it has begun to imperil your health, Lou, welcome to the club.

You've arrived.

#12.

Define "A Social Drinker"

Q. I've never been drunk in my life, my husband and I never had children, so I've always worked, and never been fired from a job. I admit I like a whiskey sour or two before dinner, a Bloody Mary before brunch on Sunday. What's wrong with that? But my husband says I drink too much. I tell him that's because he's jealous.

In his drinking years, I went to too many Al-Anon meetings not to have learned that alcoholics are controllers. You have to learn to live your own life, and not let them dictate to you.

Last Sunday, I told him if he does not want to drink, that's fine. I'm all for that. But I'm a social drinker, I told him. Please don't interfere with one of the minor pleasures in my life. He said I was not a social drinker, and that I was in denial.

Bill, who's right?

A. Dear Ms. Social: One of the rules for serenity is don't get between an addict and his fix; whether it's booze, food, gambling, whatever, and never, never between a quarreling married couple. So please don't appoint me your marital umpire. But perhaps this can help:

In 1981, the National Council on Alcoholism came up with this five-point definition. Social drinkers:

1. Never, on any occasion, have more than four drinks.
2. Never get drunk.

3. Do not drink on occasions that involve precision machinery, automobiles, and/or children.
4. Never drink more than they intended.
5. Do not get upset if long periods go by without a drink.

Yes?

I've known people who occasionally get drunk at Christmas or New Year's Eve, and others who get cranky if they can't have their martini, glass of wine, or Cinzano and soda before dinner every day. Despite what the National Council says, in my book none of these facts alone defines them as alcoholics or even heavy drinkers. Let me repeat, that's merely my own opinion. If you want an official five-point yardstick, there it is, above.

Here's another little test people have found useful. One of the hallmarks of addiction is once you have a drink in you, you become unpredictable to yourself. The test is this: Tell your husband that you're going to have two drinks every day before dinner for the next fifteen days. And that's what you do—neither more nor less. If you are an alcoholic, you won't be able to stick to it.

But, PS, Ms. Social: I suspect whatever test you take or mark you score won't end the trouble at home. All those Al-Anon meetings, and while you talk about control, you never mention *co-dependence?*

To put on my alcoholic Dr. Laura hat for a moment, I'd suggest *that* may be the heart of darkness you and your husband are skirting. It was one of the cracks in both my marriages and so I've gone into the idea at greater length perhaps than any well-focused booze book should. (For more about co-dependence, see Q. #53).

#13.

In Vino Veritas?

Q. Why are some people cheery drunks, while others become sullen and get into fights? You know the old saying, In Vino Veritas? Is it true—that alcohol brings out the hidden truth?

My name is Celeste, I'm twenty-nine and Tim is thirty-one. When he's sober, he's easy and loving. After a few drinks, he becomes some-one else, Dr. Jekyll and Mr. Hyde. Does this mean he's that way down deep, and alcohol merely brings it out?

One night after a fight, I took a taxi home. He followed me to my apartment, and in a drunken rage, broke the door down. He said it was because he loved me so much, he could not stand having a barrier between us. Now he's asked me to marry him. I want to marry the lov-ing, gentle Tim, not the person he turns into. Which is the real one?

A. "In vino veritas? No. In vino *bullshit*," says John A. MacDougal, D. Min., a United Methodist minister who is also Manager of Spiritual Guidance for Hazelden in Center City, Minnesota. "Alcoholics and addicts have a real self and a drunken self. Our drunken self is based on our drug of choice and our particular personality rut. Once we find our drunken rut, we tend to stick with it, but it is not who we really are."

John, who along with Bowen White, M.D., is author of *Clinician's Guide to Spirituality*, goes on: "With stimulants such as speed or cocaine, our feelings are absent except for alertness, a sense of bulletproof invulnerability, paranoia, and anger . . . followed by 'crash and burn.' With downers such as alcohol, heroin, painkillers, and tranqs, our feel-ings get distorted into personal favorites: The Romantic Drunk, whose bumper sticker reads, 'No One Is Ugly at 2 A.M.' The Defiant Drunk. His sticker says, 'Of course I'm drunk. Did you think this was a stunt car?' The Abusive Drunk: 'Guy with Chip on Shoulder Seeks Sweet Sexy Girl to Dump On.' Pitiful Drunk: His car radio is permanently tuned to songs about crying, loving, and leaving, and resentful drunks love talk radio, the more hate- and anger-filled the better.

"None of this is real," John goes on. "I'm reminded of *Die Fledermaus* where an actor drinks champagne and sings, 'You, you, you, I will be forever true to you, if in the morning we still remember.'

"In early sobriety, we are no longer distorted. However, to be all our creator intended, it's good to take all 12 Steps and make them our way of life. And remember, in romance, we attract people who are about as recovered as we are."

To which Caron's Sharon Hartman wisely adds: "I've learned to watch for little throwaway phrases. When Celeste says 'after a few drinks' a significant personality change takes place, a red flag goes up in my mind. Especially when accompanied by a violent act like breaking down a door."

Celeste, to sum up: A definition of addiction that you'll find over and over again in these pages calls it behavior that may have begun as fun, but which continues even after the fun is gone and it's begun to damage our health or job, our relationships with those we love. Play this over in your mind. Before you say yes, ask Tim to agree to an alcohol dependency evaluation by a qualified expert.

—Or, did you call me in a last forlorn hope, afraid you already know the answer?

#14.

Am I an Alcoholic/Addict? (Revisited)

Q. When we have arguments, my husband says it is because I'm an alcoholic. He says, "Lilly, a lot of hidden anger comes out in you after you've had a drink or two."

My feeling is that he doesn't think it proper for "a lady" to drink at all; he is very hypersensitive and old-fashioned. I tell him if he'd drink with me, we'd get along better. But when I am alone with my thoughts, sometimes I think maybe he is right. How can I know if I'm just an occasional heavy drinker, or an alcoholic?

A. Close your eyes and imagine you're having a medical consultation with a doctor who knows you very well. He looks up from your chart and says, Lilly Jones, you've had your last drink.

How does that make you feel?

For most people, the reaction would be, Not even a cold beer on a hot day in July? Oh, well, if it's a matter of life and death, that's not too high a price.

At a rehab, when they said that to me, I felt a chill. Oh, no, I said—*never?* Never to drink again? That was death.

Addiction narrows the world. Drunks and dopers cannot imagine life without chemical acceleration. As W. C. Fields used to say, "Far too nice a day to spend out of doors," and he'd head for the bar.

Addicts lie. To themselves first. I lied to the first doctor who ever said that to me because while I then knew very little about alcoholism, I did know that if you admitted to it, you could never drink again. Telling her the truth meant the end (!) of good times. You bet I lied.

In Q. #6, I talk about a feeling I had in my drinking days—I had only one endlessly loyal friend who would never let me down. If I could just live through the current argument or difficulty, get past this time when someone—usually my weeping wife—was berating me for boozing so much, if I could bear her tears five minutes more, wait it out until she shut up, I could go around the corner and find my secret friend, a pint of gin, and I would be all right again.

I have never yet met an addict who did not have this belief.

As they like to say in AA, alcoholism is the only disease that tells you that you're okay—that if these interfering other people would just leave you alone, you'd be even better. The great turning point in recovery comes when you come to believe, in your heart and soul, that this secret friend is not your friend, but an enemy who wants to kill you. To get to that point, denial must end.

Lilly, you've taken a first step. Still in denial, but at least open to the notion that perhaps you have a problem with drinking.

That you think if your husband drank with you it would make the relationship better shows you've got an additional problem, one I don't think you as yet understand. You're asking him to enter into enabling co-dependency with you. That he is resistant to the idea is a plus for your marriage. (For a more detailed discussion on enabling and co-dependency, see my talk with Paul Ehrlich, Q. #53).

We think a drink oils the wheels of conviviality. Yes, by lowering social constraints and diminishing our sense of tact. Lilly, want to see how alcohol might be affecting your marriage? Try this: Don't scare yourself by saying you will never drink again. How about deciding to lay off for just thirty days? My bet is you'll be amazed by how much easier to get along with that "hypersensitive and old-fashioned" husband of yours suddenly becomes.

PS. Worried you might be an alcoholic? The Caron Foundation, a top rehab (of which I am a 28-day graduate), offers day or night 800 telephone help. Phone them right now—see Q. #88.

Or do the self-diagnostic tests you'll find scattered throughout these pages, starting with Q. #6.

#15.

Why Can't I Hold It Anymore?

Q. In my career, I was a well-known journalist, one of the first women reporters to go to Vietnam. My friends used to call me a whorehouse drinker: That's where I'd go to keep on drinking after the legal bars closed. I've always prided myself on being able to drink like a gent, but lately things changed.

In your terms, maybe I was an alcoholic. But I never lost a job or missed an assignment, so I hope you will allow me to call myself Heavy-Duty Drinker (or HDD, a play on my name).

I never married, maybe because as Margaret Bourke White once said, I never met a man as interesting as a war. Maybe it was because you don't marry the kind of man I met in bars.

What I'd like to discuss is suddenly one glass of wine and my speech slurs and I find people looking at me funny. I had a martini in a restaurant with friends last week, and fell on my ass. Charles de Gaulle called old age "a shipwreck." I'm not that old yet, but why can't I hold my liquor anymore?"

A. *(I owe my discussion of this question to a conversation with Matt Ridley, when he was a guest on my show, and to a further reading of his brilliant book,* Genome.*)*

The new studies of the human genome show that the capacity to digest alcohol largely depends on an enzyme manufactured by genes on chromosome 4. This can be a valuable trick. Fermented liquids do not carry germs. "The devastation wrought by various forms of dysentery during the first millennia of settled agricultural living," Ridley writes, "must have been terrible." People whose genes weren't adept at handling booze died out: evolution at work.

As late as the nineteenth century, people crowded into cities were wise not to drink the water. The rich drank wine, beer, coffee, and tea. Prince Albert, a temperate, abstemious soul, drank the water in London and died. But foraging, nomadic people did not need the sterility that fermentation brings.

Living at low densities, their natural water supplies were clean and safe. "So it is little wonder that the natives of Australia and North America," Ridley writes, "were and are especially vulnerable to alcoholism and that many cannot now 'hold their drink.'" You do not tell us, HDD, that you are a Native American, nor would I guess you are. If your genome was not expressing those genes that manufacture alcohol dehydrogenases, you would not have been able to do your kind of heavy-duty drinking. I think, though, you've already begun to guess that the answer is one you don't want to know.

With age, your liver loses the capacity to oxidize (burn up) alcohol. Sometimes it can seemingly happen overnight, and even whorehouse drinkers like you can be knocked flat by a single glass of beer or wine. I'm sorry to say, HDD, that you probably never are going to be able to drink like a gent again. But then, neither can I. I suspect neither of us ever did. Nor can either of us fight the accumulating years.

What we can do is look for a way of life satisfying without chemical lift. My first step in finding it was to fly the Atlantic in a blackout. Paradoxically, I look back at that as one of the best things I ever did: It woke me to the trouble I was in. Your first step may be that episode of falling down drunk in a restaurant.

We are both writers, so let me end with a word about language. Or perhaps, literary stance. Yours seems to be bravado. If you heard a man talk like that, you'd laugh at him for childish macho posing and call him Hemingway Lite. What makes you think arrested development sounds better coming from a woman?

The question isn't why can't you hold it anymore, but why should you want to when it's begun to harm your health, your social life, your literary style, and self-respect? Before you try further research on how hard a bottom do you want to hit, do a little reading first: Q. #26 discusses going cold turkey versus going to AA and/or a rehab. I chose a rehab and hope you will too.

#16.

Drinking Makes Me Feel Normal

Q. Bill, I'm Louise, twenty-seven years old. My father died of cirrhosis, and my mother brought me up to believe that if I ever tasted a drop of alcohol, my life would be ruined and I'd go straight to hell. I guess I'm okay looking, but not the soft, warm kind of woman that men take to. I'm shy, edgy, not easy in my own skin. I tell jokes wrong, and when other people tell them, I laugh at the wrong places. I don't know how to do life. I just don't fit in.

Last week, one of my friends arranged for me to go out on a blind date. I was so nervous, I threw up before we met. But when I met Tommy, it was in a bar, and he didn't even ask did I drink. "Glad to see you," he said, and ordered drinks for us both. Usually I feel like a spaceship dropped me on the planet Earth and I have to pretend to be one of the natives. Bill, from the first drink, it was wonderful.

For the first time in my life, I felt normal. I had fun, it was fun for Tommy to be around me, it was an evening I'll never forget. When I think of my future, this may sound awful, but I see myself drinking the weeks and months and years away with Tommy.

I often hear you say that if someone is having a good time drinking, and not in trouble with it, hasn't lost a job, broken up a marriage, none of that . . . you congratulate them and say go on their merry way, they need no advice from you. But maybe something in me doesn't quite believe it can be all that easy.

Isn't life meant to be enjoyed, and if a drink makes me feel "together," like I'm part of the human race at last, what's wrong with that?

A. Most people find alcohol one of the minor pleasures in life. Perhaps one out of eleven goes on to become addicted, many of these becoming hooked with their first drink or hit.

In these people, the brain does not naturally produce adequate levels of dopamine; they are born low in capacity to feel simple everyday pleasures. Give them their first hit of a dopamine-enhancer, it's like falling in love. (Does this mean there's an "alcohol gene"? See Q. #24, and I'd read #15 too.)

There's a radio station out of Los Angeles that has a morning talk show that I like. Bill Handel is the very funny host from 5 A.M. till 9, after which (!) he goes to his office, and conducts a successful legal practice for the rest of the day. Talking about his teen years one morning, he said the first time he experimented with drugs, the feeling was so wonderful, he was like someone who won ten thousand dollars his first day at the track.

"I chased that feeling for years," he said. He never caught it again, the price of the chase began to be too high, and he stopped. That's how he can keep two successful careers going at the same time.

One of the definitions of addiction I like is feeling there is something out there—booze, sex, money, cars, fame—if I can only get enough of it in here, in me, I'll be fine. If you're like Louise, who says it takes alcohol to make her feel normal, the inevitable progression of addiction comes to mind: It's going to take more and more alcohol as the years go by to get you to that state. Like Bill Handel, you'll chase it for the rest of your life, but get there less and less often, while all the troubles that come with addiction will mount up and grow worse.

Like Bill Handel, most people would stop. People like me, and I suspect you, Louise, merely say, I don't have to stop, I just didn't drink enough, next time, I'll drink more.

The playwright Eugene O'Neill once wrote, "Man is born broken. He lives by mending." And the mending he chose to feel normal and together himself was "God's good creature rum." He died an alcoholic.

Using bourbon or gin to feel more "together" is like getting high to fight depression. The next day, you're more anxious and depressed than ever—because your real problems have not gone away in the night, but there they are again in the morning, grinning at you like demons—and you drink again to blur out that feeling.

That kind of vicious circle is the hallmark of the alcoholic life—drinking in an effort at curing something wrong you feel in your heart and soul, your psyche, and your life.

Let me end with this, a kind of self-test I heard during a lecture when I was a facilitator at Scripps McDonald:

Do you remember your first drink? How did it make you feel?

If you reply, For the first time in my life it made me feel normal, like other people—take it as a warning bell. In the UC Berkeley "Alcohol & Drug Abuse Studies" catalog, it estimates "that more than one half of clients in alcohol and drug treatment have coexisting psychiatric disorders." Better read the questions about professional help, Qs. #36, #37, and #71. There's likely to be more working in your psyche than alcohol alone, and my belief is you'd be wise to supplement your 12 Step AA program with a little psychotherapy.

#17.

Mixing Pills and Booze

Q. I once heard you say that it was mixing pills with gin that got you into a hospital. And you always see these warnings on prescription drugs, even on cough medicine. *If you take one of these, don't drink.*

But I've found that if I take a drink with just one or two Benadryls or Tylenol tablets, I get a very nice little cheap buzz. And if I buy even the cheapest vodka, and add one of my husband's high blood pressure pills, Bill, that's like New Year's Eve.

None of this has led me to the terrible conclusion you warn against. Sometimes you sound like those government warnings against pot—a lot of people too old to have a good time, and they don't want anyone else to have one either.

If you can't afford a lot of high-priced, prestige label alcohol, what's wrong with taking it with a pill or two to make your dollar go further?

A. Go to a drug wholesaler, and buy a list of chemicals that any biology teacher can supply you. Allowing for inflation, the latest price I heard is that they would cost about $11.95. Put them together in the right way, add a lot of water, and you get a totally unexpected result: an incredibly complex live human being.

The parts are greater than the whole.

This works with chemical intoxication too.

Here's how they put it when I was doing my twenty-eight-day rehab trip at Caron. Say a shot of booze holds three units of drunkenness. And that a pill or painkiller holds three units too. If you take them together, they don't add up in a simple way to six units of high.

Potentiation was the word they used back then. Nowadays, we speak of *synergy:* The parts multiply their effect, and you get nine units of drunkenness . . . and it sets in a lot faster than you are ready for.

Mrs. Mixer, you began by mixing alcohol and "one or two" Tylenols or Benadryls. In almost the next breath, you've graduated to higher-voltage experiments, using your husband's high blood pressure pills.

It sounds like your use is accelerating.

Speeding up . . . one of the prime indicators of the onset of addiction (see Q. #6). You're playing with mysterious and dangerous chemical forces. Your nice little cheap buzz may soon turn into a cyclone.

#18.

Am I an Alcoholic/Addict? (Part III—Denial Wears a Thousand Faces)

Q. Hi, my name is Barry. I can handle booze, take it or leave it alone. Once in a while, I overdo it a bit, but then I go on the wagon for a week or two, not a drop of wine, no booze, no beer, no trouble, and I feel all the better for it. An alcoholic has to have it every day.

I've never been fired from a job, no car wrecks, we own our own house, and I'm never behind in mortgage payments. Doing okay, right? But my wife still says that I'm an alcoholic. A lot of fights around the house about it, but since she's so critical of almost everything I do, I can't take her seriously on this, but I still feel guilty. Which make me mad, and then maybe I drink *at* her—as they say in AA—over that. Is there some objective measure of whether you are an alcoholic or not?

A. "Denial is not a river in Egypt," began the first orientation lecture I ever attended in rehab, "but a lot of people build themselves palatial, twelve-room houseboats and live there for years, maybe the rest of their entire, unhappy lives." Barry's question is a classic statement of the case—you can hear it, theme and variations, in almost any bar, almost any night, almost anywhere in the world.

What made it difficult for me to see that I was an alcoholic was this: I had become unpredictable to myself. I could stop in at a bar at the end of the day, have a drink, and go home to dinner with my wife. I was just like anyone else. See?

This ignored the fact that I could stop in the same bar the same time the next day, order the same drink, and wake up three days later in Bermuda . . . so high only dogs could hear me.

Denial is seductive, you lie to yourself and don't know it. Earlier, I've described how, at the end of my drinking career, I flew the Atlantic in a blackout, and then boozed and pilled my way into two hospitals in ten days. When I awoke in the detox ward of Roosevelt Hospital in New York City, a doctor came to see me.

"Do you think you're an alcoholic?" she said.

I didn't have to read her nametag. I knew who she was. She was the end of fun.

"Oh, no," I said. "Sometimes I overdo it a bit, that's all. I'll be more careful next time, maybe just drink beer."

Quite a concession, I grandiosely thought, coming from me.

Wasn't I the big-time gin drinker . . . a high-paid liquor copywriter at one of the biggest ad agencies in New York . . . hadn't I written in my "Saloon Society" column in the *Village Voice* about how to lose weight: the famous Martini Diet—pass out before dinner? For a long time now, I'd led my life three drinks closer to the moon than most people dared. Danger, glamour, fun—how could all that stop?

When I was a facilitator at Scripps McDonald, they developed a four-point questionnaire, a diagnostic tool for screening alcoholics and drug addicts. In the privacy of your own conscience, Barry, you can use it yourself. (Reproduced below with permission.)

1. In the last three months, have you felt you should cut down or stop drinking and/or using drugs? Yes? No?
2. In the last three months, has anyone annoyed you, or gotten on your nerves by telling you to cut down or stop drinking or using drugs? Yes? No?

3. In the last three months, have you felt guilty or bad about how much you drink or use? Yes? No?
4. In the last three months, have you been waking up wanting to have an alcoholic drink or use drugs? Yes? No?

These seemingly simple questions have been carefully thought out. Each revolves around a very important building block of addiction. Each affirmative response earns one point.

One point indicates a possible problem. Two points indicate a probable problem. If you've taken this test, and answered honestly, congratulations. I don't think you would have taken it if you didn't already know-without-wanting-to-know the answer. And hedging, rationalizing, or qualifying your answers—sometimes out-and-out lying to yourself—that tells you a great deal too.

Whatever your score, you've taken a big step in breaking through the first great barrier to recovery. Getting past denial.

Incidentally, if you want to check the results you just got, there is a better known and more detailed self-test available. Just phone your local AA chapter and ask them about their 20 Question test, "Are You an Alcoholic?" You don't have to be a member, and it's free.

PS. If you've read this far—my feeling is you don't need 20 Questions to tell you what you already know. If you're sick and tired of being sick and tired of the fights, the tears, job loss, broken promises, and police action, see Q. #26: Would a rehab be right for you? For some authoritative facts on choosing the right one, and how much will it cost, see Q. #27 and Q. #29.

#19.

Blaming Others: It's Not My Fault

Q. You'd drink too if you had a rat ex-husband like mine. He ran away with some twenty-seven-year-old high-tits after I gave him the twelve best years of my life.

A. Let me see if I understand: You got twelve years older, but he did not? That would make me drink too. You better read the next question below.

Q. You'd drink too if you had a crappy wife like mine. She loves to argue and find fault. To get a compliment out of her is like getting her to write a million-dollar check. There's never any peace in the house. Gin gives me psychological separation from her unending intrusiveness.

A. Aren't you the guy I heard at a meeting last week? He said he'd come to realize he was powerless over alcohol, and "that my wife had become unmanageable."

I think I know her too. Isn't she the one who puts her foot on your throat to pin you down and pries your jaw open so she can force the gin down, no matter how much you hate it?

She must be very attractive, to say nothing of being a bigamist too. A lot of men seem to be married to her.

Your question raises an important issue for addicts.

Blaming others.

> . . . when we are sick in fortune—often the surfeit of our own
> behavior—we make guilty of our disasters the sun, the moon,
> and the stars; as if we were villains by necessity, fools by heav-
> enly compulsion . . . an admirable evasion of whoremaster man,
> to lay his goatish disposition to the charge of a star.
> —*Shakespeare*, King Lear

Properly understood, AA's seemingly simpleminded mottoes encap-sulate the rule-of-thumb wisdom of generations and millions of drunks. One I like says when you point the finger at someone else, three point back at you. Charlie did it, Louise did it, the devil made me do it, it's never my fault.

The gain in blaming others is that it allows you to ignore the blind spot in yourself: the maddening role your drinking plays in the actions of these other people whom you deplore. Blaming others, focusing on *them*, allows you to keep on drinking, doping, smoking . . . your addiction remains cozy and warm, untouched and unthreatened.

Fault-finding is first cousin to blaming others. When something goes wrong—even before something goes wrong—the faultfinder prepares for the ex post facto court of inquiry that has been sitting forever since childhood at the back of his heart. It's someone's fault, someone will be found guilty, and you better accuse someone else first. Fixing whatever it is—the objective fact plays distant second to the subjective need to make sure the blame is not tagged on you.

Example: Faultfinders and blame layers do not ask, Has anyone seen the key?

They say, Where did you put the key?

And so it goes: a boring, Johnny One Note life of unending repetition. I didn't do it, it's not my fault, you did it, I couldn't help it . . .

Little wonder, then, that accusatory arguments inevitably follow, and pretty soon you're both yelling so hard, thinking up so many wonderful reasons to prove you are 100 percent right and the other 100 percent wrong, that neither hears what the other has to say . . . which frustrates him/her all the more.

The argument escalates.

A life, as they say in AA, of drinking *at* people who just can't seem to understand the blame is all theirs. If all this sounds familiar, here's what I've found works better than blaming and yelling. At least once a week—and immediately when either one of you feels an argument is about to break out—have a prearranged, pre-agreed signal . . . maybe a raised hand or the word "Halt."

Everything stops for a structured, thirty-minute formal talk along pre-agreed rules.

Whoever calls the halt gets the floor first. Let's say it's you. You get ten minutes *without interruption* to state your side. She gets the next ten uninterrupted minutes to say what's making her unhappy. By this time, you both have cooled down enough to actually listen to each other. The final ten minutes is spent discussing how to fix whatever it is that's just come out.

If it's a good marriage, you will discover the grievance is like a nail in the shoe. Something so immediately painful that all else is forgotten, but nevertheless a minor pain, not innate to the body of the union, and which can be fixed with a little attention.

(My marriages were the other kind.)

And while you're making rules for arguing, think about these two:

Rule 1. No generalized global statements that assail the other's character and value. Look out for *always* and *never*.

Here are some dandy examples.

You're always so perfectionistic, I can never do anything right. You're always the first to attack me in public, to disassociate yourself from what you tell the world is my clumsiness or stupidity. You always want to put me down. You always have to have the last word.

Sound familiar?

Cut it out.

Phrase your argument with specific instances, and above all, *in terms of how it made you feel*. "When you corrected my grammar at the dinner party last night, it made me feel like a six-year-old."

Rule 2. No ancient history. "I'll never forgive you for the terrible thing you said to my mother last year. You just rush ahead, you never think how what you do will affect me. You got drunk at our wedding, and you just don't care." Last year is gone. Don't rehash old grievances. Keep it in the here and now. "When you brought your old college roommate home for dinner last night without warning, I felt unprepared, wearing the wrong clothes and unattractive."

Put like this, what other answer can there be but "I'm sorry, sweets. I won't do it again"?

Two simple rules. If there's any love left in the house they'll work more often than not. They do in mine. But if you're one of those who'd rather be right than happy, often wrong but never in doubt it's someone else's fault—better get married soon as possible so when you get divorced you're not too old.

#20.

You'd Drink Too If You Had Money Troubles Like Mine

Q. After being sober for almost three years, I got fired from my job, and had to take another one making 40 percent less. I'm Ted, forty-four years old.

I never thought at this stage of life it would be hard to meet the mortgage, but in fact we may have to sell and go back to renting. My wife is pissed off—she says at the situation, but I know it's at me. I hate being at my crappy new job by day, and I hate to go home at night.

The only pleasure I have these days is to stop off for a drink or two by myself when I leave work. Please don't give me the old lecture about the one or two drinks speeding up. After three years of sobriety, I've learned control. I have a lot of résumés out, and have signed up with some top headhunters. When I'm making a decent salary again, and my money worries are over, it'll be time enough to think about stopping drinking.

A. This question is a restatement of Q. #3, but since it comes up so often at any 12 Step meeting, let me go at it from another direction. At an AA meeting in Malibu, I once heard a thirty-year-old industrial chemist, new to sobriety, describe what brought her to an awakening. "For a long time, I'd had this daydream about the perfect new car. A two-door white Chrysler Le Baron convertible, with just the right sound system, red leather seats, and all the rest. I had this picture of myself, wearing just the right white mini skirt maybe riding just a little high up on my thigh, just the right red bandana in my hair, a sunny day, Julio Iglesias on the CD . . .

"I got a great new job, saved up, and at last one day went to the dealer's, signed the papers, they gave me the key and I drove out. I hadn't gone ten miles before disappointment set in. The new Chrysler wasn't as big a kick as I had imagined. *Next time I'll get a Lexus!*

"It was my sponsor who pointed out this was addiction: When something we want out there doesn't satisfy, we don't think let's look in another direction, maybe inside ourselves. We think what went wrong is I didn't get enough of that stuff out there, *I need more!*"

On the morning after, hung over, in trouble about the rent or with someone we love, we don't think I've got to cut out drinking. We reach for a Bloody Mary or a line of coke and start all over again. My guess, Ted, is if you think that after three years of sobriety, you've "learned control," I don't think you're sober yet. You may need a better job, yes—but you need even more an awakening of the spirit.

Remembering how fond was my friend Polly S. of quoting Edna St. Vincent Millay—and how strongly she identified with her—I recently brought home *Fatal Interview,* Nancy Milford's wonderful biography of perhaps the best-known American poet of her generation. The Jazz Age Madonna might be another title, and Polly once told me of a famed three-way frolic Millay conducted with Edmund Wilson and the poet John Peale Bishop. On the occasion, and at La Millay's invitation, the two friends together took her to bed—dividing their attentions to her at the waist—all the while discussing who got the better half. The story was recently told again, by another biographer, Mark Epstein, who breezily goes on to suggest such episodes may well have been inspiration for the famous line, "My candle burns at both ends."

Polly herself led a gaudy life when young, shipped off by her parents at ten or twelve, married three or four times—twice, I think, to a gambling man she adored. Early in this book, when Polly says she herself broke the candle in half and set fire to all four ends, was she telling me, in her veiled and understated way, that she could have given Ms. Millay cards and spades and trumped her still?

Poets notoriously die poor, but in the Depression winter of 1931 Millay's books sold an amazing 50,000 copies. Add that she also won the Pulitzer Prize, and you might think, like Ted, that with fame, fortune, good looks ("supernaturally beautiful" said Edmund Wilson), and all the romance she could handle, life for Millay would be complete.

Instead, Milford writes Millay's last poems are ". . . marked by a sense of overwhelming loss." A longtime devotee to gin martinis, Egyptian cigarettes, and "⅜ gr. M.S. (morphine) hypodermically delivered," Edna St. Vincent Millay was found dead at fifty-eight, "fallen to the bottom of a flight of stairs at home," her neck broken. Ted, do you think rich, famous, and beautiful Edna Millay died sober?

None of this is to deny money is the first value. If I'm hungry and can't afford a meal . . . if I'm outside in the rain because I can't pay the rent . . . I'm not interested in some Beverly Hills crooner singing me Christmas carols that the best things in life are free. Money—rightly—is all I can think of. "First feed my face," as Brecht liked to say.

Money can also take you to Paris for a romantic weekend or fix the toilet by paying for a plumber, but a few weeks ago, I met Bev for lunch at a Noah's Bagels not far from the *Chronicle* offices. Two guys I believe were sportswriters were at the next table, talking about a twenty-one-year-old football player. He'd been signed right out of college by an NFL team, six years at something like $9 million per.

"When I got to his house for the interview," one guy was saying to the other, "he'd just bought his seventeenth Mercedes-Benz. He already had three Ferraris. 'Shit,' he said, first thing when I walked in the door, pissed off, no joy there, 'Now you.' The guy's moral imagination never went past a picture of himself driving a brand-new car out the showroom door so he did it seventeen times." (For Freud's take on why money doesn't bring happiness, see Q. #3.)

"What addiction teaches us," Polly used to say, "is if you're trying to fill that hole in your stomach with the wrong stuff, you can never get enough." Some of the great American Nobel Prize–winning writers, Steinbeck, Hemingway, Sinclair Lewis, Faulkner, all died prosperous, at the peak of their fame and drunk. When I could not sleep last night, I heard a 2 A.M. news bulletin, Beatle George Harrison dead of cancer at fifty-eight. They played an in memoriam sound bite of a late seventies interview. "All your life you wanted to be rich and famous," Harrison said, "and when you become rich and famous you realize that's not it, there has to be something more."

Money and fame did not keep Darryl Strawberry sober, nor Robert Downey, Jr. Our SUVs grow bigger, our marriages shorter, and on the radio this morning, the report of a Hollywood starlet marrying a race car driver in Scotland, "cost of the nuptials, two million dollars." If we were not happy in a six-thousand-square-foot house, why do we think we'd feel better in a twelve?

Are You Addicted? Getting Past Denial

In this morning's *Chronicle* I read that the greatest medical break-through yet toward a cure for Alzheimer's belongs to a biotech corporation that not only refuses "to share its research with other scientists, but [is] actually suing them for patent infringement." We Americans have never been richer nor more angry. Road rage, airline rage, courtesy and politeness are taken to be the mark of losers—hate and fury are the staples of prime-time talk shows. We have all the material pleasures of which daydreams are made, and howl our disappointment at finding them so empty. The word "meretricity" comes to mind. It means falsely glittering.

Forget "The American Dream" ads in the *Wall Street Journal,* and the TV commercials of handsome white-haired couples riding their retirement yacht contentedly into the sunset. If you're new to Wall Street, the first broker you meet will give you the inside dope. What are the real values that rule the market? "Fear and greed," he'll tell you with a smile, proudly showing what a realist he is. But do you really want those to be the dominant emotions in you life?

In San Francisco recently, I saw a Washington Mutual outdoor sign.

The Only Thing Better Than Money,

it said,

Is More Money!

True if you have the values of an insurance actuary to whom my life and your daughter's death are merely profit and loss. Want to see how close greed is to addiction? Just substitute your favorite chemical pleasure for the word "money" in the billboard above.

Freud's famous formula for a happy life was "love and work." I've been too deluded in love to try to write about it yet—"operatically stupid about women," is the description recently used in another context—but for the rest, I see a distinction between what Freud meant by *work* and what the world means by *labor.*

Labor is an equation in a bargain. You rent or lease out your hands and brain by the hour, week, or year; the bargain is how much of your life do you sell for how much money. Labor pays the rent, feeds the kids, buys gas for the car . . . but then it's Thank God, it's Friday, and before you know it, Oh, no, not Monday again. . . .

Freud's notion of work is defined as self-chosen: spiritually satisfying in that you add your heart and soul to hands and brain and make yourself whole. In a recent newspaper column, the psychiatrist Dr. Gordon Livingston said it more simply than that: Find something to do that makes you forget the clock.

There were days when I began working on this book after breakfast. The next thing I knew, Bev was saying, Why don't you turn on the light? Such escape from the insistent, narrow thrust of the childish ego into a timeless loss of self is the nirvana we found in booze and dope. The problem for us now, Ted, is to find something we care about as passionately. In *The New Republic*, December 31, 2001, Martha Nussbaum writes, "For evil is very likely to begin in the inner world, with the struggle of love against infantile egoism and ambivalence, the laborious effort to form patterns of thought and action that defeat narcissism and acknowledge the reality of other people." I believe the life of the spirit is the one Ms. Nussbaum so eloquently describes and addiction means the struggle lost.

This evening when you leave your crappy job and head for the bar, remember that the wisdom of millions of drunks accumulated by AA over the years says you're deluding yourself if you think your drinking will stop when you have more money. Money can do a lot of things. It never kept anyone sober.

Three days ago, as I began writing this chapter, hijackers flew two Boeings into the World Trade Center in Manhattan, demolishing the twin towers with enormous loss of life. When a call for blood donors went out, people who had never been to New York, disliked New York, and who made jokes about New Yorkers, immediately lined up across the country to give blood, and if their hospital collection point was swamped, made appointments to come back whenever they could be taken. No planes were flying, so structural engineers in Wyoming and Louisiana, medics and nurses in Virginia, steelworkers in Kansas got into their cars and drove to New York to volunteer their help.

I saw an interview with a firefighter who'd come up from Philadelphia. "Won't your wife miss you?" he was asked. "You go out with men on a call," he said, "maybe you walked into their firehouse ten minutes ago, but now they're your mother, they're your wife, your family; nobody thinks of anything but helping each other get the job done." Money for victim relief poured in by the ton, and armed forces recruiting stations were besieged with people wanting to sign up.

You may call this patriotism or idealism . . . I believe it was, if only for the emergency moment, a purpose in life grander than yourself, a more deeply satisfying feeling than the counterfeit joys of making money while afloat on a sea of booze and dope, the unending masturbation of showbiz and trivially entertaining yourself to death—a chance at last to break free from the narrow and forever tyranny of me, me, me.

Commenting on why the attack brought Pearl Harbor so immediately to mind, Harvard historian Ernest May said it was not just the fact of surprise. It also reflected "the idea that this, too, would . . . unite us. I think people were reaching for that." Posters proclaiming "United We Stand" sprung up on every wall.

Our economic system pits people against each other, the competitive "war of all against all." It may be the most efficient ever invented, but in the end is it anything more than getting and spending? It does not satisfy a basic human desire, the one that brought the Philadelphia fireman to New York for no pay: the exaltation of spirit that comes from working together for a noble goal. Here was an instance of community, of human solidarity—emblematic of the kind of group morale that is the healing force in 12 Step programs. When AA speaks of a return to spiritual satisfactions, this is what is meant. Honor and altruism are in us all, one of the joys of life to feel and answer their call. Too bad it takes a national catastrophe to awaken it because by the time this book comes out I think we will see—I hope I am wrong—that kind of external awakening does not last very long.

PS. It is now six months later, and writing in *Time*, Roger Rosenblatt, an intelligent man not devoid of irony himself, said that post-September 11, "The Age of Irony" was over—the hip notion that "detachment and personal whimsy were the necessary tools for an oh-so-cool life" had been found wanting. The altruistic spirit of which I wrote immediately above, he tells us, will now reign supreme.

The *Boston Globe* too editorializes that the grim events of what we have by now snappily learned to call "9/11" have "brought growth, too, and a deeper understanding of just how fragile life is, and how what we often take for granted—the kiss good-bye in the morning, the chat with a friend, the Saturday soccer game—is what matters most." And *The Oregonian* writes: "Something deep inside has shifted."

Yes?

I don't know how it is in Boston or Oregon and will of course accept Roger Rosenblatt's testimony that nobility of feeling is rife in Rockefeller Center, where he works, but out here where I live? Autos still do go by flying (torn and dirty) flags but this morning's news is—in the finest traditions of *après moi le deluge*—Enron execs paid themselves billions while wiping out their employees' pension plans . . . people are suing each other for the T-shirt copyrights to "Let's Roll,"—the slogan of those people who died on the hijacked plane that crashed into the Pennsylvania countryside . . . the sign at the motel next door to the radio station displays a giant American flag with the slogan "Thank You for Travelling," and a new TV ad I saw last night tops even this glorious concatenation of patriotism and business as usual. "You wanna fight terrorism?" says ex–LA Dodgers manager Tommy LaSorda (head shot, extreme CU). "Go out to the ballpark and buy a big foot-long hot dog."

You know, I think maybe Roger Rosenblatt was right.

Tommy spoke with no irony at all.

#21.

Oh, My God, My Kid's Smoking Pot!

Q. My name is Ralph. I'm thirty-two and was awarded custody of my twelve-year-old son, Ferris, when his mother was found unfit (heroin). He's a levelheaded kid, but still misses his mother. One reason I guess is because living with me isn't all that easy; I have a bad temper.

But, Bill, when I came home from work two days ago, my God, there was Ferris and another twelve-year-old, smoking pot. I threw the other kid out, and almost yelled the house down around Ferris's ears, but when I calmed down, I remembered I smoked some pot too at that age. I *know* his mother did. Was I lucky it stopped for me there? For how many kids is smoking pot a gateway drug to all the rest?

A. The message slip at the radio station merely said, "Call Ralph, wants to talk off air." I remember feeling vaguely irritated when I phoned, as if I'd known this Ralph before in some dim, Proustian past. What was this tide of resentment he resummoned in me?

Parents notoriously lose credibility when they try to frighten their kids off smoking pot by delivering the gateway drug lecture. "Ninety-nine percent of heroin addicts," they say, "smoked pot first." Et cetera. Yes, and 99 percent also drank milk and rode in a car before they ever lit their first joint. Are Elsie the Cow and the family Buick Riviera gateway drugs too?

Post hoc, ergo propter hoc: a mistake in freshman logic. No matter. One puff—parents thunder—and you're hooked. You start with pot and that opens the gate, inevitably you go on to heroin and crack, die early and in jail . . . and on and on. Since their children have already been smoking dope for years with no visible ill effects (yet) by the time Mom and Pop think they're old enough for this lecture, the kids just smile and say sure, sure, whatever, and the old saying, *Don't trust anyone over thirty!* gets another generational lease on life. Things were different when I was growing up.

In those days, nobody wanted to be hip or cool, the words unknown in their current meaning. People wanted to be *respectable*.

Divorce was a scandal, for movie stars only. Men wore hats front to front, women wore gloves in the street, no four-letter words in the movies. *Ladies* had not yet become an insult, *gentleman* meant something more than carrier of the Y chromosome and in insurance company surveys women declared their dream man was not Mr. Buns O' Steel but, in the phrase of the day, *A Good Provider*.

But such respectability came at a price, putting a premium on hyprocrisy and role-playing plus institutionalizing co-dependency under the slogan, *Togetherness*—which was *McCall's* magazine smarm for lives of quiet desperation. On the other hand I never met anyone in those days who couldn't read.

Characteristically, a big advertising image of the time was The Lord Calvert Man of Distinction: gray-haired captain of industry, dark blue suit, window behind him showing factory chimneys belching smoke— the epitome of "respectability." His opposite, the closest idea then to being hip or cool was "bohemian," meaning, outside society. A pejorative word in those days but now, when even the guy at your bank offers you a toke while helping you shade an application for a car loan, no longer much in use.

And then came the sixties and the Baby Boom: the profound sociological revolution we are living through still. Society decided it no longer wanted to be respectable but to be young. Teen agency no longer was merely a time of trial for families to live through, the smart-ass kid with acne became the cynosure of our manners, morals, and commercial arts. And didn't the engines of commerce rev up!

The Boomers were a brand-new, well-heeled, huge and cohesive market for clothes, clubs, music, movies, shoes, games . . . How do you sell someone something? You flatter him for having the good taste to buy it. How do you flatter someone who has done nothing? You flatter him for being young and the cameras enshrined the mindless rebellion and knee-jerk attitudes of the fourteen-year-old boy as the sign of—new phrase— being with it. What advertiser was going to spend millions to tell kids listen to the hard-won wisdom of their parents? Nobody made money that way. Tell the kids instead what was important was to know the latest Rock Top 40—*that* was how you made money.

Booze? That was *old*, what your parents did.

I was in the Haight during San Francisco's 1967 Great Summer of Love, and can remember thirteen-, fourteen-, and fifteen-year-old runaway kids, not two minutes off the Greyhound and already asking, "Hey, man, where do we score some dope?" For most of them, a passing phase. Those kids are in the boardroom today, in Wall Street, the law offices, and the United States Senate, running giant corporations, running the world. But a lot of them too are dead. And so while I do not want to give the impression I feel even some booze and dope use must lead to addiction, neither do I want to seem to condone their use by kids. Trouble is, many people who grew up in the sixties continue drug use even when parents themselves.

"A twelve-year-old boy with a heroin-addicted mother is going to be in emotional pain whether he seems 'levelheaded' or not," says Lindley Hainsworth, Addiction Counselor at Oasis Treatment Center, Anaheim, California. I had asked her about "Ferris" (above). She had no comment on the kids I saw in San Francisco, but agreed with me that "lots of young people experiment with alcohol and pot and never go on to heavier drug use."

"How does Ferris's mother being addicted to drugs enter into the boy's prognosis?"

"That means he's predisposed to addiction himself."

"Can the father play a role in changing Ferris's pot use?"

"That's more urgent than the kid's use of pot. What are the boy's feelings about his addicted mother? If she is clean, sober, and available, she should be brought back in some role into the boy's life. And how does Ferris feel about living alone with his dad? The boy's pot use seems to have come as a total surprise to Ralph. How much attention is he paying to his boy?" How much, indeed, I thought to myself, and like an iceberg sliding into the sea, a memory of my own, frozen in time, slid into view. Ralph reminded me of my father and I wondered if it was too late too for Ralph and his son.

Growing up with my father was like growing up on the slopes of a volcano. A seething cauldron of a temper, you never knew what would set him off. I can remember huddling in bed at night, frightened at hearing him roaring at my mother. "Philip, please, Philip," I can hear her still. "Please, Phil, you're frightening little Billy to death." "He's a level-headed kid," my father would roar on. "He'll be all right."

Yes?

By the time I was thirteen or fourteen, my father's temper had already lost him his two eldest sons and he began to make some tentative gestures toward friendship with me—taking me to the ballgame, buying us hot dogs, asking what I thought of the left-handed pitcher. I never enjoyed these trips. It was too late. I never knew when his rage and anger would again erupt. He could never regain my trust. He had a heart attack while I was in the army.

The Red Cross flew me home. My mother and one brother met my plane. "He keeps saying that when he sees you again," my mother said, "he will be all right." What can that mean? I thought. What he had always expressed to my face was that I was just one more of his disappointments. *Bill, you're eighteen years old,* I said to myself, *and a soldier. When you see him in the hospital, ask him what that means. Could he really have missed you?*

The question was never asked. My father died that night, silent and alone—as mysterious and frustrating in death as he'd been in life.

I remember another time, Polly and I walking along under the palms facing scrabbly Smathers Beach in Key West. Without warning, I had been served divorce papers in New York the day before. "Polly, I swore growing up I'd never be like my father, but there I was, red-faced and yelling—"

I'd thrown the toaster through the microwave window.

I said I felt ashamed.

"Have you had a drink?"

"No."

"So far so good," Polly said. "When your Dad died, when you saw his coffin being lowered into the ground, Bill, what did you feel?"

"Relieved."

"Better do something about that anger of yours. Want that to be your epitaph too?"

And so, Ralph, I'd like to say that to you. Perhaps your son's pot smoking is less a problem than your own addiction to anger. When you die, do you want your son's epitaph to be that he was relieved you were gone? Some therapy might be in order, and before it's too late, be a father to your son.

#22.

Bill, My Mother's Turning into a Lush!

Q. My mother's father died of alcohol, and so she never drank her whole life. She's sixty-four, I'm forty-four, my name is Hank. When my father died, my mother moved in with an old friend, a widow too. Last year, when my mother had a bad cold, her friend said a hot bourbon toddy would make her feel better. My mom's been drinking ever since. . . .

At first I thought, well, she has so few pleasures left . . . why not let her drink the best? I bought her some Bottled-in-Bond Old Crow. Then her doctor called me up and bawled me out. He said mom's on high blood pressure medicine, and shouldn't drink at all. The last time he saw her, she was banged up and bruised. My mother's become a falling-down drunk!

I'm not a member of AA, but I got hold of a lot of their literature. It made sense to me: If you think you can slow down, you're fooling yourself. You have to cut it out entirely. But when I asked my mother to read the stuff—I even offered to go with her to an AA meeting—she said she was old enough to know what she was doing.

I can't tell you how many fights we've had about her drinking. The last time I saw her, I was so sick at heart that I slammed out. Bill, my mother's killing herself. What can I do?

A. In his memoirs, André Malraux describes how, nearing eighty, he went back to the village where he'd been born. He looked up a boy-hood pal, now a priest. As I remember it, the great French novelist said to his old friend, "Pierre, in my life, I've seen wars, plagues, revolutions, the inside of prisons, the death of kings, the fall of governments. You've been a priest for over fifty years. You've heard thousands of con-fessions, but rarely traveled more than twenty kilometers from the house where you were born. What have you learned?"

"There are no grown-ups," said Father Pierre.

Remember the Haight-Ashbury Summer of Love, San Francisco 1967 . . . fourteen-, fifteen-, and sixteen-year-old runaway kids, get-ting off the Greyhound bus, asking for the nearest place to score some dope . . . the eighteen- and twenty-year-olds who made up the slogan, "Don't trust anyone over thirty . . . ," the kids who were there, who turned the whole world onto rock-and-roll, sex, and dope?

Where are they now? They are the Boomers, the fifty-year-old gen-eration in the Senate today or in the front office and running the banks, no longer in rebellion, but running the world.

"They're the grown-ups now," said Terry Haynes, a clinician specializing in mental health services for older adults in the county where I live. "And one of the clouds in their sky is that their parents are getting old, and often need their children's care. The sad joke is that the generation who, as you say, turned the world onto sex and drugs and rock-and-roll—how appalled they are to learn their own, once strait-laced parents have become addicted in their senior years."

I told Terry that in my years in recovery circles, no matter how often I've heard that old theme song that a drink is one of the few pleasures left in an aging parent's life, I've never yet met an addict at any age who was not overjoyed at being released from bondage to chemical pleasure. I went on to ask if, in his work, he often ran into cases like Hank and his mother.

"Often enough to have worked out a little strategy. By the time I see people like these, they're at loggerheads. Mom is not going to take orders from this kid she can remember she once had to diaper. Instead of siding with Hank (as Mom expects), and sternly forbidding her to touch a drop, I come in as her white knight.

" 'I know how hard it would be for you to stop,' I say, and then to her surprise, merely ask her to slow up a little.

"Bill, when my client is sixty-eight, any little gain is a plus. Of course, I have to handle the son too, and explain what I am doing: Half a loaf is better than none.

"I don't expect absolutes but when Mom sees I'm not threatening to cut her off entirely, a bonding process begins—the two of us against her hard-nosed son. In time, that may allow me to get her to join a senior support group, *maybe even wean her from alcohol entirely*."

"Is there a lesson here for others worried about their parents?"

"As Mom and Pop get older," he said, "high blood pressure pills and other medications play an increasing role in their lives. The abuse of alcohol can aggravate a whole slew of maladies like heart disease, arthritis, glaucoma, diabetes, pancreatis, colitis, gastritis, and ulcers. Their liver is slowing up, unable to oxidize alcohol the way they are used to. So more and more, these problems come up. The lesson is, very often, a professional third party, someone like me, can see a way out of the mess that the people enmeshed in it cannot."

"Where does someone reading this book find a Terry Haynes?"

"Every county in America has a mental health service," Terry said. "Pick up the telephone book. Start there."

#23.

Am I an Alcoholic/Addict? (Last Time)

Q. Maybe my favorite quotation from Omar Khayyam is the one that goes something like, "I wonder what the vintners buy/Half so precious as what they sell." So you see, I'm not one of those who come crying to you for help.

You can call me Al. I drink and do drugs when I'm happy, I drink and do drugs when I'm sad. I do it because the sun is out, or because it's raining. And in between I drink and do drugs because they make me feel better.

One of my favorite jokes, the guy goes into the Magic Liquor Shop and the sign says "The Forever Full Bottle of Gin, It Never Runs Out," and the guy says, "I'll take two."

I'm twenty-nine years old and I feel the meaning of life is found in a few rare and intensely poignant and exuberant moments, and all the rest is boring time filling up the in-between. Booze and dope get me through that. Without them it would be too dreary to get out of bed in the morning. In other words, I *choose* to drink and dope.

Friends keep coming around—blue-nosed Good Influences, I call them—who try to tell me that I am an alcoholic or dope fiend. Are you going to be another Good Influence, Bill, you too going to tell me that I'm addicted?

A. Al, do I detect an unspoken desire to be a poet or writer yourself? If we're going to play favorite quotations, let me name one or two of my own. The first says, "Eat, drink, and be merry for tomorrow we die." To which, Dorothy Parker (I think) replied, "Alas, we never do."

Rarely do we drunks live fast, die young, and make a pretty corpse. Instead, we get old and fat, suffer strokes, run out of friends, lovers, money, and jobs and end up ugly and homeless.

Despite your bravado, Al, something like that must be on your mind. Else, why call me? But I don't see my role as going around, diagnosing you as addicted or not. I can give you some signals that mark the path, and, after that, you tell yourself.

To begin, Al—what you tell me about drinking is close to what I used to feel myself. I once wrote a column for the *Village Voice* (later published in book form) called "Saloon Society,"—weekly, I hope high-spirited and humorous, sketches and vignettes on the life my friends and I led "three martinis closer to the moon" in the bars of Greenwich Village (see Q. #1). I've just reread some of those old pages. Were my drinking days really that much fun?

Drunks romanticize drinking and memory often lies, flatters, or forgets the bad times, but luckily I have an accurate and sober witness to call upon.

"Booze never made you angry or sullen, you did not change personalities. You never got into fights," says Beverly Lovejoy, who was still called Bartlett on a long ago night in the White Horse (Q. #3) when I turned to see her raise her arms to knot a scarf at the nape of her neck and I fell in love and things went on from there—one of them being the pleasures of drinking together.

In time we came to that point in the developmental and biological pas de deux where the girl thinks maybe it's time to get married, and the boy thinks well, maybe not yet. The jazz critic Nat Hentoff once wrote that Billie Holliday never sang an unhip note in her life. Beverly never said an uncool word. There was no poison, ultimatums, or deadlines, no tears or reproaches. Bev was beyond all that from birth.

"You see that boat?" she said to me one night, pointing to a ship I later learned was the *Hanseatic*. We were in a taxi speeding along the West Side Highway, the great ocean liners of the world docked right there in the heart of Manhattan, alongside the elevated road. "I have a reservation next month, sailing for France. You can join me if you wish." I saw her off with champagne, and I've described how one of my rueful *if onlies* over the years was that I did not stay on board. I went back to the White Horse instead and had a drink.

Time went by. She married some other people. I did too. And then (after a parenthesis of some thirty years), one hurricane-laden Florida afternoon she phoned from California and invited me out for a visit. I got in my car, drove three thousand miles and never went back, selling my little Key West house on the phone ("Yes, the pots and pans and books, the sofas and beds, the CD player and TV, if you have no use for anything, the clothes in the closets too, give them to the Salvation Army.") That was seven years ago and we are partners today both in life and in a house—a break in the past mended, my life healed and come round full circle. It was Bev's idea that my radio program could be the basis for this book, and she was my first reader, first editor too.

In the years when we were apart my drinking speeded up and became pathological. Bev's slowed, and today she can have a martini or a glass of wine before dinner and—true mark of a nonalcoholic—not even bother to finish it if her mood changes.

Bev goes on: "I remember one Saturday morning, you called up our friends and told them you had just signed a contract, come out to Lüchow's and help you celebrate. Maybe a dozen people showed up and you bought us all champagne and oysters. There was no contract but you had a good job and wanted everyone to feel as guiltless about spending your money on food, booze, and good times as you did.

"Very often," she added, "we'd bring them all home with us, the party'd go on till Monday morning. You'd drink some Yoo-Hoo (a chocolate milk drink popular in those days), some aspirin for your head, get in the shower and come out, clean, combed, shaven, gray flannel suit, button-down white shirt, and off to work. You were like a four-color ad for drinking."

So to answer you, Al, in your own frame of reference, I would say that I too, at twenty-nine, did not drink out of stress or sorrow, but out of exuberance, a desire to transcend the dailiness of life: the laundry and grocery shopping, taking out the garbage, and going to the dentist. Alcohol was a great and good friend who would never let me down.

I was bulletproof.

Yes?

I may have been drinking for the fun of it, but in the end (Q. #1 again), that did not keep me from drinking my way into two hospitals in ten days. Alcohol is a drug, perhaps slower in its addictive powers than others, but drink enough, long enough, and it does not care why or how you started, it takes physiological and psychological hold of your system. Two questions come to mind.

First, granted that she weighed fifty or sixty pounds less, Bev's drinking, for her weight, matched mine. Why did she always remain cool and beautiful even if we drank till 3 or 4 A.M. when they closed the bars, how was she able to slow up without even thinking about it and is now able to drink moderately and with enjoyment?

Second: Why was I the one who ended up addicted?

Dr. Abraham Twerski is the founder and medical director of the famous Gateway Rehabilitation Center in Pittsburgh, Pennsylvania. He is also a rabbi, a psychiatrist, chemical dependency counselor, and author of the book *Addictive Thinking*, the best guide I know to understanding your own self-deceptions. I sent him the above to read, and asked for his comments.

He said my caller (Al) reminded him of a patient, "Clancy, who felt the difference between an alcoholic and the nonalcoholic is that for the former, alcohol adds color to life. 'My life was like the area around St. Helena after the eruption,' said Clancy. 'Everything was covered with gray. My wife was gray, the kids were gray, my job was gray, my car was gray . . . I couldn't stand a gray world and alcohol gave it color.' "

Dr. Twerski, whose books often focus on the alcoholic's problem of low self-esteem goes on: "A world in which a person sees no ultimate purpose for oneself is a gray world, which may be intolerable. . . . Alcoholism and drug-addiction are testimonies to the failure of hedonism as a philosophy of life. Without an ultimate purpose, the world can indeed by intolerably gray."

For an answer as to why my drinking speeded up and became addictive, while Bev's slowed down and became purely social, I turned to my wise and acerbic friend, clinician Larry Bouchard.

"Bill," he said, "the answer to why Bev didn't get as drunk as you, why she was able to slow down, lies in the realm of genetics, brain chemistry, individual biology, etc., meaning, 'nobody knows.' The literature is filled with people given potentially addictive painkillers like Demerol, morphine, codeine, etc., because of cancer or back trouble, and after they're cured, they just stop taking the painkillers with no trouble at all. Not all people will become addicted. On the other hand, thinking about why you speeded up: Well, I've heard your rap about being a happy drunk often enough not to believe it."

He went on: "What do we know from your story (that I've heard many times)? We know that your drinking turned pathological and ruined your marriage, or so you would have us think. If you'd level with yourself, I think you'll find the dissatisfactions and pressures that led to heavier drinking were the same 'legitimate sufferings' you drank to avoid in the first place. I would say that instead of facing what was wrong with your marriage, you hid from it in booze. The more you hid the more dissatisfied you both became. By the way, experience tells me your wife no doubt used your drinking to avoid underlying conflict too! But the drinker always takes the rap."

"Are you saying we lived together in a more or less make-believe marriage, each holding secret resentments—"

"Each holding resentments," Larry finished my sentence, "until it blew up in divorce. The sad paradox is when an alcoholic like you, Bill, is lonely, he isolates. Liquor and resentment build a wall around you, you're alone in there with your smoldering anger. You're alone even when you're in the same room, the same bed with someone."

"I never said my wife made me drink."

"No, you chose that yourself, chose what you thought was the easier, softer way."

All true. Thanks, Larry.

I'll close with this. If, like Al whose phone call began this discussion, you feel alcohol is just too much fun for you ever to become addicted, let me recommend a little four question self-test—it's on Dr. Twerski's rehab Web site: Gatewayrehab.org. It's private, you score yourself on your own computer, and if, while the test is still up there on the screen, you have any questions about interpretation there are 800 numbers right up there too: Phone and talk to a trained, live human being about do the results you just racked up really mean you.

Al, you might be wise to take it, let's say every year on your birthday. Alcoholism is a progressive disease, one that notoriously tells you that you're all the better for your drinking. If your score doesn't creep up with time, you need no advice from me. Go on your merry way. But if you see your score first inching up, then zooming, you may want to talk to me again. I'm on the air every week.

*   *   *

PS. I just gave this Q&A to Bev to read for the first time. It made her laugh. "The reason I didn't fall into the same states of disrepair as you," she said, "was because you were so busy ordering another round you never noticed I'd already switched to club soda."

#24.

"I Didn't Have a Chance, It's in My Genes"
Is Alcoholism Inherited?

Q. I've been reading the new research that says alcoholism runs in families . . . in our genes. Shakespeare said character is fate, but science says character itself is written in our DNA. My father's joke was, Kevin, you were born into the CIA: Catholic Irish-Alcoholic. He was telling me why he was a drunk, why his father was too, and also three out of four of my uncles.

I'm not an alcoholic yet, but I don't have a chance, do I?

A. Genetic inheritance cannot be denied but even that is mutable. Take the wolf, ancestor of the dog. Generations of selective breeding have changed not only lupine physiology, but psychology too, from that of a killer into that of a pet whose greatest desire is to love you and have you love him. But, Kevin, while that's a fine old sad Irish song of doom and destiny you're singing, I hope you'll tamp down the self-pity long enough to listen to a more hopeful tune.

After ten years of intensive study of the human genome, we now have evidence that notions of strict genetic determinism in Homo sapiens are exaggerated. The discussion that follows leans heavily on Francis S. Collins, Lowell Weiss, and Kathy Hudson, writing in *The New Republic*, June 25, 2001. Collins is Director, Hudson is Assistant Director of the National Human Genome Research Institute. Weiss is an executive at the Morino Institute, Reston, Virginia.

"(O)ur genes play a major, formative role in human development," these writers say, "—and in many of the processes of human disease; but high-tech molecular studies as well as low-tech (but still eminently useful) studies of identical and fraternal twins make it perfectly evident that our genes are not all-determining factors in the human experience."

As my friend Larry Bouchard said earlier, people don't get sober listening to lectures on brain chemistry, and so I don't think it is necessary to go into detailed discussions of serotonin, dopamine receptors, the "long" D4DR gene and all the rest of the new findings revealed by study of the human genome. If you are interested, let me recommend the superb *Genome* by Matt Ridley.

Suffice to say that some of us are born with, on the average, what might be called low levels of feel-good brain chemicals. These are the risk takers, thrill seekers, and long-shot players because these activities boost the brain's level of those chemicals.

Born, as legend says, a drink or two behind.

It does not take much introspection to number myself among them: I love to ski, and if freelance writing isn't economic high-wire acrobatics without a net, what is?

This does not mean we are doomed to become death-defying Evel Knievels, or bottom out as no-hope, Lower Depths drunks. We may inherit a *propensity* for something—that does not mean we must *become* that something.

You may be born with good foot-eye coordination. That does not mean you will be a major league soccer athlete. You have to start early, want to put in the hours of practice, etc. And if you live in a country where soccer isn't played, all you have is a nonnegotiable talent that will never be fully developed, and of which you yourself may be only dimly aware.

A more obvious example: Science and laity alike have long known that there is an hereditary factor that increases—enormously—someone's propensity for violence. It is the Y chromosome. If a violent act is committed, the odds are very great that the person committing it will be a carrier of the Y chromosome, that is, male.

But we cannot therefore say that all Y carriers, all males, must be seen as lacking in free will, or can be assumed, ipso facto, to be inherently possessing violently criminal intent.

Inheritability is not inevitability.

". . . [T]he case of the Y chromosome," write Collins, Weiss, and

Hudson, "is an almost absurd extreme. In the vast majority of cases, genetic factors exert a much smaller influence on patterns of behavior."

You, Kevin, may have a genetic propensity toward alcoholism. That does not mean you are doomed to be one. In *Genome*, Matt Ridley puts it like this:

"(N)o gene is an island . . . Each one exists as part of an enormous confederation called the body . . . The brain, the body, and the genome are locked, all three, in a dance. The genome is as much controlled by the other two as they are controlled by it. That is partly why genetic determinism is such a myth. The switching on and off of human genes can be influenced by conscious or unconscious external action."

Kevin, sing me no more sad songs. You're just giving yourself permission to become a drunk. Whatever your genetic "CIA" inheritance, you do not have to become an alcoholic or doper. You can choose to stop.

#25.

"My Doctor Is No Help"

Q. Bill, you sound pretty well informed, and certainly well meaning. But the road to hell is paved with good intentions. You can call me BK. I'd just feel safer talking to people more professionally trained than you or any 12 Step guru. Where can I go for a discussion of whether I really am an alcoholic? And if I am, what treatment options are available other than the ones perhaps you know about and recommend on your radio show?

A. By all means, BK, talk to your doctor first. Sometimes it does take the authority of a medical man to persuade addicts and alcohol abusers they're in more trouble than they thought. Caveat: In the *San Francisco Chronicle* (February 11, 1999), Dr. Peter D. Hart Research Associates and The Recovery Institute report that 82 percent of physicians report they avoid addressing the problem of alcoholism in their patients, and that more than 60 percent felt their med school training left them ill prepared to either diagnose or treat the disease.

This accords with the experience of a lot of drunks and dopers I've met over the years. AA and NA meetings are filled with people who got started on pills by their doctor and thought it was their guarantee they would never get hooked.

"Doctors want to be able to do something medically," says Keith Humphreys, Assistant Professor of Psychiatry at Stanford University. If you feel your M.D. wants to get rid of you in the eleven minutes his accountant says is the optimal amount he can profitably spend with you . . . write you a prescription for your "nerves" or "anxiety" . . . and tell you to give this coded payment slip to the receptionist, please, as you leave, good-bye—well, perhaps you better look elsewhere.

That being said, "the surprising fact," says Keith Humphreys, "is that the vast majority of people who get over alcoholism do it without treatment at all." But my feeling is if you've read this far, you do want help. My first recommendation still is go to an AA meeting. But here are some other options:

1. There are many forms of treatment. All start with self-admission that you are an addict. To see if you are indeed a member of the club, there's a simple test. Get the famous checklist "Are You an Alcoholic?" at any AA meeting. It's free. (And I promise if you want to just pick up the list, say it's for "a friend" and walk out, nobody will pull a gun and make you stay.)

    For even more privacy, there's a test on the Internet. Click your mouse to: www.niaaa.nih.gov. That's a test you can do alone.

2. For a medically informed discussion of various approaches to ending addiction, go to the Web site for the American Society of Addiction Medicine: www.asam.org.

3. There are 12 Step meetings that bore me and make me wish I had never stopped drinking, others that were uplifting and a lot of fun. Find one you like: www.alcoholics-anonymous.org.

4. Support groups help. Don't feel you have to take the first one that comes along. I find some so groping and depressed, I leave after ten minutes; others lively and interesting. Do a little research.

    PS to BK. Try: www.mentalhelp.net/selfhelp.

    PPS to Canadian readers. The Centre for Addiction and Mental Health (affiliated with the University of Toronto) runs a very comprehensive Web site: www.camh.net. Or phone: (800) 463-6273.

How Do I Stop?

Infatuation . . . ," writes Barbara Tuchman in *The March of Folly*, "is what robs man of reason . . . the Greeks had a goddess for it, named Ate . . . her mother was Eris, or Discord, goddess of Strife . . . The daughter is the goddess . . . of Infatuation, Mischief, Delusion, and Blind Folly . . ."

The words came back to me at a recent AA meeting when I heard some woman say, "I was infatuated with Jim Beam, he was the guy I went home with every night . . . I was in love with crack cocaine."

Sound like you? It sure sounds a lot like the way I used to be. The fun is long gone, and your use has turned pathological and grim. Divorce, lost jobs, lost houses, lost families, auto accidents, and police and jail time, thoughts of suicide fill your life. You hate what you're doing and swear each time not another drop, never another line—and here you are, drinking and using again.

This section details firsthand steps that worked for me and for addicted people I've known over the years. They can for you too.

How to stop—at last, and for the rest of your days.

#26.

Rehab vs. Cold Turkey?

Q. I am forty-seven years old, my job is on the line, and my wife says she is going to leave if I don't stop drinking. I've tried to quit on my own, even gone to a couple of AA meetings, but I was already drunk when I went, got drunker when it was over. Sometimes I use a little coke to get me going in the morning. I am desperate enough to think of going to a rehab. Would my job insurance cover the cost? My Dad says be a man, quit moaning and just quit. Does cold turkey ever work?

A. I've known quitting cold and on your own to work, but it's hard and lonely. And Desperate, if you've been a big user, it's dangerous too. You may need to come down with medical help. But if you do try, experience shows what rarely works is what I hear in your words: some vague desire at the back of your head to quit someday soon.

As a practicing addict, it's hard for you to take advice, but as they say at AA meetings, your own best thinking is what got you here. First step: Get that vague desire out from between your own two ears, and give it some concrete, external structure.

Once a month, I devote my radio show to teenagers. "I made a bargain with my Mom," one sixteen-year-old girl said on the air. "We printed out a contract that I designed on the computer, and I signed it. It said I hereby promised to stop smoking pot on a specific date. I signed it with my father as witness."

"Did it work?"

"All it did was put into paper and ink a promise I had made to myself inside. But it made the whole thing more real."

I think she got it right. You have to do more than merely *want* to stop. Make the commitment out loud. Tell it to loved ones and friends. Name the specific date. One simple idea: Write down the following 4-D steps and keep them in your pocket. Any time you feel tempted to drink and/or use, get them out and read them again:

1. Delay. The immediacy of the desire will pass in time.
2. Deep breathing. It'll clear your head and even maybe give you a little bit of a healthy buzz. Once again, it's delay at work.
3. Drink a glass of water or chew some gum. In my own early days a bit of chocolate helped—but led to trouble too (See Q. #48).
4. Don't brood over it. Do something else. Take a walk, go to an AA meeting, call a sober friend and say you need help.

Simple rules, but effective. However, Desperate, for people like you, I'd suggest something else. Your question about rehabs opens the door to what I feel is one of the most important things I can say.

I've described flying the Atlantic in a blackout and drinking my way into two hospitals in ten days. When I came to in the second, a doctor came to see me. She suggested I go to a live-in rehab. I knew so little about alcoholism I said to her, "What's that?"

When she told me, I laughed. "You actually think some bunch of holy rollers are going to turn me around in twenty-eight days?" But there was something about her—something ironic and fine that saved my life. Within two minutes, I believed her. Dr. LeClair Bissell, one of the most remarkable people I've ever met. She was also connected with a rehab in Pennsylvania, and that's where I went. With the exception of one fifteen-day relapse at the six months' mark, sober ever since.

Twenty-eight days? Why couldn't I have learned all I needed—faster—by reading a book? Maybe by talking to a doctor, or a recovered drunk? Going to AA or by becoming a patient of LeClair Bissell (I later learned how eminent she was) and talking to her? What happens at rehabs? Why do they work better than anything else I know?

I often asked that of people who run rehabs, of addicts who've gone the twenty-eight-day route themselves. The answer often is, "I don't know why it works, but I left floating on a pink cloud. I can't put it into words but it's magic." Not as dumb an answer as one might suppose.

The important stuff that goes on at a rehab is indeed nonverbal. It is not processed through the brain by means of words. Ever read the lyrics to a popular song without listening to the music? The words alone are often flat and trite, even silly. Put music behind them, they take on enormous power . . . magic.

Patients at a rehab attend scientific and medical lectures on addiction, get pounds of literature on the subject, come away with hard, factual information about their life predicament. All this is fine, but the words merely reinforce what they already knew: This chemical stuff is bad for you. It will kill you. Cut it out.

They can't act on it. What is missing is motivation, the power to put that hard, factual information to work . . . the music.

How do you stop, not only today, but for the rest of your life?

The rehab I went to was then called by a historically apt but silly-sounding name, Chit Chat, in Wernersville, Pennsylvania (called the Caron Foundation today). More to the point, it called itself "a therapeutic community." That resonated with me—we helped heal each other. It's the existential experience of going through the rehab live-in process with a bunch of other addicts and drunks—all of whom want to stop too—that changes the self. The heat and intensity melt down the fraudulent old identity as a supposedly cool, sophisticated drinker/doper. A new identity struggles to be born.

Looking back now, I feel that what goes on operates on an almost unconscious level, and has little to do with information, willpower, cognition, science, medical fact, words, or philosophy. You don't have to understand it—you don't even have to be intelligent—for it to work. Living there, being there—the music never stops.

Let's say you have a waiter, a poet, and a stockbroker. There's a war, and you tell them: Run up on that beach and take out that machine gun emplacement.

Fat chance.

The military long ago learned a practical solution to that problem. Group morale—esprit de corps. "Group cohesion," is the official term favored by the American army. Give recruits a uniform and a number, strip them of the superficial marks of who they used to be. Put them through the intense rigors of basic training, hardships they suffer equally, and together. You're in the army now. Group morale buoys them up, loyalty to an entity bigger than themselves, they become bonded as a regiment, welded into a company and a squad—an identity stronger than they ever felt on their own.

"Run up on that beach and take out that machine gun emplacement!" is the order. Group morale heartens them, pride in their new identity as one of a band of fighting brothers keeps them going even in the face of death. They do not want to let the others down. They run up on the beach. The machine gun nest is taken out.

One of the rules for newcomers to AA is the injunction to make ninety meetings in the first ninety days. An effort to build identification with the group as quickly as possible. A very sound idea. But rehabs do the same thing in twenty-eight days, and do it, in my experience, more often, more lastingly. The music, the intensity of the live-in experience changes your perception of who you are.

Entering a rehab, you feel like a new kid showing up first day at school. With your old rules, signs, and landmarks gone, the primitive power of territoriality enters: You're low in the pecking order. Better take your clues from the people who were here before you.

What are all these strange new slogans in the air? "The First Drink Gets You Drunk," you hear someone saying. What does that mean? "Easy Does It." Isn't that too stupid to be freighted with the heavy meaning these people seem to put on it? But these are the rules, and the Number One Rule here—you quickly see—is that the people most admired are the ones everyone feels are going to "make it"—stay sober—on the outside once the twenty-eight days are over. "Stick with the winners," people in rehabs enjoin each other, hang out with those most strongly determined never to get drunk again.

Before you got to a rehab, your friends boasted about how often they got blasted, wasted, high, or drunk; the most admired were those who drank or doped the most. Group ethos—peer pressure—made using the cool thing to do. In this society you've just joined, that's turned upside down: Losers are people who drink and get high.

Nor are the people saying all this Goody Two-Shoes. They're not preachers, not your mother or Aunt Sally. They are hard-core drunks and dope fiends just like you used to be, they've been there, people whose experience you must respect. No longer are you fighting addiction on your own. You're one of a huge, successful fellowship, an army of people who've won over booze and drugs and want to keep winning after they've left rehab. Esprit de corps.

Why do women who would never think of going into a bar by themselves like to go to male strip joints like Chippendale's when they're in a gang? Think about going to a football game by yourself. It's okay, but not too much fun. Now think of going to the same game with a bunch of friends, all rooting for the same team. An entirely different experience. It's a kick, and you want to do it again.

Nor does group morale affect only people in the stands. Hard-headed bookies in Las Vegas factor it in when figuring the morning line. Is the team playing at home, with thousands of partisan fans cheering them on? On a sports talk radio show I listened to last night (I needed something boring to put me to sleep), they asked Pittsburgh's Lee Flowers why the Steelers' defense was playing so well this year. Did Flowers answer with talk about a superior game plan, some technical discussion of Os and Xs? "We're playing like band of brothers," said Flowers, "If you need help, you know the other guys are with you." Call it spirit, confidence, or momentum—group morale plays a dominant role in who wins the game down on the field.

To go back, Desperate, to the question you first asked—yes, I would advise going to a rehab. Living twenty-eight days away from everyone you know, stripped of your old haunts and habits and marks of who you used to be, and hanging out with the winners, is like going to 280 AA meetings in twenty-eight days. The intensity of the live-in experience maximizes the odds in your favor, speeds up development of group morale, the bonding process that my years of sobriety tell me is at the heart of staying sober and enjoying it too.

Some rehabs are wonderful, others less so. What does it cost and choosing the right one are questions too important to kiss off with just this one try. See Qs. #27, #29, and #30.

#27.

You Got Any Proof Rehabs Work?

Q. My name is Benny, a carpenter, twenty-nine years old. When I listen to you talk about rehabs, it's very smooth and rah-rah, but so far, all I hear is that—advice and more talk. Maybe I have a suspicious nature—I haven't yet heard you cite any hard figures on do rehabs work.

A. This question came in on my voice mail at the station, but I'll answer as if on the air.

You don't exactly say you're worried about being addicted yourself, suspicious Benny, but why else call me up? The good news is that sounds like you're worried, and not too far into denial. Otherwise you'd have said the hell with it and had a drink.

Success rates and hard figures are difficult to come by—even the best rehabs treat them as confidential. But there are some I've been able to put together. I think they offer evidence that a good twenty-eight-day rehab maximizes the odds for getting sober and staying that way too.

In a study of 1,083 clients admitted to Hazelden between 1989 and 1991, Dr. Pat Owen of Hazelden, and Randy Stinchfield, University of Minnesota, report that a one-year follow-up showed 53 percent remained clean and sober, another 35 percent had reduced their alcohol/drug use.

The Betty Ford Center too spends a lot of money on follow-ups. In the April 2000 issue of Findings, the Center reports that 120 patients were asked if they'd like to participate. "Twenty declined, 100 agreed to receive and participate in monthly phone calls. Fourteen months later, 79 out of those 100 graduates were still clean and sober."

Not a very large statistical universe, of course, and one has to ask, Did the twenty decline because they knew they were not going to stay sober long? But on the whole, an encouraging estimate, close to results of other top treatment centers. (Figures for 12 Step programs are understandably hard to come by too. I myself believe the ones that say the success rate for AA alone is maybe 20 or 30 percent—less than half that of a good rehab.)

Statistics can be manipulated toward almost any end you like, including doing nothing. "I haven't made up my mind yet, all the figures aren't in." But some of the most important decisions in life are made on insufficient evidence.

Is this the right time to buy a house? Should I marry Sally? The one certainty is that addiction is progressive. If you keep looking for reasons not to do anything about it, it will get worse.

#28.

"I Never Got Laid Sober in My Life"

Q. I'm visiting friends in the Bay Area and just heard your show driving through Sonora, on our way to ski at Dodge Ridge. Bill, I heard your name and thought I'd call. When I tell you my San Francisco friends are Paul and CoCo and that I used to be a dancer in a world-famous company, I think you'll remember me too. Let's say my name is Tom and that these days I'm a choreographer of some note. Here's my life.

Imagine I get a commission for a new dance, perhaps from the Rio de Janeiro Opera. I fly down there alone, and spend two or three months living in a hotel, working on the commission and rehearsing sixteen, eighteen hours and more a day, and going back to the hotel alone at night. I can't speak the language but I'm so revved up I need to drink myself to sleep.

Competitive pressure in the dance world is intense. So is my own perfectionism: My standards are very high; nothing I do is good enough for me. I'm one of those who just don't hear compliments paid them. Kind words fly past my ear as if meant for somebody standing behind me. I always feel I'm a fraud or fake; whatever success I had with my last dance, well, that was a fluke, a mistake, and next time they'll find me out.

I once went to a pretty good shrinkess, and she told me this perfectionism is at the heart of why I drink. In fact, she refused to go on seeing me professionally unless I joined AA. But perfectionism is built into my art. If I ever let myself get complacent or sloppy in my work—well, there's always a ton of young new choreographers waiting to take my place.

By the time the show opens I can't bear to see it. The new dance may get rave reviews, but I'm not there to take a bow. I'm drunk in some bar on opening night with some hot new guy, both of us getting drunker on our way to bed. And when I wake up, my agent phones and says there's a new commission waiting for me to do the same thing all over again in Osaka.

My liver has begun to act up, my blood pressure is dangerously high, and my doctor says at my age—I'm forty-two—that's not good news.

He's another one who wants me to stop drinking. And maybe he's right about one thing. It's taking me longer these days to get over my hang-overs, and I missed a commission last year because one of the board members said something about drinking was making me bad-tempered and hard to work with. And maybe toughest of all, I think booze is beginning to play hell with my potency.

But, Bill, you see, my work and art and how I make my living, my fear of failure and my love of sex—these are the basic elements on which I have built my life. Take one away, the others collapse, and I am diminished.

How can I stop drinking? I never got laid sober in my life.

A. Tom, you don't know what you've been missing.

What's the first thing people do when they meet? "Let's have a drink." Somebody once asked the famously boozy roue, John Barrymore, to describe his worst sexual experience. "Magnificent!" said the drunken old ham.

But art and science, Shakespeare, and Masters & Johnson, all agree: Odds are, Barrymore was telling a lie. Alcohol increases self-confidence and eases inhibition and so may heighten a man's desire. Notoriously it diminishes his performance. You're not the first guy, Tom, to find too much drinking leads to disaster in the bedroom, nor the only one who, next time out, does it again to quiet apprehension of failure, and it gets worse.

Maybe there's one democratic thing to be said for good ol' Jack Daniels: He's an equal opportunity killjoy—just as blue-nose when it comes to disenhancing pleasure in the human female.

My friend Larry Bouchard recently told me about a famous experi-ment. A group of college women volunteered to take a raft of booze on board and then sit through some porno flicks. To scientifically quantify their degree of arousal, pulse pressure was measured ("How do you get that job?" said a friend whom I am too high-minded to name) at the vagina.

The results were instructive: The intrepid volunteers *said* the more they drank, the hotter they got, but the dials and meters said no, their true physical arousal went measurably down. But then, we never did need more evidence that alcohol is a liar, did we?

Maybe, Tom, you're telling us some of your own.

The way you tell your story, it sounds as if you drink too much only when you are far from home, alone, "not able to speak the language," under pressure to choreograph another new and marvelous dance, poor me, etc.

But you also tell us your "shrinkess" fired you because you were drinking—not in some faraway foreign country—but at home, showing up at her office drunk enough, often enough, for her to feel (correctly) she could not continue to treat you. The condescension and diminishment in the title you give her tells me her words hit home, but you did not want to hear it.

All of which adds up to denial even within your own poetic terms of confession.

You know you drink too much, but don't want to know it. You want to go on drinking even though your M.D. wants you to stop, even though it has begun to interfere with your potency and health, and lately with your career too: one of the prime definitions of addiction.

You tell your story so well, I suspect you're hoping I'll say, My dear, poor Tom, you are the exception to the usual rules for ordinary people. Your dedication to a noble art, the way you make your living, the joy you give the world, your lonely nights, all, all entitle you to keep on drinking. Go, you have my understanding and blessing.

Even if I did say it, alcohol would not.

Let me hasten to say, I do remember you, I know and admire your work. I think I understand something of the vicissitudes of the artist's life. None of that matters. My bet is that as your therapist told you, you suffer from insatiable perfectionism, a "sadistic superego" as Freud once put it—an enemy lives within your own breast, an overly strict conscience that does not like you, nor wish you well.

You may think you have outgrown the values, rules, and standards laid down for you in childhood, but I am also Freudian in this: They do not go away. They lay up there in the dark at the back of your brain, the harsh, unconscious, and demanding voices of your past—probably

Mom and Pop—alive and well and come back now as your overbearing conscience, telling you that you're no damn good, never will be.

Result: bitter, rankling, unending low self-esteem. One of the prime reasons people dope and drink.

I agree that the intense, lonely way you practice your art and make your living puts great pressure on you to drink. Addiction is seductive, remembering past good times, forever holding out promises of even better ones to come. You're pretty good at rationalizing, but while you're ruled by addiction, it is very unlikely you will see past those blandishments.

My best advice is get to a rehab. Qs. #26, #27, #29, and #30 will tell you why. Use the time there to get your priorities right. As they say in AA, are you willing to do whatever it takes to get sober?

It's a hard choice, but it's yours. Maybe you will choose to find a new profession. Maybe you will choose to die. At the end of my own drinking career, I used to laugh and say I hoped I'd die dead drunk in a nightclub, champagne on the table and the bill unpaid. I was giving myself permission (disguised as a joke), to keep on drinking, even if it meant I would die. Half the people I used to drink with made the same kind of jokes, and are dead.

Tom, a last thought before we say good-bye: If I hear you right, you take your sadistic superego as a mark of superiority. The false pride and grandiosity, the self-inflation that's fueled by booze will most likely make you think that's where your uniqueness lies, the quality that's made you a world-famous figure.

Thought of that way, it's hard to beat when you're fighting it alone in the arena between your ears. With your own unsleeping perfection-ism forever riding you down, my hunch is despite all your talent, you live with the nagging, frustrating feeling that the glass is forever half empty, self-acceptance so close but still forever just beyond reach— like sucking on a chocolate Hershey Kiss with the silver wrapping paper still on.

A knowledgeable therapist, experienced with this kind of stuff, can be a shrewd ally, speeding up the process of getting rid of all that old-time baggage. I'd suggest you read "Dual Diagnosis" (Q. #38).

Tom, good luck. I hope we meet again. I hope you think you're valuable enough to save.

#29.

Bill, You Never Said What Rehabs Cost

Q. I was listening last week when you gave figures to show rehabs maximizes the odds on recovery. I'm Marcus, thirty-four. My wife thinks I drink too much and maybe I'm beginning to think so too. Your talk was persuasive, but did I miss something?

Isn't AA set up precisely to help you get sober, and isn't it successful with millions of people? What's more, meetings are free, and you go as your schedule allows. My question about a rehab is, can I afford the money, and since I'm an independent contractor (in CPA jargon) can I afford the time?

Would you go over again the reasons you feel AA alone does not do the trick? And second, you never did give a specific dollars-and-cents answer about rehab costs.

A. I never said AA alone does not do the trick. I said going to a rehab maximizes the odds. That's because AA and rehabs go at the problem of newcomers very differently.

When someone decides to stop drinking, s/he's just about as unlikable as s/he will ever be again. You see them at the back at any meeting, maybe dirty or half drunk, skeptical, suspicious, filled with self-disgust and yet half-ass arrogant too—AA may be fine for these other simple people who maybe now and then have a glass of wine too many, but it will never work for so hardened a drinker/doper as me.

And AAs respond in kind.

Why should they immediately warm up to someone like that? The newcomer is just one more in the passing parade . . . people who come to one or two meetings and then drop out, never to be seen again. "Keep coming back," the old-timers say, and after the meeting, go out for *coffee and* together. The newcomer feels bored, angry, and left out, and over a drink, tells the bartender AA is a lot of crap.

Rehabs go at it differently. When I got off the bus in Wernersville, the Chit Chat station wagon was waiting to take me to "the farm," as I soon learned to call it. I asked to stop at a drugstore for toothpaste.

The driver accompanied me inside. "We don't want you buying after-shave or anything like that with alcohol in it," and it came to me that these people had a lot of down-and-dirty experience in a drunk's wily ways—that I was not going to be alone in my fight to get off booze.

Sober, I would resent such interference. As a drunk, frightened of myself, it came across not merely as well meaning, which had never done the job for me yet, but as structure, wisdom, and expert care.

At the orientation lecture later that day, the speaker said, "The nearest bar is two miles down the road. Our gates are never locked, walk out and have a drink any time you like. But when you finish, keep on going to the Greyhound bus station. There are people dying to come take your place. We are a therapeutic community, we help each other stay sober," and the feeling warmed me again; this was where I belonged, I was one of them and I was not alone.

None of this says there aren't numberless people who never went to a live-in rehab, people who did stop through AA alone. This is merely my witness: I believe Chit Chat gave me a running start toward sobriety I would not have found by myself. Now the question of costs.

The counselor who gave the orientation lecture about a therapeutic community that first day was Jerry Shulman, who ran the place with dedication, wit, grace, and vast knowledge. One of the pleasures in writing this book was to find him again, and ask him to go into the economics of recovery (below). After you've read it, I will come back with a final word of my own.

PAYMENT FOR TREATMENT
Gerald D. Shulman, M.A., M.A.C., FACATA

Part of your decision on a treatment center will depend on how the treatment provider will be paid. Payment mechanisms include:

- Private insurance including Blue Cross/Blue Shield plans, commercial insurance, and various options for HMOs and PPOs. Coverage will be determined by the specifications of the contract.
- Medicare, which is a federal system providing both inpatient benefits (Part A) and outpatient benefits (Part B) if the premiums have

been paid for this benefit. Medicare is available for people over 65 or those who have been disabled for at least two years and on Supplementary Security Disability (SSD);

- Medicaid, which is a state system of health care reimbursement for people who meet certain low-income criteria. Medicaid reimbursement policies, which may be called other things in different states (e.g., Medical Assistance), vary from state to state.
- State funding other than above is often available, either to pay for the treatment of a particular individual at a specific treatment program or for funding the operation of the treatment programs;
- Direct first-party payment in which the patient or other concerned persons pay directly for treatment, which can be considerable, particularly for the more intensive levels of care.

Be aware: There are often copayments for treatment which is reimbursed by insurance (as well as the need to meet a deductible amount of the policy), so even with insurance, there might be hundreds or thousands of dollars at issue. ALWAYS ask the treatment center about your insurance coverage, if you have it, and exactly how much will be owed beyond what the insurance covers.

More: Treatment programs often provide free assessment, but there's a potential conflict: The assessor may look at only those levels of care offered by that particular treatment program. For an objective referral:

- *Physicians,* including psychiatrists who specialize in addictive disorders, may be found by calling ASAM (the American Society on Addiction Medicine) at (301) 656-3920;
- *Psychiatrists* who specialize in addictive disorders may also be found by calling APA (the American Psychiatric Association) at www.psych.org or phone (888) 357-7924. Ask for a list of Board Certified Psychiatrists with Subspecialty Certification in Addiction Psychiatry;
- *Psychologists* who specialize may be found at www.apa.org or by calling the American Psychological Association at (800) 374-2721 and asking for the names of Division 50 members in your area.

* * *

Final word to Marcus: If you're still asking, can I afford the time, can I afford the cost—ask yourself how much money have you spent on your addiction, how much time pursuing chemical pleasures . . . and how much is the rest of your life worth?

If you still say you can't afford to go, ask yourself this: Do you really want to get sober?

#30.

How Do I Choose the Right Rehab?

Q. I'm thirty-three and been drinking (doing some pot, a little crystal too) since I was fourteen. Let's say my name is Doubtful. After my third DUI, I finally had to admit that I'd "crossed the line," as they say in AA. I believe I'm an alcoholic, and have gone to a half dozen AA meetings. But I'm doing hard-time sober. The old-timers say I'm "white-knuckling it." I'll admit right here thoughts of suicide cross my mind—*ideas that never come to me when I'm drinking.* And so after a week or two sober, one time forty-seven days, I can't resist taking another drink, and getting some ease from these black thoughts that way.

Another thing old-timers say bugs me. "You didn't become an alcoholic overnight," they say. "The same amount of time it took you to cross the line—that's how long it's going to take you to reach full recovery." Bill, say what you like about booze, you take a drink, you feel better right now.

But I can't keep getting DUIs and all the other things that go with drinking. I once heard you say your twenty-eight days in rehab were like compressing a year's AA into one month. My medical insurance would cover it. But I am not sure I can afford the time. And like anything else, there must be good rehabs, and bad ones. How do you choose a good one?

A. The drunk looks down with detestation at the drink on the bar, the coke addict chops a line on a mirror and hates what he sees—in the moment before they lift that drink, snort that line, the problem seems so simple. *This is my last one. Then I'll stop.*

As the sign on the wall says, Free Beer Tomorrow.

And tomorrow never comes.

"Why not?" says the addict's family. "Why can't he Just Say No?"

"Because," says Dr. Dave Moore, "chemical dependency is a progressive life disability, affecting your total personality. It's a primary disease: You must put recovery first. It's chronic too: You're never 'cured,' and must plan for a lifetime of recovery. The problem isn't in the addict's glass, nor in the smack in his spoon. It's in himself."

Before joining the faculty at the University of Washington, Dave was Director of the McDonald Center rehab at Scripps Memorial Hospital, San Diego (where I was once a facilitator myself). He ran the place superbly, and in my dealings with him I found he combined ease and clarity of explanation with a vast command of technical knowledge. I had him on my show several times as a guest, and now that he's back in academia, turned to him for an objective answer on how to choose the right rehab. I will quote him at length because he's not only a guide for the addict thinking about entering a rehab, but for his/her family too, wondering how they can help.

Dave went on: "I once directed the largest outpatient treatment system in the Northwest—for people who won't go for twenty-eight-day round-the-clock, live-in rehabilitation. Like AA itself, a good, sound idea—"

"But not first choice," I said, "for someone asking your counsel?"

"Doubtful's best bet is to enter residential treatment and begin to plan a whole new self, a whole new life. So many of my friends send their children off to a summer basketball camp, a residential training program, or a church retreat for a month. Then, when it comes to something far more important than learning to dribble, navigate a computer, or spend time studying scripture—they say they can't afford a month's residential treatment to begin recovery from addiction.

"Choosing the right rehab," said Dave, "opens a door into a community of recovery: medical, social, and vocational services staff, faith community, and families of other recovering persons. I'd choose one with at least fifteen years' experience, and run on the 'Minnesota Model' endorsed by the AMA. It is also important that there is outside review. The two national accreditation bodies are CARF (Committee for the Accreditation of Rehabilitation Facilities) and JCAHO (Joint Commission on Accreditation of Health Organizations)."

"Any red flags to look out for?"

"Something you wrote yourself, Bill, goes to the heart of the one caveat I'd name. ' . . . A good rehab operates on an almost unconscious level, and has little to do with information, willpower, cognition, science, medical fact, words, or philosophy. You don't have to understand it—you don't even have to be intelligent—for it to work. Living there, being there—the music never stops.' By music, you mean a sense of union, of group morale?"

"Yes," I said. "Where did the problem come in?"

Due to economics, Dave said, "Some rehabs are forced to accept court-mandated or otherwise publicly funded patients. These people often resent being there, and their negative attitude undermines the group morale that's at the heart of the therapeutic process—everyone united to reach the common goal of sobriety. If the number of publicly funded patients is more than 30 percent, that's a red flag."

"Does it matter if the rehab is big or small?"

"This is where numbers enter again," said Dave. "Are there enough people to feel truly like a community? Twenty people in a facility for thirty feels full and bustling. Twenty in a facility built for seventy feels like rattling around in an empty warehouse. You won't get the human heat, the nonverbal music as you call it, that melts resistance and denial."

"I once heard you say the daily experience in group is the engine that drives treatment, the addict's most powerful agent for change?"

"In a good program," he said, "you spend at least two hours daily in group, facilitated by a counselor in recovery too. The groups should be gender separate. The only exceptions: seniors or relapse-prevention groups where the persons have been through treatment before."

This brought memories of my arrogance at my first group therapy session at Caron. "Hadn't I stood at the very bar in the White Horse where Dylan Thomas drank himself to death? Hadn't one of my favorite writers, Scott Fitzgerald, told Edmund Wilson that alcohol fueled his prose? I had some childishly romantic notions about booze and a writer's life. When I mentioned this in group, I thought, well, they're going to see that I'm different. They laughed at me."

"That's the power of the group," Dave said. "If one person had laughed, you might have got mad. The whole group laughing?"

"I joined in," I said, "that grandiosely stupid illusion gone."

"Exactly," Dave said and went on to his second point to look for in picking a rehab. "Visit the program. Best time is evening when the residents are on their own. They will be your 'family' for perhaps the most intense twenty-eight days of your life. Are you attracted to some and are there others who, yes, revolt you? Good. We need to learn to relate to a wide, wide range of alcoholics and addicts."

Dave went on: "Talk to some of the program's alumni to see how they feel. Gratitude and involvement demonstrate: a) the program has maintained trust with its graduates, b) you'll belong to a network yourself when you graduate, and c) the program is at the center of a 'community of recovery' and nurtures such alumni involvement."

"Third, the best programs (e.g., Sundown M Ranch, Caron, Hazelden, Betty Ford) are led not by M.D.s, but by their chemical dependency counselors, *the overwhelming majority of whom are in recovery themselves.* None of this is meant to say there need not be a good medical director to supervise the patients' medical recovery needs.

"Fourth, does the program director have background as a counselor and is s/he in recovery? Will your own primary counselor be a recovering person? Is there a psychologist on staff or is the staff physician a psychiatrist? Most mental health problems clear up with standard chemical dependency treatment, but when people like Doubtful talk about ideas of suicide, it's wise to have a professional who can detect what we shorthand as dual diagnosis problems—those requiring mental health assistance even once sobriety is attained."

I told Dave I had never been to a 12 Step meeting until I was in rehab. "That was for winos. I was above all that."

Dave smiled. "A good rehab introduces you to regular in-house 12 Step meetings, and works through resistance to going to meetings after you've left treatment." The talk logically turned next to aftercare, which I had been trained to facilitate at Scripps McDonald.

"I saw firsthand how valuable it can be for people newly out of rehab." Dave said the most important feature of aftercare is the quality of group therapy that is offered. "It should include a number of persons who are there voluntarily, once again, not simply court-mandated.

There should also be family counseling sessions arranged over the first six months of aftercare."

I said that at Caron I'd been struck by Sundays, when families would visit. "You'd see people coming together after years of pointless wrangling and bitterness. Some marriages came back together, some people decide they would be better off apart."

Dave said the best rehabs today have gone even further in integrating family with treatment. "Before you sign up, find out how many of the residents have family that attend the family program. There should be an opportunity for the safe sharing of feelings between a recovering person and their family. Sometimes this is done in just a family session (often called a "conjoint") and sometimes in group (often called a "knees to knees" session because the family members sit face-to-face and knee-to-knee, surrounded by other group members).

"There should be opportunity for the family to visit one day a week and, if possible, to attend an Al-Anon meeting while the resident attends an AA or NA meeting."

We were coming to the end of our talk. I told Dave that while I'd had some figures from the Betty Ford Center on their success rate, I felt the data relied on too few cases.

"What do we know for sure?" I asked.

"Here at the beginning of the new century," Dave said, "we have about three decades of treatment research on people who go through private residential treatment centers. By private, remember that I mean a residential program with no more than 30 percent publicly funded patients. In such well-run programs we can expect these outcomes within the first three years:

- 4–5 out of 10 patients will remain sober
- 1–2 out of 10 will have a serious relapse but regain sobriety
- 1–2 will have a very shaky sobriety and a poor quality of life ("dry drunk") between relapses
- 2–3 will resume active use and progress rapidly toward an early death or institutionalization

"The figures are significantly worse," Dave said, "in a program that has fewer of the components we've been talking about. My best advice is *not* to rely on the addict's HMO to dictate which treatment program they enter. There is no reason a family cannot pool their resources and send the addict to a program with higher probabilities of success. Amortize that over a lifetime's sobriety, it isn't much to pay."

"Finally," I said, "is there one book you would recommend an addict to read for more detailed advice?"

Dave did not hesitate. *"I'll Quit Tomorrow,"* he said, "by Vernon Johnson—the definitive primer on chemical dependency treatment, and an exact description of how group should work. In my own signed copy, which, as a recovering person, I often open, this is the last thing he wrote:

"In families where recovery is successful, a truly new life may begin. Parents and children will find a new affection in their understanding and trust of each other, a new depth in their open communication with each other. One survivor felt he had been blessed by this whole new life. 'Thank God I'm an alcoholic!' " he said. 'I just might have missed knowing and appreciating life as it is now.' "

#31.

"Sponsor? Who Needs a Shoulder to Cry On?"

Q. Call me No Smoke, twenty-two years old, sober five months. One thing I learned early in AA is that I was smoking dope as a crutch . . . to get me through the hard places in life. Through working the 12 Steps, I've learned to clean up my act, apologize to people I've hurt, and face the future on my own sober two feet. Having a sponsor seems to me to be going backwards, another crutch to get me through the hard places, a shoulder to cry on. I don't need that.

When I told that to some guy at a meeting, he said, No Smoke, when you're home alone with thoughts like that, you're in a war zone and the enemy is listening. He said I'd be better off if I had a sponsor to help deflate my ego, which he said was busting out all over the place. Bill, when I listen to you on the air, you rarely mention a sponsor. Do you have one? Have you ever been one? I bet you don't believe in them yourself.

A. When I think back to getting out of rehab, I can see now everything they told me about finding a sponsor as soon as possible was
true. But hadn't I been exceptional all my life? I could do it on my own.
I didn't want to drink right now, true. But who knew about later? In a
few months, maybe a year, I'd make a calm and rational decision about
that for myself. I certainly did not need to argue that self-evident
proposition with any know-it-all sponsor. As you can see, No Smoke, I
was a dumb, smugger, more self-satisfied version of you.

And so when I came to the six months' sober mark at 3 A.M. one
New Year's Eve without having had a drink, I knew I had alcohol licked
and the idea of celebrating the victory with a glass of champagne
seemed just right. (If this seems nutty to the casual reader that merely
proves you're not an alcoholic.) Let's play the conversation the way it
would have gone if I'd had a sponsor.

Me: *"I'm going to celebrate six months' sobriety by having a glass of champagne."*

Sponsor: *"You're suffering from an irony deficiency, Bill. You better have
your head candled."*

Without a sponsor, the debate went on between my own ears. The
relapse lasted the worst fifteen days of my life. I can see now that old
habits of infantile omnipotence, fear of dependency, and false pride
were at work. I have not made that mistake since.

Years later, discussing this relapse, my friend Polly said, "A good
sponsor would have seen right off that you hadn't fully accepted the First
Step—you never really believed yourself powerless over alcohol. You
know how you can often give yourself good reasons for doing this or
that, and they sound fine until you say them out loud to someone else? A
good sponsor is that sounding board. Bill, if you'd taken your First Step
with a sponsor, he would have heard the smugness, the rampant ego, and
the lie in your voice. Steps Two through Twelve," she went on, "are
worded with wiggle room. 'We came to believe . . . continued to take
personal inventory . . . tried to carry the message . . . , etc. The First is

the only absolute imperative: *You are powerless over alcohol and can't ever again drink.* You don't get that right, the other eleven don't matter."

This ends the conventional (and more important) part of this Q&A because Polly was by then my sponsor, the best I ever had, which completely goes against everything in the AA manual. If there is one precept everyone agrees on, it's that men should have male sponsors, women women. If you want to read on, what follows is my own opinion born of my own experience.

Of all Freud's disciples, it was perhaps Melanie Klein who took the darkest view of human nature, and her great book *Envy and Gratitude* goes far to explain the nastiness of much in life. When we meet someone of generosity and accomplishment, she says, the healthy course is to admire them, be grateful to know someone of such stature. Instead, she says, all too often we resent and envy them, want to belittle them, look for flaws, *reduce* them to the same small ugly species we feel we are inside. Even if they love and make us happy, we envy their power to make us miserable by taking that love away.

These are the resentful people who bite the hand that feeds them, and she tells the famous story of the viper who stings to death the eagle carrying him across the flood. "Why did you do it?" says the eagle. "I'm going to die, but you're going to drown." And the viper says, "I couldn't help it, it's my nature." Rather than admire the eagle's generosity and strength, the viper's envy caused them both to die.

One of the graces addiction takes from us is generosity of heart. We grow self-centered and cynical, lose the quality of admiration. What made Polly the right sponsor for me was the admiration in which I held her. I admired the way she played the cards she was dealt in life, admired the dry-eyed gaze with which she faced whatever came next, including her own imminent death. You know how compliments from some people slide right past your ear, as if meant for someone standing behind you? When I asked Polly to be my sponsor, she said, "Only if you will be mine."

A compliment I will never forget. I have not had a sponsor since she died, and do not think I ever will. "If you ever feel like taking a drink," she once said to me, "call me up first. Give me a good reason to do it, I'll come around and have one with you."

No Smoke's intuition nailed me on one point. I myself am rarely a sponsor. Given how central to most people's recovery is faith in a Higher Power, that should not be surprising. In Q. #41, I've described my dissent from all that. So if ever asked, I suggest they find someone more closely in accord with their own beliefs.

And finally, if pressed I say, if I don't have a sponsor myself (not since Polly died), how can I sponsor you? It would be hypocritical—do as I say, not do as I do. "But if you think a talk might help," I often say, "one drunk to another, call me, we'll take a walk and go from there." Afterwards, over coffee, I might say something like this:

In my years in AA, I've seen that people who bring only their rear ends to the meeting and not their hearts and minds, who sit at the back of the room, rarely speak, and dart out as soon as the meeting is over—they're the passing parade. After a while, they don't come back.

The people who make it are the ones who sit in the front row, help with coffee or clean-up, speak up, volunteer, and offer their phone numbers to newcomers. *And get sponsors right away.*

They listen intently at meetings and when they hear a speaker they like, often ask her to be their *temporary* sponsor. In time, as they come to know and admire the sponsor, her life and above all, the quality of her sobriety, temporary becomes permanent.

To admire someone means you want to be like her, right?

#32.

"This Sense of Impending Doom"

Q. I'm nineteen years old. When I woke up this morning, I had this old, familiar sense of impending doom. Like there's a hole in my stomach. The only way I ever found to get rid of it is to take a drink. Two vodkas, maybe three, and it's gone.

How Do I Stop?

I've been listening to you off and on for a couple of months because sometimes I wonder if I might be turning into an alcoholic. So I thought I'd phone before I have that first drink.

Where does this feeling come from? Is there any other way to fill that hole if you don't drink? I'll hang up and listen to your answer on the radio.

A. Ah, that sense of impending doom.

How often have I heard those words at AA meetings, especially when people come back in after a relapse. "I had this empty feeling in the pit of my stomach, and I knew a drink, or a line, some crystal meth, a heroin slam would make it go away."

If you're wise, Ms. 19, you'll get yourself to a 12 Step meeting tonight. Because I suspect, since this is Saturday morning, that the unspoken half of your story is you spent Friday night in a bar or drinking alone. Tomorrow is Sunday. Want to wake that way again, the sense of impending doom one day worse?

Before she died, my friend Polly told me something Jung once said (a quote, incidentally, that I have more than once since heard too from my friend, the wise Larry Bouchard): "All neuroses stem from man's attempts to escape life's legitimate sufferings." For the word *neuroses*, substitute *addictions*—and there we are, 19, you and me.

Bad things happen—your own fault or not. Your dog gets run over . . . your boyfriend grows cold . . . a pimple popped up on your nose the night before the prom . . . you got fired or did not get the big job . . . your father does not like you . . . Polly comes down with cancer and dies.

These are our appointed, legitimate sufferings. We have to feel them, go through them, integrate the disappointment into our life, and come out on the other side—I think the saying is *sadder but wiser.*

Growing up is another.

We bury our dog and go through the process of deciding whether it would be wise to get attached to another one if grief feels like this . . . We cry for the lost boyfriend but in the end, well—there are other fish in the sea. We try a new hairstyle and go out to see what life offers. If someone dear to you dies, there is no answer, and we learn we have to accept that too.

The alcoholic instead says, Have a drink and forget it.

Yes? We have that drink, and yes, feel we've gotten over it.

That's the lure of alcohol or drugs. The pain is gone. We seem to have skipped right past our legitimate sufferings. Three cheers and let's have another.

But the relief is only temporary. We sober up. There it is again. We know the answer. Drink some more.

The heartbreak, the stupidity of addiction is: If you're trying to fill a hole in your life with the wrong medicine, you can never get enough. Most people would say, well, that doesn't work—let's try something else. The addict keeps doing the same thing, thinking next time it will be better. The drug—the wrong medicine—becomes habit, our prime problem solver. And the unfinished business, the integration of the unfelt pain, the unmade decision, is again delayed—forever after hanging around at the back of our lives.

(That's why people say alcoholics suffer from arrested emotional development.)

Remember in school when you got a homework assignment Friday to turn in Monday morning? If you're anything like me, you put it off, put it off, and the sense of impending doom grew and grew in your stomach as the hours ticked away toward Sunday night. You watched TV, spoke to your friends on the phone, ate too much ice cream or candy . . . (fill in your escape methods here).

These only eased the feeling temporarily, helped you forget you had unfinished business to attend. When the ice-cream-and-candy fix, the telephone distraction, the TV marathon was over, the hour was later, and you felt worse.

Monday morning that much closer.

Unfinished business.

Impending doom.

Addiction is "cunning, baffling, and powerful." It turns your perception of reality upside down. *You don't drink because you have a hole in your stomach. You have a hole in your stomach because you drink.* The best answer I know to your question, Ms. 19, is another question: What hole in the pit of your stomach are you trying to fill with vodka, which of life's legitimate sufferings are you trying to escape by jumping into the bottle?

#33.

Self-Esteem vs. Self-Inflated Grandiosity

Q. I've been slamming heroin since I was fourteen and have the jail time to prove it. You sound like a know-it-all on the radio, but you're just an old-timey drunk. Your experience is totally different from mine. What makes you think you have anything to say to me?

A. The concept of self-inflation, of grandiosity, is so important in talking about addiction that the 12 Steps are often described as a program for ego-deflation. People with a sense of self-worth are embarrassed by bragging but clutching at any straw to show "superiority," Slammer is emblematic of an old AA bit of wisdom: Addicts are megalomaniacs with an inferiority complex.

Slammer even offers his jail time as proof he ranks higher on the addiction scale than I do. Says Scott Munson, Executive Director, Sundown M. Ranch treatment center, "What a contest! I've seen people pursue this need to be 'important' to amazing lengths. If they can't be the best of the best, they will be the worst of the worst. 'I've been to jail more times than you, and for worse crimes, etc.' "

"After twenty years working in the chemical dependency field," says Sharon Hartman, a Program Director at Caron, "my feeling is hell is hell, whether it is alcoholism, drug addiction, or any of the other lovely monstrous heads that addiction can raise. But with addicts, I take what is given. If Slammer feels comfortable at this stage relating only to drug addicts, then NA meetings are probably best for him."

AA long ago recognized that the guy who has to have the biggest car, the blondest blonde, talks the loudest, and never tires of telling you how rich or smart he is—he doesn't have a big ego. He has a big *false* ego. He may be the epitome of the LOOK AT ME ethos of our time, but behind all that booze and dope and showing off, he feels worthless. He cowers behind his front like the Wizard of Oz, afraid his crappy soul is about to be found out. Where dope and booze enter is

they allow people like Slammer—who know this about themselves—
to pretend they do not. A bit of chemical joy singing in the veins and
self-doubts vanish, grandiosity reigns, and King Canute orders the
tides to recede.

I sometimes think children are born knowing there's madness here
at work. When I was a kid, one of the most damning things you could
say was that someone was "conceited." The Greeks spoke of *hubris,* the
madness and pride that goes before a fall . . . triumphant emperors riding in victory through Rome would have a slave in their chariot whis-
pering, *Remember you are mortal* in their ear . . . medieval kings had court
jesters licensed to tell them difficult truths that flattering courtiers kept
to themselves . . . and Buddhists wisely talk of *unselfing.*

But intoxication goes the opposite way.

"So what if you're a little high," your favorite drug beguiles you.
"Another guy might be afraid to drive in this condition. But you can.
You're *you.*" Freud said there was something nostalgic about grandiosity, a desire for return to "infantile omnipotence," that early time when
we could do anything and nothing we did was wrong. The rest of us
call this, in an adult, a fraudulent front. And so this empty boasting is
not only dangerous to sobriety, it is a vital clue.

Slammer is right about this. A lot of AA old-timers look down their
noses at "drug addicts." So, I suspect, did Bill Wilson himself (see Q.
#58). But as it becomes understood that cross-addiction (booze *and*
speed, pills *and* pot *and* you-name-it) is more often the rule than not,
this prejudice is breaking down. If you've read this far, you know "alcoholic" and "addict" are used almost interchangeably in these pages. For
instance, I often say I am addicted to alcohol.

"What might be of further interest to someone like Slammer," says
Walter Reed, a talented marriage and family therapist in Sonora, California, "is that addiction does not necessarily depend on taking mood-
altering substances into the system. Gambling, for instance, runs the
same predictable route as any chemical addiction, and basically, the
same 12 Steps which give the drug addict or alcoholic his greatest
chance for recovery work for the gambler too. If Slammer continues to
take heroin addiction as a sign of his superiority, his prognosis is not
good. He will continue to be isolated in false grandiosity, unwilling
and unable to share the healing group identity offered by AA or NA."

Walter went on: "There is this to be said for Slammer's argument. To get a drink is easy and legal. Heroin is illegal, and so right from the start, it's an addiction of a more desperate order. But to say you and he have nothing in common is to duck the real issue. Pot, alcohol, or smack, crystal, or any other chemical, the Steps to recovery for any addiction are the same."

#34.

Why Is Crack So Hard to Kick?

Q. I'm seventeen years old, and some kids in my class say the high on crack cocaine is so intense that it is the hardest drug of all to kick. Is that true?

A. In the early nineties, when I wrote a purportedly humorous column for a Key West newspaper, I got to know the owner of a nearby art gallery pretty well. When I wrote about him, I used to call him Harry—intelligent, a Stanford graduate, decently involved not only in the arts but also in local elections, civic welfare, zoning, the environment, etc. He got married shortly after he and I met, a terrific girl, and they bought one of the best houses in town. Prominent citizen, leading member of the community. And then he discovered crack.

There went the house, the marriage, the art gallery, all he owned. He was left penniless. This was while I was mostly in New York, going through my own interminable divorce. Back in Key West one day, having an iced tea with Polly S. at a Duval Street sidewalk café, along came Harry. We invited him to join us. Scrubbed and shorn, about forty pounds lighter than I remembered. He'd given up crack for the blessings of a charismatic, fundamentalist church, "all praise to sweet Jesus," and was on his way to work.

"What kind of work you doing these days, Harry?"

"Dishwasher at a Cuban restaurant, Oh, Lord, how I love Jesus."

The month was July, temperature and humidity on the street both in the upper nineties. I remember wondering what it was in the back kitchen of the restaurant. "Harry," I said, "the house and wife gone, the art gallery, your place in the life of this town . . . any regrets?"

"Bill, you ever tried cocaine?"

"Yes."

"Crack?"

"No."

"Bless me, Lord, I feel You near me. Bill, the crack was worth it."

He left.

"Two varieties of religious experience," said Polly.

No, I never tried crack but the question of its profound addictive powers often comes up. A cover story by Sharon Begley (*Newsweek*, February 12, 2001), "How It All Starts in Your Brain," seemed to go right to the point—knowing and concise, backed by quantitative research.

Mass General is one of the half dozen most prestigious hospitals in America, and at a study done there by Dr. Hans Breiter, Ms. Begley describes how some confirmed cocaine addicts (volunteers, and how!) were given party doses of the drug. Then they were hooked up to an fMRI, which detects active regions in the brain. The fMRI showed "cocaine made a beeline for the pleasure circuits, turning (them) on . . . *and keeping them on*" (italics added).

In another study, at Massachusetts's McLean Hospital, crack addicts were again hooked up to an fMRI tube, and shown a video.

First, two minutes of monarch butterflies . . . no hum. Eight minutes more of what might be called military-and-industrial-strength drug porn: scenes of users ritualistically cooking crack . . . addicts buying the stuff . . . smoking it. At the moment of testing, none of the subjects were chemically high but "it was as if," Ms. Begley writes, "a neurological switch had been thrown: Seeing the drug scenes not only unleashed in addicts a craving for crack, but also triggered visible changes in their brains as their anterior cingulate and part of the prefrontal cortex—regions involved in mood and learning—lit up like Times Square."

Says Dr. Scott Lukas, who led the 1998 study, "The brain regions that became active are where memories are stored. These cues turn on crack-related memories and addicts respond like Pavlov's dogs."

Says Nora Volkow of Brookhaven National Lab, "Drugs of abuse increase the concentration of dopamine in the brain's reward circuits," more intensely than eating a Cordon Bleu dinner or even winning the lottery. (Other studies, however, show the brains of nine out of ten men are, alas, hard-wired in so callow a manner that the mere sight of a pretty face does light them up to the same gaudy degree as cocaine. "And the tenth man," Polly S. once remarked, "is interested in the first nine." If only Mother Nature and Father Evolution had devoted more time to the earnest study of Germaine Greer!)

To get a more direct answer to Seventeen's question, I e-mailed John O'Neill, who teaches pharmacology at the University of Texas. He felt the difficulty in ending a crack habit was "not so much dependent on the drug itself as on the genetic, and consequentially neuropsychological vulnerability of the addict."

Editor of *Findings/Sci-Mat*, a newsletter published by the Betty Ford Center, John added that he'd "seen people at Betty Ford damn near die trying to kick alcohol who got no big high from cocaine." He finished by referring me to his friend, Carlton Erickson, Pfizer Centennial Professor of Pharmacology at the University of Texas.

"Pharmacologically," Dr. Erickson began, "crack and cocaine are equally addicting. Many people believe crack is more so because it hits the brain in bulletlike bursts that users really like. While statistics from the National Institute on Drug Abuse (www.drugabuse.gov) indicate that only 17 to 18 percent of either cocaine or crack users become 'addicted,' our experience is that cocaine dependence is indeed the most difficult to treat. No one knows why except that cocaine seems to 'hijack' (not a scientific term) the pleasure pathway to the brain more powerfully than other drugs."

So, Seventeen, there's only anecdotal evidence to answer your question. One professor of pharmacology says crack addicts are "the most difficult to treat," another says some users never get addicted to it at all. Perhaps the last word belongs to Walter Reed.

As he said to Slammer in Q. #33, and which I suspect holds true for you too—alcohol or smack, crack, crystal, or any other chemical joy you choose, the Steps to recovery cannot be begun too soon no matter what your age and for any addiction are the same.

#35.

Crossing the Line

Q. When Sandy and I met I was married to someone else, and the affair was a little risky and naughty. We got through it by saying to hell with trouble, we'd face whatever happened together. We were always meeting in bars, always in a part of town where nobody knew us. I'm afraid we drank a lot. But that was fifteen years ago, and now it seems like the most romantic time in our lives. We're married now, two children, but sometimes I want to have that extra cocktail with him—"get a little looped before dinner" was how we used to put it in those days. You know, Bill, relive those exciting times.

Sandy says we're beyond the age for that kind of drinking. They're downsizing at his company and he says he can't afford to go into work with a hangover. I think maybe he's afraid of turning alcoholic. In fact, sometimes I think he's already had one or two before coming home from work.

I'm Barbara, forty-four. Sandy's forty-six. At our age, how much is it safe to drink?

A. Barbara, Barbara, Barbara . . . you're like the woman I heard in a commercial last night, saying her wish list is a mascara that won't run, blue jeans that *really* fit, and if only her husband would act like a boyfriend again. In your forties, children, and in your second marriage, my guess is Sandy's right about one thing. That time is over.

At your age, the liver has begun to slow down (see Q. #15)—you can't burn up alcohol the way you used to. If he's worried about his job, and is secretly drinking to allay his fears, that's trouble too.

But for the record:

The National Institute on Alcohol Abuse and Alcoholism says if you have four or five drinks at a time a couple of times a week, you're at risk. When I was at Scripps McDonald, I heard a doctor put it like this: Alcohol reorganizes the brain, even for people who have no genetic predisposition. Maybe you're drinking for the fun of it, he said, with no stress in your life at all—but drink enough, for long enough, and you are very liable to become addicted.

What did he mean by "drink enough?"

The safe amount at which the National Institute draws the line—mark of the "moderate" drinker—is two drinks a day for men, one drink for smaller-bodied women. If you're saying to yourself right now—*Oh, no, that little? That can't be right,* listen a little harder.

That's an alarm bell ringing.

Before we say good-bye, Barbara, let me play your alcoholic Dr. Laura for a final moment. Is there more wrong with your marriage than how much or little your husband wants to drink with you?

Perhaps a good look at your life is in order. First, what are your dissatisfactions in this marriage? Why do you think whatever they are, it's Sandy's fault for not easing them?

Most of all, why think the answer lies, not in yourself—perhaps in your apprehensions of mortality—but in a glass?

#36.

Right and Wrong Way to Do an Intervention

Q. My father is a retired doctor, in his sixties, and I'm afraid drinking himself to death. He says because he's a medical man, he knows exactly how much alcohol the human liver can oxidize per hour, and he never exceeds that. True, he does not drink before 6 P.M., but every night at 6:01 P.M. the cork is out of the Cutty Sark, and he begins.

And while he does start with an exactly measured one ounce of scotch, pretty soon he is slugging them down without measure, and the next day he denies that is what happened. The truth is he drinks till he passes out.

My mother is worried sick, and I am afraid to bring my children to visit their grandfather. I went to an Al-Anon meeting, and someone there suggested we do a formal family intervention, but I'm afraid that would anger my father into drinking even more. Or getting so mad he will never speak to us again.

What is a "formal family intervention," and do they work? Does "formal" mean you need professional help to do it right?

A. A formal intervention is when the family and friends of an addict gather in a prearranged and highly structured manner to face the addict with what he is trying to deny: that he is killing himself, hurting the people who love him most, and if this does not change, there will be consequences he may find unbearable to pay. My own experience is that I botched the first intervention I ever tried.

It began with a tearful call from Sally, wife of an old friend.

"Bill, Perry's locked himself in the guest bedroom; he's been drinking four days. I can hear him cursing the world. Can he have a gun or something in there? You remember Charlie, our son? He just said, Mom, why don't we just put some rat poison in Dad's scotch and put him out of his misery. He's never going to stop before he dies."

"I'll be right over."

Perry and I had once worked together at an ad agency while I still lived in New York. Drinking pals and more, the friendship continuing long after I'd given up the business and gone off to pursue life, love, art, booze, and marriage (with a contract for a novel in my suitcase) in Europe. When I returned, I looked him up, and while the old feelings of friendship remained, they were hard to sustain now that I no longer drank. So I had not seen him in some time.

I do not think I have to describe Sally's state when she answered my ring at her door. Charlie, the son, would not meet my eye—to him, I was just another of Dad's drunk friends. I did not stay to talk to them long. (My first mistake.) Sally nodded at the guest bedroom door. I knocked and said my name. Perry let me in. I'd been sober about five years by then and had no qualms about making a Twelfth Step call. I knew it all.

(The second.)

Red-eyed, disheveled, the room around him reeking of booze, vomit, and stale sweat, Perry looked at me, glass in hand. "Bill," he said, downing a half water glass of scotch in one, and giving me a wry smile, "Have one with me. I can't stop."

I didn't join him, but going there alone was the third thing I did wrong. Drunks are charming and persuasive, and old habits sometimes can be reawakened. AA tells you *safety lies in numbers.* If you're going to make a Twelfth Step call, take a sober pal with you.

What I had in mind was that Dr. LeClair Bissell, who had persuaded me to go to a rehab myself, had just been funded by a grateful patient. She'd bought the palatial old Billy Rose mansion on the Upper East Side, and opened Smithers Center, New York City's first rehab. Since I believe so strongly that a rehab is anyone's best chance for recovery, I'd already phoned Smithers and knew they had a bed.

At the end of his rope with his drinking, his family, and with me, Perry let me persuade him to go. But as the old saying goes, anyone persuaded against his will is not persuaded at all. He left Smithers after three days, off again on another drunk.

You see them at almost any AA meeting: people arrested for DUI and ordered by the court to attend a dozen or so meetings or face an even harsher penalty. They sit at the back, silent, sullen, and resentful, broadcasting the signal: I don't belong here with you rummies. They get the hell out the minute the meeting is over, and I know more than one case where there was an angry rebound: They get in their car and head straight for a bar.

Before I was a volunteer at Scripps McDonald I assumed that people who came in to a rehab because of intervention would be like that, in a poisonous rage, too resentful for treatment to work. But I came to see that if correctly done formal interventions are more successful than I would have believed. One of the people on staff at Scripps whom I most admired was Gil Jaramillo, who gave me my earliest on-the-job training. I've turned to him for help with this question.

"I know just how your friend felt," Gil said. "His feet took him to the rehab; his heart didn't want to be there. The emotional symptoms for someone in Perry's state are anger, self-pity, self-disgust, and depression. Unbearable stuff. The only remedy he knew was alcohol. Since he didn't want to be in the rehab, he didn't give it time to work. He wanted relief, and wanted it fast. He went out and got drunk."

Gil went on: "At the end of my own addiction, I was doing a daily ton of crystal. I'm six foot five, close to two hundred and sixty pounds, but was walking around high on meth, a quart of tequila in hand, plus a machete and a loaded gun—and you know what, Bill? Scared to death. Did I want to stop? Hell, no. The only reason I let my family persuade me to go into Scripps McDonald rehab was I thought they would teach me how to slow down and drink with control."

Gil stayed on at Scripps McDonald after his twenty-eight days, and is now approaching his first decade sober, a highly regarded member of the staff. Among Gil's trained specialties is intervention. I asked him where I'd gone wrong with Perry.

"First of all," Gil said, "you were too self-centered and too sure you knew it all . . . you walked right past your two strongest allies, Perry's wife and son, people he loved. He listened to you because of your old friendship, because you'd been there yourself, and you cared enough to make the call. All fine . . . but not reason enough for him to change in his heart and soul. So after a few days, he walked out of the rehab and found a bar."

"What should I have done?"

"Worked as a team with the people to whom Perry had deep ties. If you had prepared them to come in with you, his wife and his son—"

Gil sighed. "But, Bill, in the case you describe, I don't think you ever had much of a chance for success. For an intervention to work, it has to be prepared more formally than just walking into the patient's bedroom and saying let's go—I have a bed waiting for you in a rehab. These days we don't think it's just the addict who is at risk. It's a family disease, and the whole family has to be involved in the recovery."

"Isn't one of AA's prime rules you have to want to stop for yourself? Do it for anyone else, even your family—it never works."

"Somebody like Perry, they're too far gone to stop for themselves. Very often in fact, in some deep, dim unacknowledged sense, they see their continued drinking as punishing themselves for being so awful. *Which they want to do!* So they will not stop for themselves."

Gil's words reawakened memories of the end of my drinking career, memories that shame me still, adolescent fantasies that nobody but me could understand the high romance of playing with death. Others might stop. I never would. To write that down even now is embarassing. In the airless silence of my own drunken mind, they were glamorous and enticing. "So the intervention interrupts the descent into total denial?" I said to Gil.

"If you'd brought Perry's wife in with you," he said, "and even more important, his son, and coached them first so they were able to put their own understandable anger aside for the moment and talk to Perry out of the depths of their heart—" Gil shrugged.

"He would have had better reason to go into a rehab, maybe stayed longer?" I said.

"We have a saying here at Scripps," said Gil. " 'We will love you until you can love yourself.' We care about newcomers exactly at the time when they are filled with the most self-loathing and disgust. Within these four walls, s/he is exposed to a new ethos and attitude, a new prime directive, perhaps for the first time ever. The other patients are all drunks and dopers too, but again and again they hear people saying, 'Stick with the winners,' and the winners are those perceived by the patients' own cool and knowing eye as most intent on getting clean and sober. What intervention does is break the rhythm, interrupt the pattern. Then something new can happen.

"When people come here after an intervention, they usually are angry, as your questioner feared, at least for the first few days. And before they leave, many confess they first went along with the intervention thinking well, hell—it'll get my family off my back. 'Okay,' they think. 'I can go right back to doping and drinking when I get out, but this time use what I learn here to get it right, and next time, do my doping and drinking like normal people, under control.' "

"What changes that idea?"

"Almost unconsciously, they begin to introject the group ethic of sobriety. They feel better, physically and mentally. When they phone home, they hear the joy that being clean and sober brings the people they love. Their head clears and they begin to care for themselves, proud of the effort they are making. Hope is reborn; they can beat addiction. Self-disgust and low self-worth give way to self-respect."

I told Gil I felt that when market research told advertisers Americans feel they've lost control of their lives, an ugly new word entered the vocabulary. "Nine times out of ten anyone who speaks about *empowering* yourself is trying to sell you something. You don't raise your self-respect by washing your hair with L'Oréal, you don't take control of your life by leasing a Toyota, you don't empower yourself by buying a more expensive lawn mower."

Gil was nice enough to smile at my jeremiad. "Those pleasures are short-lived, false, and fleeting," he said, "and behind the expensive façade, you know you're a fraud. Self-esteem is built by doing something you yourself think is admirable. Kicking addiction is exactly that. You can see the revelation in the faces of people in rehab: I don't have to live that stupid way, I don't have to lose my family, I don't have to be ashamed of myself, I don't have to die."

Here's Gil's step-by-step rulebook for doing an intervention.

ONE. GET THE RIGHT MIX OF PEOPLE.

Gil says they have to be willing to risk the addict's anger, risk the very relationship itself. The intervenors can be wives, husbands, relatives, coworkers, friends. This is not the place for anger and old recriminations, says Gil. "Whoever they are, the message they carry is, 'I love you.'"

TWO. NO SPUR-OF-THE-MOMENT STUFF.

Each participant writes a script in advance . . . thinking out the words, getting it right . . . exactly what they want to say. No generalities like, *You were always worthless, never any good.* Instead, cite specific examples of addicted behavior (i.e., "You drove the car with the children in it, dead drunk." "You threw up all over my boss's wife." Etc.) No deadly and endless catalog of all the sins the addict committed since the world began. Three or four are enough.

Share your feelings. Describe honestly how badly these incidents made you feel. "Very important," says Gil, "do *not ask questions.* That just gives the addict a chance to argue back, feel sorry for himself, rationalize and deny. All of which throws the intervention off the track."

THREE. CONSEQUENCES: HARD-NOSE THERAPY.

This is the hard one. Each participant has to carefully think out in advance a heartfelt consequence: "If you don't go into a rehab, I will divorce you." Not let you see your grandchildren, fire you, etc. No empty bluffs. Addicts are wily. They will ferret out any ambiguity in what you feel or say.

FOUR. DO THE RESEARCH IN ADVANCE.

Get all the facts on insurance coverage, treatment facilities, costs, payment options, length of average stay, visiting days, etc., in advance. Know the plan of action you will ask the addict to take, maybe even having a bag packed, ready to go. When I worked at Scripps McDonald, my feeling was the interventions that worked best were those in which the addict went into a rehab the same day the intervention took place—right after it ended if possible.

The addiction wants to live and flourish, and like cancer, which I think it resembles in so many ways, does not care that its life may mean the death of the host. The addiction will throw up all sorts of barriers to the threat intervention represents. Team members should help each other think up possible objections, excuses, and questions— *Who will walk my dog? I can't afford the time. How do I explain this to my boss?*— and come prepared with answers.

FIVE. SURPRISE.

Don't ask the addict to, "Meet us at this time and that place." He's liable to get in his car and disappear for one last binge. The best idea is surprise, and very important, Gil says, "Someplace other than the addict's house, workplace, or office."

SIX. REHEARSE.

Don't come at this cold. It's hard to do, and a life is at stake. Says Gil, "I like to have the interventionists secretly meet and go over their questions with each other, making suggestions and comments to help strengthen each other's resolve and ability to do the job right." Gil also suggests that the team members read their scripts aloud at this meeting. "Rehearsal is very important. That way, it comes out right when the chips are down."

Adds Gil: "Once the script is written, and maybe amended at the rehearsal, it is very important for every intervenor to understand that's it. On the day, no impromptu variations, additions, or subtractions. Stick to the script."

John Seaman is a professional interventionist, who works closely with the McDonald Center at Scripps Memorial Hospital. "If there are young people under eighteen in the family," he says, "it's better they not be at the rehearsal. Certain accusations may be shouted in the heat of the moment that it would be better for children not to hear. A wife yelling, 'You dirty so-and-so, you cheated on me with my best friend.' Or a husband to wife: 'I'm not even sure this child is mine!' That kind of thing would be inappropriate for the children to hear."

SEVEN. BATTING ORDER.

At the rehearsal, decide who is going to speak first, second, etc. "This is where it might be wise," Gil says, "to have a trusted and cool-headed clergyman or professional interventionist present—once again, to make sure nothing will be said that will be detrimental to the children." To which John Seaman adds, "I think it works best when, after careful rehearsal, the patient's children speak last. Their love and fear are so transparent and guileless, that the patient can't resist. 'Okay, I'll do it.' The words just jump out of their hearts and lips."

I asked John Seaman how successful did he feel interventions were. "My experience over the years," he said, "is almost nine out of ten people intervened upon in this way agreed to enter treatment."

Final note: All the above sound slippery and tough? It sure is. My advice: Don't try it alone. Many rehabs have trained, professional interventionists like John Seaman on their staff, ready to guide you through this very emotional process . . . perhaps even be present at the intervention itself. Look in the yellow pages and call one near you for their recommendation. All else failing, call the 800 number on the last page in this book.

Good luck.

#37.

"Psychiatry Takes a Drunk and Turns Him into a Basket Case"

Q. Sometimes I like what I hear you say: If you're a drunk, it was your hand that lifted the glass, nobody holds your jaws open and pours the gin down. Et cetera. Then, other times, you go into this business of dual diagnosis. The poor dear had to drink because his mother wouldn't put sugar on his oatmeal.

I'm Olsen, and went through rehab in the sixties, so I'm sober far longer than you. What I learned back then was called Reality Therapy, and it's still true: All that Freudian stuff about evil Mom and absent Dad—that just helped you blame others for the mess you made of your life. That kind of psychiatry turns drunks into moral basket cases.

Bill, I don't think you help anybody by helping them evade their own responsibility.

A. Reality Therapy, as famously expounded by Dr. William Glasser, does not accept the concept of mental illness. Whatever you do, it's your will, and your responsibility. Dick Caron, founder of Chit Chat, the rehab of which I am a graduate, once wrote, "Whether the (addicted) patient thinks he is Napoleon, is running berserk, or having nervous headaches, the common cause is inability to fulfill two essential needs: to love and be loved, and to feel worthwhile to themselves and the people around them." No psychobabble nonsense, no soft excuses, *I had an unhappy childhood, it's not my fault,* etc. The answer to that is, Your story is sad and may even be true, but the past cannot be changed. What can be changed is your behavior. Do you want to change that or do you want to remain unhappy the rest of your life?

Says Scott Munson, Executive Director, Sundown M Ranch, one of the top rehabs in the country, "I think it is important for psychologists and psychiatrists to understand the mistrust of those professions by many people in AA. Chemical dependency is a *primary illness,* not the result of another disorder." Treating alcoholism as a symptom of something else does not work.

I too believe the goal is indeed to be able "to love and feel loved, and feel worthwhile" too, but I am not sure you can get there by sobriety and cognitive therapy alone. Can you *will* to change your feelings? What if you do change your behavior, put down the glass, and still find yourself profoundly unhappy at what sobriety offers?

I'm not so sure Reality Therapy works for, let us say, the clinically depressed, whose brain chemistry, drunk or sober, is awry, and certainly unreachable by any act of will. These often are the people you find white-knuckling it through AA meetings and through life.

Maybe their 12 Step program brought them sobriety. They're still not "happy, joyous, and free." And if not, the dangerously easy next step is: Where's the payoff, why remain sober?

The advances in pharmaceutical science since Olsen and I went through rehab say you don't have to live that way.

How realistic is that promise?

See the next page.

#38.

Dual Diagnosis: White-Knuckle Sobriety

Q. I sometimes hear the term "dual diagnosis" brought up in AA and NA meetings. My understanding is that it means you have something wrong with you—something more than drinking—something *psychological* that just being sober alone can't fix. This makes the old-timers angry. Doctors and psychiatrists don't know anything about addiction, my sponsor once said to me. "Jerry, all you need is a good program," he said, "and to work the 12 Steps." His feeling is that if the straight AA gospel was good enough for Saint Bill W., it ought to be good enough for me.

I picked up a dope habit when I was in the Gulf War, and it changed into alcohol when I came home, but I've been sober now for forty-one months, and life is not, as the promises go, "happy, joyous, and free." In fact, my wife, who hated my drinking, sometimes says now I was easier to live with when I drank, and after our last fight, she even offered me a gin-and-tonic! What do you do if you're sober, going to meetings, and your life still doesn't seem to be worth living? As Peggy Lee used to sing, "Is This All There Is?"

A. When I lived in Key West, there was a guy—I'll call him Ned—who would ritually stand up at meetings of the Anchors Aweigh club. Pain written on his face, and getting up all his courage, he would say, "I have a right to be at this meeting."

Don't I?

It was heartbreaking. Even though sober, he felt so low and unworthy he did not think he had a right to be in the same room with so elite a society as us busted skulls, drunk drivers, unfaithful wives, runaway husbands, thieves, liars, dopers, and reformed felons. I spoke about him to a psychiatrist friend of mine.

"Since you are not quoting me by name," she said, "I'll allow myself a guess. I'd say odds are that Ned was the unwanted child of a young, unmarried mother who let him know every day of his life that he was a burden to her, that she wished he'd never been born."

She went on: "It sounds like there's an underlying clinical depression at work on Ned that he'd been self-medicating with booze. He tells us his habit began during the Gulf War. In World War I, they called it shell shock. In World War Two there was 'combat fatigue.' Since Vietnam, we've called it post-traumatic stress disorder. Call it what you will, it often causes addiction and later relapse. My bet is Ned is a case of dual diagnosis: There's more wrong than alcoholism alone. Being sober, using the 12 Steps, that rarely does the job alone."

I said that the rehab I went to ignored all past history. "They called it 'Reality Therapy.' We don't care if your mother loved you, the orientation lecture said, or your father beat you up. Don't sing us any sad songs from long ago. That cannot be changed. We deal with the here and now, and your here and now is you're an addict. Let the past go, change your behavior, we start there."

"And very right too," my psychiatrist friend said. "Common sense says, well, if alcoholism is at the root of Ned's problem, get rid of that, and the depression will cure itself. But the sad fact is that we've learned that for people like Ned, or your caller, Jerry, it does not.

"I have a nineteen-year-old patient," she went on, "who is addicted to meth. She was molested by her stepfather when very young, and her trouble is, whenever she goes off crystal, she is consumed by a rage so total, it frightens her. It's a vicious circle: The fury that scares her, the urge to murder the bastard, all that hides behind the addiction. So until I can get behind the addiction, nothing else helps.

"Jerry is ahead of my patient, in that he is sober," she said. "I have the greatest admiration for AA for helping him accomplish that."

"What about the old-time AA Nazis whom he speaks about?" I asked. "They won't even take aspirin for a headache, calling it 'just another drug.' How do you answer people like that?"

"Bill," my friend said with a laugh, "you sound like an old-time AA Nazi yourself. Those people would hate what I'd say next. If Jerry were my patient, I'd put him on Prozac. It would help him make his feelings of depressed self-esteem reachable by psychotherapy."

"In the end, then, the solution to Jerry's problems is in himself?"

"At the moment, Jerry is victim of his unbalanced brain chemistry. He's fighting with a hand tied behind his back. It's unfair. Prozac therapy tilts the odds back in his favor. It would enable him to become the moral agent for his own change. What's wrong with that?"

#39.

Post-Traumatic Stress and Relapse

Q. My husband Rollie served in Vietnam, and came home with a mild drug habit. When we became engaged, I told him I did not like it, and he quit . . . or maybe he merely turned to alcohol. Except for some violent flare-ups of bad temper, we had a good marriage for a long time, but in recent years, his drinking has steadily grown worse. His temper too.

Last year, he checked himself into a rehab . . . stayed the twenty-eight days . . . and began drinking again almost the day he got out.

I heard the beginning of the show you did last week on post-traumatic stress disorder. You had some doctor on. He said PTSD often leads people who had fought in Vietnam first into addiction and later into relapse. The talk frightened me very much. Does this mean there's no hope for my husband?

A. As with anyone who goes into the Army, almost the first thing that happened to me was a battery of tests, one of them for mechanical aptitude. On a scale of zip to one hundred, I scored maybe an eleven, which is the category that says, Don't give this soldier so much as a pointed stick, let alone a weapon. So they lost me in what is called military intelligence, and the only stress I suffered in my Army career was the Abandoned Dance Hall Bar & Grill, in Hopkinsville, Kentucky, on a Saturday night.

But if I don't know much about the stress of combat, I do know all I need about relapse (see "My Last Drink," Q. #76). And what I know is this: It is as close to hell as I ever want to go, the worst two weeks of my life.

What's in a name? In World War I, they called it "shell shock." In World War II and Korea, "combat fatigue." After Vietnam and the Gulf War, it was "post-traumatic stress disorder." Now, with our new War on Terror, will the malady be given still another title?

No matter. The name changes, but the suffering is real—the topic of PTSD, combined with addiction and relapse increasingly important. So I turned once again to my friend, mentor, and a practicing psychotherapist, Larry Bouchard, once an Air Force combat photographer in Vietnam, later assigned to the Army for clandestine missions about which he remains vague to this day.

"Right off the top," said Larry, "let me give you a minority opinion. I think PTSD is maybe the most misdiagnosed or overdiagnosed disorder going today. A guy comes in to see a psychiatrist or someone like me because he's addicted, and can't stop. Then, if he's a Vietnam vet, it's very easy to go right past his rocky marriage or oppressive child-hood—both of which could be the unresolved issues that keep him drinking. He's a Vietnam combat vet and therefore, Bingo!, we pin this red-hot diagnostic label on him. PTSD, ta-rah . . ."

"You're saying there's no such thing?"

"No. I'm saying it's misunderstood, and its symptoms falsely attrib-uted. Whether it's getting your new bicycle stolen the day after Christmas," Larry said, "or having your closest comrade shot through the eye beside you at 'dinner,' the grieving process is the same.

"There are seven distinct and equally vital stages," he was writing them down for me on a paper napkin. "First—Denial. It didn't happen. When I look in the backyard again, the bike will be there, probably behind a tree . . . or, he isn't really dead, the medics will fix him. Sec-ond—Anger. If I find the kid who stole it, I'll stab him with a rusty spear, I'll eat his liver . . . or, I'll blow away every fucking gook and all his friends. Third. Bargaining. Please God, when I wake up, let the bike be there, I won't ever tease my little sister again. Fourth. Accep-tance. No use moaning . . . It's gone. Reality is beginning to set in."

Larry went on: "Steps 5, 6, and 7 begin a form of meditation, the ego removed from the process. In the fifth step, there's an experience of melancholy and loss. It was such a wonderful bike. I loved the way the sunlight glinted off the red fenders. Ah, well . . . Sixth stage is res-olution. Well, it was a wonderful bike, but life goes on. Maybe I'd bet-ter get my homework done for tomorrow. And hope enters in the seventh: Maybe I'll get a better bike for my next birthday."

"What if you don't finish the entire seven-step process?"

"Sooner or later, bad things happen, mostly later. PTSD used to be called 'delayed stress syndrome.' It was abandoned because it implied the victim had a choice as to when to process stress. If you're already using alcohol and/or drugs to escape life's difficulties—delayed stress is a way of life."

"You saw people go through this process in Vietnam?"

"Some did, some stuffed it. When I was living with the Army, I saw guys coming back from the sharp end of the war every day. One grunt, tall and stringy, full of heart and fun (we called him Greenbean), he had a wonderful family back home. Never interested in dope or booze. He set the tone for guys like him. Back from a recon mission, they'd barbecue some ribs, maybe drink a beer, maybe not, play their guitars, and tomorrow go out and do it again. I saw Greenbean come walking out one day, carrying his best friend in his arms. Carrying him three hours. The medics had to tell him, put the guy down, Greenie, he's shot through the head, he's dead."

"You're saying he didn't drink or dope over that?"

"And I don't think he ever will," said Larry, a staff sergeant in Vietnam but who ended his career eighteen years later a captain. "Terrible things happen to everyone. But people like Greenie, who come from families who loved and supported each other, learned to process these events and come out the other side, healed and even stronger. We aren't born knowing this stuff in our genes. What Greenie did was make a song about his friend dying, played it at the barbecue that night, cried a lot, and went back out to the war again the next day."

"He processed the whole thing in twenty-four hours, all seven steps?"

"He'd learned how to resolve internal conflict from a functional and effective family that wasn't stuck in denial and unresolved conflicts of their own. You know how people will not take a ten- or twelve-year-old kid to a funeral home to see their dead grandparents? They think they are 'protecting' their kids. They are aborting and perverting the learning process. Healthy families grieve well, and teach it to their kids," said Larry (who, incidentally, I know is the father of three wonderfully well-adjusted young men).

"How," I said, "how does any of this apply to Mr. and Mrs. Rollie?"

"Listen to her words," said Larry. "Rollie had a 'mild' drug habit. He 'merely' turned to alcohol. 'We had a good marriage,' she says. I believe they had a good-looking marriage. She's in denial, which deepens his isolation and demands he continue drinking to numb the pain and inevitable loneliness that brings. Maybe he experienced terrible trauma in the war. Maybe not. The question for therapy remains: Did he go 'through' the trauma? Or did he just encounter trauma, put the mandatory grieving process on hold, get back to the States and then repress it completely—attempting to escape the suffering that genuine grieving would entail. Of course, the booze and dope would be prime movers here.

"Now he's home, where it's safe and there's time to let feelings surface and he has time to brood about them?"

"But he can't," said Larry. "They're too painful, too real, too raw and

141

unprocessed. That's where PTSD enters, but when I met guys like Rollie in my job, many were *predisposed* to use maladjusted ways of handling stressors, starting long before they went to Vietnam. I bet Rollie came from a troubled family, one as deeply into denial as Mrs. Rollie. That's why he married her: He felt at home with her."

"If Rollie were your client, what would you advise him to do?"

"I don't know the quality of the rehab he went to, but it sounds like he's still stuck somewhere in unresolved grief . . . probably anger and/or bargaining and no one has detected that. Probably, as his wife says, he's still burning with unresolved, unforgiven anger. I call that resentment, which is the number two cause of relapse, right after over-confidence that you have addiction beat.

"If you didn't learn how to process grief and loss as a kid, one of the best ways I know is to get a good AA program, get a good sponsor, and do the 12 Steps, over and over until they are integrated into your worldview and daily life. All lives have loss, and all people experience trauma. The ones who have the mental tools to get through life's sufferings . . . e.g., lean on friends, share feelings, cry, laugh, go bang garbage can lids, curse God till it hurts—in other words, go crazy for a while—these people go on to the next phase and live life as it comes. The ones who delay it or try to escape it suffer ten-fold the original trauma in countless other, seemingly nonrelated areas of their lives, including the compulsive insanities of addiction."

"Larry, one of the reasons I like to talk to you—this stuff rolls out like a textbook. Is this what you learned in college or your psychotherapy practice, or did it happen in your own life too?"

"When the movie *Platoon* came out, vets were advised not to see it alone. *Take another vet with you,* we were told, *because it's all there except the smell.* Tough guy that I thought I was, bulletproof—I went alone. After twenty minutes, the smell was there! I knew I had work to do 'someday,' but, Bill, I put it off. Someday, I thought, but I'm busy right now, ordered a beer, and let it go. I even volunteered to work on a committee verifying spellings, ranks, home town, dates of birth and death, for names going up on the Vietnam memorial wall—one of about 120 from all five uniformed services doing the work."

"You paid a visit to the wall?"

"Yes, finally. I did that verification work for five years but never went to see it myself. I hid . . . staying busy, helping others, externalizing my focus so I wouldn't have to look inside. When I finally did visit the wall, something changed. My anger finally dissipated into the ether. The meaning of 'it takes what it takes' came home. I just never believed I was actually carrying all that shit. Others knew it, but I never did. Isn't denial a bitch when you don't know you're doing it? I hadn't finished my own grief work until that visit—a visit to the memory and pain of the loss of thirteen cherished comrades, a reconciliation to the idea of their death, and when it comes, to my own. Suddenly their lives had meaning, not their dying but their living . . . and so did mine. And there on a hot, muggy, sweat-filled D.C. evening in front of total strangers—just suddenly—there was hope. Resolution and then hope. Real, undeniable, breathtaking hope."

"You saying all those years, you were going through a kind of repressed PTSD yourself?"

"Yes, sort of."

"When did you leave Vietnam?"

"January, 1972."

"When did you visit the wall?"

"June 30, 1999," said Larry.

"Twenty-seven years?"

Larry said yes.

#40.

Booze and Incest

Q. Bill, you had some feminist support group on your show last week, talking about their drunken father or creepy Uncle Louis or whoever. I'm Albert, an over-the-road trucker, fifty-two years old. You ever get tired of hearing young women get up on shows like yours or in AA meetings and say the reason they drank was they were molested as a kid? I never heard of anything like this when I first joined AA nineteen years ago, but nowadays, 'incest,' that's all you hear. Isn't it just another exaggerated fad excuse to keep on drinking?

A. To answer this one, I had lunch with the psychiatrist friend whom I quoted in the Q. #38. "You have wide practice among young women," I said. "Is it possible Albert is right—all this talk about sexual child molestation is sort of a copycat, one-size-fits-all excuse for anything that goes wrong—'Be sorry for me, my stepfather did terrible things to me when I was a kid'?"

I said I remembered reading that when Freud began his practice, he was flooded with similar stories of young women patients who said they were being molested by their fathers. "In the end," I said, "he decided these were not actual events, but a kind of frightening wish fulfillment daydream on the part of girls overly in love with their fathers. Freud said it had to be oedipal 'phantasies'—he could not believe middle-class, nineteenth-century Vienna was fucking its daughters."

My friend stopped smiling.

"That's one of the places Freud took a major wrong turn," she said. "Memories of incestuous events come up again and again in the early lives of addicts I treat. Remember when we talked about dual diagnosis? People who remain troubled, and need psychotherapeutic help, even after they've stopped drinking and using dope? Victims of early incest are high on that list. The sad fact is that almost invariably their lives are suffused with shame, each one thinking she's the only one to whom so awful a thing ever happened . . . and what's worse, that it is her fault. You would be doing a service to your incest survivor readers if you firmly informed them no, they are not the only ones, and no, it is not their fault."

Let me shamefacedly admit to some masculine bias I may share with Over-the-Road Albert (above), or at least with Sigmund Freud. I phoned Scott Munson and asked, in the host of clients he's seen go through Sundown M. Ranch in his years as Executive Director, did he believe all these feminine stories about incest? "Bill," he said, "the numbers and percentages change according to who you talk to, but one thing is clear: Yes, a large percentage of girls raised in homes with chemically dependent adults are molested."

I got more conformation from my friend, the therapist Lynn Telford-Sahl. "No less than Dr. Karl Menninger himself," she told me, "once complained about Freud's wrong turn, 'Why, oh why couldn't (he) believe his own ears?' Menninger then went on to say that 75 percent of female patients at their famous clinic had been molested in childhood by an adult. "In my own experience," Lynn went on, "when I was working as an in-patient counselor for Starting Point in Sacramento, the statistics were about one in four."

"What does the secrecy surrounding these acts do to the child?"

"The little girl *knows* something's wrong, her feelings tells her so, the bond of trust between parent and child destroyed. However, to keep the secret and survive the violation she has to shut off her intuitive knowledge, her body knowledge—disassociate from her own experience. (I'm using the female pronoun because it happens to girls more often than boys.) This allows the child to survive, but causes a huge disruption in healthy self-development. Drugs and alcohol act as either numbing agents against the humiliation and shame—or if they are too numbed down—helps them *feel* something, anything. Incest has been going on forever. The reason Albert didn't hear about this stuff fifteen years ago is, it wasn't out of the closet yet. Women were still too isolated and afraid to talk. But he's right about one thing: *Anything can be used as an excuse to keep drinking.*

"The victim mentality that says 'I can't help it' is part and parcel of the learned helplessness of many incest survivors, but can't be dealt with until the woman realizes getting sober is the beginning of the process to work through what has happened to her, not the end."

#41.

The "Higher Power" Business Puts Me Off

Q. A few days ago, I went to my first AA meeting. A woman got up and said she could never have gotten sober without her belief in a higher power. Two others said the same thing. But all that God talk made me feel I didn't really belong. My feeling is that the logic in AA's famous "Chapter to the Agnostic" would flunk Freshman Philosophy 101, and I've never had a religious emotion in my life. Will I never overcome my addiction unless I find some program less religiously oriented than AA?

A. In the years I've been sober, I've heard this question often enough. I'm going to answer at some length because it expresses emotions I've felt myself. Let's start with the first big hurdle I faced when I turned to Alcoholics Anonymous for help: the 12 Steps themselves.

When I called AA world headquarters in New York City while writing this book, they firmly regretted that if I was going to publish under my full name they could not give me copyright permission to reproduce the Steps. I will go into my feelings about AA's famous insistence on anonymity more fully in Q. #58, but you can find your own copy of the Steps at any AA meeting, in your library, or on the Net.

What is pertinent to this discussion is that if you read them, you will find nine references to a capitalized Deity and one to prayer—for someone like me, ten steps backward for every twelve forward. I remember thinking getting sober their way was going to be a long road, and perhaps not mine.

But I've been around AA too long now not to see for most people strong religious belief is indeed instrumental in getting clean and sober. My difficulties with the Steps are merely that—*my* difficulties. Therefore, for a more positive guide through this aspect of the Steps, pick up any of the books they give away free at most AA meetings. If I have not totally disqualified myself in your eyes, I would especially recommend *Twelve Steps and Twelve Traditions*, by Bill W. himself.

My friend Lynn Telford-Sahl is a therapist and author of *The Greatest Change of All—A Spiritual Novel*. She puts it like this: "I grew up in an alcoholic home myself and in my fifteen years of practice, worked with a lot of wounded folks, including me. One thing seems really clear. In order to be truly well, people need to feel life has purpose beyond just having what we want for ourselves, something bigger than our own little ego-centered world . . . Jesus and Buddha and many others have demonstrated this human potential. It is what makes life meaningful and worth living. This is our Higher Power."

More conventionally, my friend Tom R. once told me he hadn't prayed in twenty years. "But when I got sober, my anxiety was so fierce I couldn't sleep, my blood pressure was through the roof. I thought the only way was back to pills and booze. But my sponsor said, Tom—go down on your knees every morning and do it again every night. I thought, baloney, but Bill, what can I tell you? It works. My blood pressure is normal, I get a good night's sleep five or six nights out of seven. For me, praying takes a lot of pressure off."

I know Tom is intelligent and honest. I also know he is sober, his recovery pragmatic proof of faith's value. So nothing that follows should be taken as an attack on religion, either in or out of AA. On the other hand, let me report another conversation.

I once went through rehab myself, a place in Pennsylvania called Chit Chat (a dumb name, but historically rooted). One of the counselors was a Jesuit, a graduate of the place himself. At the end of his twenty-eight days he called up the Order and said, Okay, what next? "Take off your collar and stay there," they told him. "You've found your life's work."

What I liked about Jack was that you could talk to him as a counselor, as a priest, or just a well-educated fellow drunk interested in literature and speculative philosophy. I told him I'd love to feel my life so important, my every action invested with such terrible majesty that if I took the Lord's Name in Vain or sneaked a cookie on a fast day it would be sadly noted by God Himself in Heaven.

"But I don't," I said.

I said I knew a lot of people who were helped by their religious belief but what it made me feel inside was alienation. Maybe all the talk about God and a Higher Power meant that AA wasn't for me?

Jack's said he often thought intoxication a kind of left-handed try for religious experience. "We call alcohol 'spirits' and what is 'getting high' but a search for spiritual transcendence over the nitty-gritty dailiness of going to work, doing the laundry, getting sick, and death? A mistaken effort, and self-destructive but a try, nevertheless, for life and ever more abundant life—which is one of religion's promises."

He smiled. "But, Bill," he said, "religion never kept me sober."

Now, years later, I've come to wonder about his choice of words. "Religion," he said. Not, "faith."

In *The March of Folly*, Barbara Tuchman writes that the gods—Zeus, Hera, Apollo, and the rest of the Olympians—"are a concept of the human mind . . . creatures of man, not vice versa . . . needed to give meaning and purpose to the puzzle that is life on earth. . . . (T)hey exist to bear the burden of all things that cannot be comprehended . . ."

It is difficult for me not to feel that "God" too is a human invention, created to bear the same burden. So here is a minority report, aspirin for the bedeviled: that small part of AA, those of us who do not think that "Higher Power" and "God" are necessarily synonymous.

Let me begin with this. AA describes itself as a spiritual program, not a religious one. I believe the life of the spirit covers a vast rainbow of ideas, religion being only one. You may feel belief in God is the first, most vivid color in that rainbow, but spirituality includes just about every value invisible to your accountant—that which is done for itself alone rather than a step toward some further, utilitarian goal.

By this definition, praying to God as a meditation within your own soul is a spiritual exercise. To pray for a red BMW, to bring a loved one home, or even for world peace is just a negotiation, like the tacit bargain you make with your boss: If I'm a good employee, you will give me a raise. Which is another way of saying what you never believed when your mother first told it to you as a kid, *Virtue is its own reward.*

How many of us thought getting sober meant the end of fun? How many found in sobriety that merely showed (as I once heard it said at an AA meeting) how narrow an idea we'd had of what fun meant? In my lexicon, fun is a spiritual value too.

Truth, friendship, beauty, marriage, family, compassion, loyalty, books, romance, art, esthetics, the beach and the sea, going for walks, going through rehab, playing baseball well, falling in love, doing volunteer work, the Zen of golf or tennis, the beauty of a tree or a child, taking care of a sick cat—all these merely begin a list of human endeavors which are at least fun, and may in time become sources of the passionate transfiguration we seek in religion or drugs, which reminds me, I left out my own personal favorite high—skiing.

I further think there is spiritual value in group morale. What psychologists call the ocean feeling is, I believe, at the heart of why AA works. Go to a football game alone, not much fun. Go with friends, all rooting for the same team, the spirit swells, it becomes sublime and thrilling. If you see a sparsely filled restaurant—no matter how good the food, your impulse is give it a miss. But fill the same place with the hum of a crowd enjoying themselves—people you don't know, won't speak to, will never see again—take your place as part of that spirited whole—you'll have a better time too.

How can Fat Farms charge money to starve you to death when you can starve to death free, by yourself? Why do expensive exercise machines gather cobwebs at home while people in crowded gyms enjoy the experience and keep coming back? Because there is spiritual sustenance, there is a kind of fun—the deep pleasures of group morale—*we're all in this together*—in doing something with other people united in a common goal. Whether that goal is pushing away from a table, singing hymns with the congregation, or encouraging each other not to pick up a drink, it's a feeling of union, of life, transcendent life.

"The Second Step says we came to believe a Power greater than ourselves could restore us to sanity," people say to me often enough. "If you don't believe that, what do you believe?" My reply is I believe the ancient Greeks were righter than they knew.

They believed the planets moved in concert, the *music of the spheres.* Pythagoras proclaimed the universe governed by the same laws as octaves in music, the proportions of musical intervals set forth by the laws of geometry and defined by the mathematics of number. Einstein indeed said mathematics was Der Alte's language, Dirac said it too, and music, said Leibniz, was "hidden arithmetic."

I believe those mathematical physicists whose formulae describe an infinity of strings vibrating in ten- or eleven-dimension space. At the few frequencies visible to us we call them quarks, electrons, mesons, and pions. Molecules are notes, human beings are songs, our dim understanding of these harmonics is what we call the laws of physics, and the sum of it all is Music, which you may choose to call God. As for me, I believe the second Step talks about G.O.D.

Group of Drunks.

Kept me sober all these years.

My Own Demur: Ironically, I believe the dying away of faith in contemporary life impoverishes us all. Charles Larmore is the Chester D. Tripp Professor at the University of Chicago. In a recent *New Republic* issue he addresses why we should want to do what is right. "That question assumes a special urgency," he says, ". . . as older religious motivations lose their grip," and we are left with prophets so sure they sit on God's right hand they have no doubt they can proclaim what S/He has in mind for the rest of us—William Bennett and his *Book of Virtues* come to mind, and may I add radio's own Dr. Laura? ("Thank you," Dr. Laura says to a woman phoning in to report some bit of conduct the good doctor likes, "thank you"—God letting Her servant know She is well pleased with her obedience to Her Law.)

The concept of grace, the fatherhood of God, avoidance of Hell, and the mystery of eternal afterlife in Heaven—all, all reified in some of the world's most glorious poetry, art, architecture, and music? Religion once seized the imagination with images powerful enough to hold their own against the counterfeit glitter of material pleasures, the immediacy of greed. But to my (again, perhaps biased) eye, and if I understand him, to Professor Larmore too, religion today seems little more than a feel-good club, one whose dues are lip service—Sunday sodalities of social identity divorced from what we do the other six days a week. We do not ask of someone, Is he good? We ask, *Is he rich?*

If you were caught short by the statement about religious values dying out, consider how society today swings between two extremes. At one pole, The Golden Rule. Do unto others. Help the poor and unfortunate. Treat each other with kindness, love thy neighbor, etc.

At the other: The Bottom Line. Don't tell me about your sick cat, that your mother is dying, or you can't pay the rent. You're nothing to me but an economic unit, a counter in the game of profit-and-loss. If I can't make money on you, you're a waste of my time, good-bye.

Golden Rule vs. Bottom Line.

Which predominates in everyday life?

We know what people say. Where do they put their money? On the cross atop the altar or the Mercedes-Benz advertised on TV?

Don't make me laugh.

Asked about his beliefs, Churchill once said, "Sensible men are all of the same religion" (quoting, interestingly enough, Benjamin Disraeli). As I said earlier, the notion of a higher power is too important in any

12 Step program to allow my personal interpretation to stand as the only one in these pages. Statistical studies sent to me by Hazelden's Dr. Pat Owen show "belief in a Higher Power . . . predict(s) reduced severity of relapse," and in my own years in AA, I've seen what might even be called bumper-sticker religion work—"Honk If You Love Jesus." How this can be true is beyond my understanding—which is merely another way of saying I'm an old-fashioned Bertrand Russell agnostic—but better minds than mine have been wrestling with these questions for two thousand years.

The biologist J.B.S. Haldane once famously said our "universe is not only queerer than we suppose, but queerer than we can suppose." He saw this as supporting his own atheism, but it can easily be read to support the idea of a Creator—a Grand Designer—of that universe.

Therefore I am pleased to have found, after diligent search, a distinguished theologian to present a religious point of view. What follows in the next pages is Father Bob's reply to the same question I tried to answer above.

#42.

The "Higher Power" Relationship Works for Me

A. "My name is Bob, Father Bob if you like, a Catholic priest over fifty, from a large Midwestern diocese, currently working in a parish 80 percent Hispanic. I've also been a professor in theology at one of our Catholic universities. And so I've had the benefit of added education beyond my seminary training. About three and a half years ago I went to treatment for alcoholism. I learned that I also had the twin disease of depression. Unfortunately, my drinking was only making my depression worse. In fact, I had almost lost the desire to go on living. I used to get up in the morning and the first thing I would say was, 'I wish I was dead.'

"Alcoholism is an equal-opportunity disease that can strike anyone, lay person or clergy, male or female, young or old, black or white, Latino or Native American, a believer in God or an agnostic. Of course, you expect a Catholic priest to have no problem with a belief in a higher power, whom I choose to call God.

"Yet, my experience when I was drinking was that I was in the midst of a spiritual crisis in terms of my relationship with my higher power. I had prayed many times that God release me from the grip that alcohol had on me. Unfortunately, I didn't really want to quit until I was in total despair, unhappy, and desperate. Why hadn't God directly intervened in my life to stop me from drinking?

"Now after three years of sobriety, I can recognize the hand of God that led me to seek help. I had been lying to my psychologist about my drinking. No wonder he had a tough time helping me overcome my problem with depression! Finally, I told him the truth and he said I was in the midst of a medical emergency. He wouldn't let me leave the office until I had an appointment with our Liquor Vicar (the priest who works with alcoholics in our diocese) to discuss going for treatment.

"I never stopped believing in God. It's just that I didn't know or want to know (I was in denial) what I had to do in order to get on the road to recovery. I knew I was powerless over alcohol. My life had become unmanageable. People I worked with and many of my friends were afraid that I might one day wake up dead, having drunk myself into a stupor. Of course, I didn't want to hear that.

"It really doesn't matter whether you are religious or not. AA doesn't back any particular religion. Christians, Jews, Muslims, atheists, and agnostics—all are welcome in AA. Remember: AA is a spiritual program, not a religious one. It's less about your personal doctrine about God and more about the recognition that there is a power greater than yourself that can help you, that can restore you to sanity.

"The one thing alcoholics have to admit is that the way they are living is insane, self-destructive, a miserable way to journey through life. Alcoholics must recognize that they don't have all the answers to life's questions, that they want to find a more healthy and peaceful way to live, and that they believe that help is out there somewhere.

"For many people, their AA group becomes their higher power. It's where they hear the voice of God calling them to live a more healthy life. It's where they get the help they need to change unhealthy patterns of living, to learn to cope successfully with stress, to have realistic expectations of what one person can accomplish with one life, and to develop the type of relationships (with the group, your sponsor, the AA community at large) that will help you to remain serene and sober.

"Much of AA spirituality reflects Christian principles of living. For example, each day we are told to take our inventory and, if we have injured anyone, to make amends for our actions. Of course, this sounds a lot like what Catholics mean when they are told to examine their conscience and do penance (make up) for their sins. At the same time, making amends and not weighing yourself down with guilt and shame over past failures is a very healthy way to live. It's dealing with life on life's terms, not on our terms.

"AA spiritually tells us to 'let go and let God' take over. This doesn't mean turning our minds (consciences) off and refusing to accept responsibility for what we do or say. It does mean that we aren't in charge of the universe. In fact, we really can't control much about life except what we ourselves do or say. And if what we do or say creates a pattern of unhealthy thinking and acting, then we've got to find a better way to think and act. I found such a way in AA.

"One of the problems in the Chapter to the Agnostic in the Big Book is that it sounds like it's trying to convince you to believe in God. Of course, it will fail at this because there are no adequate proofs for the existence of God. You accept God's existence on faith. When I was studying philosophy in college, our professor reviewed the five famous proofs for the existence of God, which go back to such greats as Aristotle, Thomas Aquinas, St. Anselm, and others. Anselm speaks of God as 'a being than which nothing greater can be conceived.' God is the most perfect conceivable being, the one necessary being without whom the rest of the universe would not exist.

"Thomas Aquinas argued for the existence of God based on the fact of motion to a Prime Mover (God). God is the uncaused cause that starts everything in motion, much like dominoes falling on a huge playing field. Aquinas also believed that contingent (imperfect, limited human) beings required a perfect, Necessary Being as their model. This Necessary Being we call God.

"Another argument is based on the premise that degrees of value require an Absolute Value. The source of Absolute Value is the Necessary Being we call God.

"Finally, the argument from the design of the universe or the argument from beauty also appeals to many people. Look at the amazing way the universe is put together. Examine the breathtaking beautiful sights in Mother Nature. This design, this beauty can't be an accident or simply good fortune. For example, take a pocket watch and take it apart. Throw all the pieces in a bag. Shake the bag up and see if the pieces will all fall back into their correct spot in order to make the watch work. I suspect you're going to be shaking that bag for the rest of your life, frustrated that the pieces won't fall together in order to create the design of the watch you started with.

"Philosophers have had a field day with these seemingly logical arguments for the existence of God: motion, necessary being, absolute value, design, and beauty. For there are ways to refute all these arguments. Moreover, once you have a strong relationship with God, you don't need intellectual arguments and debates to convince you that you are a spiritual as well as a physical person. All you need to do is dialogue with your higher power on a regular basis.

"This past weekend I celebrated a quincenera (a ceremony blessing a young person on their fifteenth birthday) in my parish. As is often the case, the young woman and her twenty-four friends (all dressed in tuxedoes or fancy dresses) arrived at the church about twenty minutes late. Usually, I'm fairly patient with people, but about a half hour before the Mass a man in the parish came over to the rectory (place where the priests live) and asked me to come over to his home to give the last sacraments to his brother, who was dying. I explained that I couldn't do this immediately, because I had a church filled with people to take care of, but I would come as soon as the Mass was over.

"Fortunately, the man whose brother was sick was very understanding and said 'no problem. Come as soon as you can.' I felt relieved that this man understood my predicament and was accepting of the response I gave him.

"However, as I paced in back of church for twenty minutes, I began to feel annoyed (angry) that I was just standing around doing nothing, when someone really needed a priest to help them. I prayed that God keep me calm and help me to celebrate with the young woman coming for her quincenera.

"What I heard God tell me was this: 'Look, this young woman is all excited about this very important day in her life. Don't rain on her parade and complain about how late she is. You know it's hard to get a group of twenty-four people together at one place at the same time. Cut them a little slack. Besides, there's nothing else going on in church after this Mass. I'll take care of the sick man until you're free to visit him.'

"I let my anger and worry go. I put the celebration and the sick man in God's hands. God would get me through this. However, life is never as smooth going as we would like it to be. There were a few things that the young woman wanted to do that she hadn't told me. On top of that, the teenage boys in the party were having a tough time paying attention.

"I got to a sacred moment in the Mass where I recall the suffering and death of Christ on the Cross and say the words 'This is my body, this is my blood.' For me, this is a peak moment in the Mass, a moment in which we remember the great love of Jesus who laid down his life for his friends. However, as I was saying these words, I could hear the boys giggling—someone was telling a joke and they weren't paying attention. Again, my first reaction to this was to get angry: 'Don't these teens realize how important this prayer is that I am saying?'

"Once again, God spoke to me this message: 'Bob, you were once young yourself. You know what it's like being a teenager. These boys are probably very nervous, uncomfortable wearing a tuxedo for the first time, probably wearing new, tight-fitting shoes. Laughter is how they're handling the tension. Cut them some slack. Smile at them. You don't want to turn them off. They may never come back to see me, if you get nasty with them.'

"The reason I share this story with you is that I find myself dialoguing with God a good deal during each day. I try to listen to what God, my higher power, wants me to do: be patient, deal with your anger, let go of control, and let God take care of things, trust in God, don't expect perfection from imperfect human beings. After all, I'm not perfect either. Don't go judging another person. Don't start taking their inventory. You've got a long enough list of things to work on in your own inventory. Leave the judging to God.

"I often leave AA meetings with my spirits raised and even a new idea or two. In fact, some of the ideas and ways of living I've learned at meetings are so good that I keep a notepad in my glove compartment and jot down some of the 'wise sayings' that stayed with me when I went back to my car. Every so often I take out that list and read it. There's a lot of wisdom there! But is this the wisdom of God?

"I think it is, but I respect those who think otherwise. At least we can agree that people who go to AA meetings walk out with the wisdom of the group, their higher power, to guide them, to keep them sane and healthy. Sure, we may not feel particularly religious. We may even think we haven't had a religious emotion in our life. That's all right. You don't have to believe in religion to be part of AA. All you need to do is to believe that a power greater than yourself can restore you to sanity and remove the defects of character that you, on your own, could not remove. While prayer may be difficult for someone who's an agnostic, reflection on what your higher power (your group) would do or say in the particular situation will work just as well.

"AA is not religiously oriented, but spiritually oriented. It helps you develop a relationship with a higher power that can transform your life and lead you to a more realistic and fulfilling approach to living each day. For me, AA has been the road that has led to peace. It can happen to you! Father Bob T."

#43.

Dry Drunks and Stinking Thinking

Q. One of the things I don't like about AA, there's this "in" crowd. They run the meetings, do all the talking, and all I ever get out of them is this mind-numbing sloganeering they pass off as wisdom. One Day at a Time . . . Take It Easy . . . It's the First Drink That Gets You Drunk . . . Let Go and Let God . . . and on and on.

I've been sober now for nine months, and after an AA meeting one night last week, when They, in their Infinite Wisdom, finally invited me to go out with them for coffee, I said to them, Well, I've been sober now for nine months. It's not all it's cracked up to be. When do the good times start?

Bill, you know what they said? "Charlie, you're a prime example of stinking thinking," and another said I was a "dry drunk"—both phrases

I've heard endlessly at AA meetings, but no one ever defines. Are they the same, and what do they mean? And, PS., Bill—if being sober is going to continue being joyless hard time for the rest of my life, maybe my drinking wasn't all that bad.

A. Marianne Peck is a marriage and family counselor who specializes in treating people who grew up in alcoholic families. She is a friend of mine and a frequent guest on the show. "When your primary relationship is with booze or drugs, when your brain is poisoned by chemicals," she says, "emotional and intellectual growth is difficult. Your relationships are mostly based on finding friends, not who might challenge you to grow and change, but who are merely interested in getting high with you."

When you're drinking, there's always a quick and easy way to handle life's problems. Fight with your wife? Didn't get the raise? Maybe just bored? Stop in a bar . . . pour yourself a picker-upper at home . . . lift a cold one with a few friends. Hey, presto!

But, Charlie, look where it led.

Freud remarks somewhere that the mark of maturity is the willingness to delay immediate gratification for the sake of a greater payoff in the future. Ten hours a week in the gym can mean ten years of more active life later. Hard study in school now earns a better career after graduation. When I was drinking, Freud's words had little meaning. My slogan was something lifted from a movie star: I want what I want when I want it, *immediate gratification isn't fast enough.* A drink or a line, and the anxious edge was taken off. And so after years of boozing and doping, I never did learn the coping skills that sober people have been learning and practicing all along.

This is not to say that just because you're sober life will be one long dream of heaven. Your dog can still get run over, the IRS calls you up and says bring all your books in for an audit, the girl you love runs off with the football star. The meaning of a "dry drunk" is you may be sober, but still have not solved the moral and spiritual problem you were drinking to escape. Six months out of rehab, I was frozen in a marriage I did not understand.

In his wise book *Addictive Thinking*, Dr. Abraham J. Twerski, Founder and Medical Director of the Gateway Rehabilitation Center in Pittsburgh, Pennsylvania, says: "Newly recovered addicts may experience anxiety and panic when confronted with new feelings they have never learned to manage. They may believe being angry means feeling homicidal, loving means engulfing someone, being loved means being engulfed by someone, hating someone means alienating the whole world, and so on. Confronting these feelings is a formidable challenge. . . . *Not knowing how to isolate a particular feeling or manage it, they just shut off their whole feeling apparatus.*" (My italics.)

Those words describe the kind of dry drunk I went into when I came out of my twenty-eight-day rehab.

When I got married, drinking was still fun for me, but I think now that I was in a state of alcoholically arrested emotional development. Other men may have been going through their single years, their twenties and thirties, trying, consciously or not, to figure out what they wanted from life, from women, from themselves—what does marriage mean. I just stepped up to the bar and had another drink.

And so perhaps I was sober those first six months out of Caron, but I still did not understand who I was, nor able to face that I did not want to be in this marriage. Without booze to lift me, I went into the numbness of which Dr. Twerski speaks.

All my unresolved questions were shoved down into the dark—stinking thinking, or in my case, stinking nonthinking, a dry-drunk way of life . . . keeping off booze by white-knuckle willpower alone.

I now think I was making an effort to distance myself, not only from my unresolved problems as a husband, but also from unacceptable feelings about my wife. *I should not feel that way about her!*

When I took that first drink on New Year's Eve, it was a relief.

As a friend later said to me, "Bill, you did not put in the work necessary to resolve your feeling about your marriage. You knew your feelings but did not want to face them. You chose instead to handle the problem as you'd been doing all your life. You had a drink."

I sometimes think marriage takes a special talent, like, let's say, the special talent it takes for the violin. Isaac Stern or Jascha Heifetz—the music is one of the wonders of life. Without talent, all the hard work in the world just adds up to sour notes. We don't demand that everyone have the talent to play the violin. Since I do not have the talent for marriage, why demand of myself that I get married?

How Do I Stop?

To get back to Charlie, my caller who asked the meaning of the term *a dry drunk.* If you reread his words, you can hear the anger, feel the-chip-on-the-shoulder attitude . . . the unreality with which he still sees the world and the people in AA. *They were unfriendly to me.*

Yes?

At bottom, what I hear is you haven't yet been able to fight back from low self-respect and low self-esteem, states which are both contributory cause and effect of addiction. *I am mad at them because they have seen to the heart of me, and know I am not the kind of person they want to go out with for coffee.*

Projection.

My suspicion, Charlie, is your truculence turned people off. Unless the meetings you go to are different from any I ever attended, I bet they did invite you for coffee . . . but in your shut-off state, you just didn't hear the words, didn't believe they were sincere—one of those people found at every meeting: sitting in the back, never saying a word, leaving as soon as possible, angrily wondering why AA isn't working for them.

The old adage is that alcoholics are megalomaniacs with an inferiority complex . . . either up or down to some nutty degree. If people buy your grandiose airs, it causes anxiety: Someone is going to say, "You're all front, a fraud." If you act out the low self-worth half of your character, you're anxious again, depressed. The power of a good 12 Step program is to get you off that seesaw for good.

AA is the only social organization I know that is without snobbery, without a pecking order or hierarchy. Nobody is up, nobody is down. Even in church . . . even in the finest charity . . . there still will be people who vie to sit at the president's table, etc. But I've been to AA and NA meetings where no one wanted to chair, and they just turn to someone, even a newcomer, and say, "Well, it's your turn, get up there and take over the gavel. Lead the meeting."

Some of the blessings of AA take time to realize, if only because they are never quite put into words. If you go to ninety meetings in ninety days, slowly it comes to you: There is no A list. Everyone in the room is equal: no one more than the lift of a hand away from a drink. It's an education in leading an unposed, democratic life—we're equals in our war against addiction—power, prestige, and pecking order relationships hooted out of court.

When I got out of rehab, I took my brother and sister-in-law to an open meeting to let them know what I was up to. Elsie was so taken by the sense of community, the authenticity of emotion she heard from everyone there that she asked if she could become an AA member "without the hassle of becoming a drunk first."

AA's promise is that in time, with the help of the 12 Steps, you will learn to handle life's unhappy entanglements . . . learn how to maintain a feeling of optimism or serenity about what's to come . . . "mellow out," old-timers say. But sometimes, the negative habits are so deeply ingrained—the word *neurosis* comes to mind—that you end up a sober pain-in-the-ass to yourself and all around you. Sober, or at least *dry*, but still in a rage, still finding life impossible to deal with on life's own terms. Magical thinking and daydreaming enters, obsessive thoughts, indecision. If only I'd done this, if only I'd said that . . .

You may be sober, Charlie, but the way I hear your thought processes, they are not. And that's why you're white-knuckling it through life. As my friend, the family therapist Marjorie Ward, puts it, "Life is full of good stuff and bad stuff. When the bad stuff seems to be winning, counseling can help."

I don't agree with many old-timey AA militants who say the 12 Steps are all you need. Some problems, some psychologies are so intractable, that counseling—professional psychological therapy—is a good idea. (See "Dual Diagnosis," Q. #38.)

Sobriety alone is not enough. Why not enjoy your life?

Recovery After Addiction, and How to Stay That Way

Old joke: "I can stop any time I want. I've done it dozens of times." Six months sober, I too thought I had it licked. The nuttiness of addiction is I celebrated with a glass of champagne. The relapse that followed was the worst two weeks of my life.

This section is about recovery, about staying clean and sober for good and ever after—"happy, joyous, and free" is the AA promise. About the right way to avoid trying it again, the right and wrong ways for families or friends to help prevent relapse.

#44.

Relapse Prevention

Q. With the help of AA, I put the cork in the booze and pill bottle six months ago, and while I'm no longer on the famous "pink cloud," I am enjoying recovery very much. I'm "Leo," and my question is about one of life's peak experiences.

It's the feeling of meeting someone new over a drink or two, and by the fourth or fifth, you both know it's going to happen, and sure enough, before long you're taking her and a bottle—maybe also a little pot, maybe a line of coke—off to bed. Is that never going to happen to me again?

A. (I owe many of the insights in this discussion to my understanding of a training lecture at Scripps McDonald, given by Terrance F. Gorski of the Gorski-Cenaps Institute.)

When I got out of twenty-eight-day rehab, freed of the obsessions and compulsions of addiction, I was floating on the famous pink cloud myself. Nifty stuff, but standard. The physical symptoms of addiction are gone . . . the shameful secret is out and dealt with . . . families reunited . . . the crying stops. No more lies and alibis, hangovers are merely a memory, a new life begins.

But I think, Leo, that you've begun to find out that just because you're sober, that doesn't mean the IRS won't still be after you, that your dog didn't get run over by a fire truck; you never will be a rock star, you didn't even get that raise in the crappy job you do hold, and the son-of-bitch next door will never turn down his TV when you want to sleep.

Sobriety makes you a more competent player; it does not guarantee you will be a winner. You're still a dress size too large, and your husband is going bald. Your wife doesn't understand you, and you're in a dead-end job. You'll be able to address these problems with a cool, sober brain, yes . . . with a bit of detachment, yes . . . but they are still there. You've discovered that even glorious sobriety has realistic limits.

The pink cloud begins to float down, closer to earth.

Very dangerous time. There is no iron rule, but in my experience, this often happens at six months to a year after leaving rehab. That's when it happened to me. With most people, dissatisfaction comes under two major headings.

They're stuck in a dead-end job, one they resent, dislike, and may even hate.

They're stuck in a dead-end relationship/marriage, one they resent, dislike, and may even hate.

Drunk or sober, that doesn't change, but now you no longer dull that painful knowledge with booze or dope.

Another form of denial usually sets in. That's life, things are not too bad, etc. Underneath, dissatisfaction rankles. Well, all that AA stuff isn't all it's cracked up to be. The rosy, first optimism of early sobriety begins to flatten. Meeting attendance drops, with a corresponding lowering of the shared group morale I have spoken of elsewhere—the heart of what keeps people sober. What's the point of being sober, if life is going to be a gray drag like this? That's the emotion I hear behind Leo's question.

The answer is, coming to terms with the disappointing fact that sobriety alone does not guarantee automatic happiness leaves you with a choice between three courses of behavior.

1. Suicide. 2. Act out your impulses (run away to Paris, quit your job, get a divorce, switch to new addictions like overeating or gambling.) Or 3. Go back to dope and booze

The first (1), suicide, is not unknown of course but too radical a solution for most people. Acting out (2) one's secret impulses is more often the choice. But divorce, quitting a job, "taking the geographical cure" by running off to start anew in Timbuktu are still drastic actions. The easiest choice, the one most often taken is (3), Go back to what you know best—tamp down the dissatisfactions of life with crack, gin, marijuana, speed, crank . . .

When you were eight, it was appropriate to play cops and robbers. At eighteen, it would be arrested development. It is hard to persuade a kid in Burger King that one day he might come to prefer Veal Prince Orloff. It is difficult to convince an addict there are more satisfying experiences than getting chemically high.

I sometimes think addicts go through life walking backward, staring nostalgically into a rearview mirror at pleasures being left behind, unaware that the next stage of development may offer satisfactions as yet unknown—but if the deeper pleasures appropriate to our new stage of life are not found, the grim merry-go-round begins turning again. Remember the rainy night you met that blonde at a bar—now, that was fun! What if I stopped in this bar right now? How much harm can one drink do?

When I hear Leo talking about "peak experiences"—when he used to drink and dope—warning flags begin to fly in my mind. He is beginning to fantasize about how much fun he used to find in booze and dope. He's just about ready to regress to an earlier stage of life in the hope of some sexual fantasy meeting with some dream woman.

Change is inevitable; growth is an option you may or may not choose. Isn't Leo's resistance to growing up a kind of dark recognition that the ironic end of all growth is a slow farewell, one by one, to the physical pleasures of this world, and at the end, an acceptance of death? Which of us is good at that?

This is where AA's much misunderstood spiritual program enters—an idea, which, as I write in Q. #41, need not be interpreted in a narrowly religious sense. (For another point of view, see Father Bob, a professor of theology who is now a parish priest. Q. #42.)

Either way, I will just note here, booze and dope are glamorous, and often enough in the short run, life-enhancing. You can't just drop them without finding an equally powerful replacement. Failing that, the siren song of addiction begins all over again. As I used to hear my friend Polly S. put it so often, "The day you stop going to meetings and the day you start thinking you alone can control your life—you may think you're sober. It's the first day of your relapse."

Freud once defined maturity as the capacity to forego immediate pleasure for the sake of larger future gain. I take Leo's adolescent glamorization of remembered addictive pleasures as a sign that a relapse is beckoning—a kind of forgetting the real pain and price of addiction, a denial that this was the very life that put him into a rehab.

Let's even say Leo's fantasy might happen to him again (though you might ask, How often does that occur in real life, and wasn't it de Maupassant who said often the best part of an affair is the last ten minutes before you ring her doorbell the first time?).

Put that on one side of the scale: a couple of peak sexual adventures. On the other side, back into the waste of addiction, return to a life of pain, strokes, and heart attack, divorce lawyers, job loss, madness, jails, and early death. No wonder so many people in recovery remember their addicted life as a form of insanity.

When I got out of rehab my wife was in London, where we'd been living for several years. I flew back, and she said she would try to forgive and forget. She did try, but I was always aware of the effort. Nevertheless, on the surface, things seemed to be going well.

I went back to work on a novel I had been writing, we reintroduced ourselves as a couple to our friends. I went on a diet and lost a lot of the booze calories I'd put on. Six months later, we were invited to a big English country house for New Year's Eve weekend.

"Will you be tempted?" my wife said. "Those people really like to drink and dope."

"I'm stuck in my writing just now," I said. "A weekend away will give me a chance to get some perspective."

We packed and went.

A gala event . . . champagne and lobster, the banquet table at the end of the room loaded with brandy, pills, pot, cocaine, speed, and some of the great red wines of the world. Help yourself. At three in the morning, my wife and I went up to our room. I said to her, See, I wasn't tempted to have a drink, not even a glass of beer. My alcoholism is over. I can handle the stuff, take it or leave it.

To celebrate, I poured two glasses of Veuve Clicquot.

I finished mine and decided against another. See, I said, all that AA business about one drink will start you going again? That's a lot of crap too. I'm not tempted to keep drinking at all.

We went to bed.

The next morning I sneaked down to the butler's pantry and poured myself a water glass of gin. I drank a bottle by myself before noon, another when we got home. My wife would never trust me again. I never finished that novel, and that marriage was over too.

Sometimes I wonder—was that at the back of my mind all along?

The moral of all this: If you find yourself fondly looking back to the days when you used to drink and dope . . . If they suddenly seem glamorous to you again, look out. Relapse lies ahead.

Find a better use for that energy—like looking to see just where your life is frustrated and blocked. Work on changing that. You may find a psychologist or family therapist helpful. Tip: Be sure to ask the prospective doc, up front, how s/he feels about AA. Look out for any who say in their kind of therapy, AA or NA is no longer needed.

And be especially careful of asking your M.D. for advice. I've said this elsewhere in these pages. I feel it important enough to repeat here: When the *San Francisco Chronicle* published the results of a nationwide poll authorized by the Recovery Institute of America, 82 percent of the doctors questioned said they felt their med school training inadequate to diagnose or treat alcoholism and/or drug addiction. Therefore they do what they know best: prescribe you some pills.

Much better idea: Call your sponsor and stop telling him things are just fine—that's denial. Step up the number of meetings you go to, and maybe best of all, find some shy, floundering newcomer, and tell him he needs a sponsor, and that you're it.

Maybe you'll help him keep sober. You'll be doing more to keep sober yourself.

#45.

Blackouts and Oblivion Drinking

Q. I don't want to say this on the air. Someone might recognize my voice. Last Sunday I came to in a place I didn't know. At the back of my mind, a heavy black cloud, memory of a fight with my husband about drinking, and slamming out to get even higher, to show him. My head was back on a sofa, some guy lying half off the sofa, snoring. Oh, no, not again. My husband is circumcised. This guy wasn't.

Oh, what a beautiful morning.

Maybe "Strangers in the Night" is the drunk's national anthem, but I was too blacked out to remember meeting the guy, let alone what happened after. I found some vodka and got it down, although it almost made me puke.

Like a million other women, I've had these fantasies of making it with an anonymous stranger, and I wanted to keep it that way. So I was careful not to look at his face, and sure enough felt that old masturbatory thrill (yes, women do it too!) thinking back to what happened. After another shot of vodka, I felt well enough to get dressed and go home.

Maybe booze encouraged me to put my fantasy into action. So

what? I've lived a little and I'll never see him again. If you can answer without a lot of male moralizing, what I want to ask, Isn't a blackout just like a bad hangover? Not much fun, but by 5 P.M., you're over it? I've had blackouts before but this one was so bad I can't even remember if I had a good time.

I hope I did.

(Signed with an E-mail address.)

A. W. C. Fields tells a story about waking up in a strange hotel at the end of a five-day binge.

The room was filthy, he says, the sheets greasy and black, vomit on the floor, the windows cracked, the washstand beside the bed caked with five days' grime. In bed beside him, he goes on, was the ugliest, dirtiest, most raddled and unwashed old whore he had ever seen, her cheap makeup smeared and caked. "In that dank, dark, muddy pigsty of a room," he says, "there was only one clean white thing. The tit nearest me."

Humor is fine, Ms. E-mail, but denial, no matter how raffish and hard-boiled, is something else. My guess is that yours, like that of W. C. Fields, is a bravado effort to whistle your way past a graveyard filled with fear. Blackouts—also called alcoholic amnesia—are a warning bell, and I suspect you wouldn't have e-mailed me unless you have begun to hear it ringing yourself. Another name is oblivion drinking, a drive to get away from conscience and fear so strong that nothing will do but erasure of the mind.

Your letter seesaws between attitude and anxiety, evidence, perhaps, that you are afraid your addiction is dangerously further along than you want to admit.

Your problems with your husband are beyond my scope, but "drinking at him," as they say in AA, will not help. Without male moralizing about your sexual fantasies, why do you have to be blackout drunk to act them out, unless you do not approve of them yourself?

Final word: W. C. Fields, who was notoriously eccentric and secretive about money, is supposed to have opened savings bank accounts in made-up names all over the country. He did this during blackouts so deep he never could remember till the day he died where the money was. That story may be apocryphal. This is not: He died drinking gin out of a douche bag suspended over his bed because he was so drunk, his hand shaking so badly, he could not hold a glass.

Your phrase about feeling "impending doom" is one I've heard a thousand times from a thousand alcoholics. It's one of the prime indicators that I talk about elsewhere in this book (see Q. #32). If I were you, E-mail correspondent of mine, and my alcoholism had progressed so far that this latest blackout seemed to me no more than *ho hum, just one of those things* . . .

Here's what I would do.

First, get myself tested for AIDS and other STDs, and for pregnancy too. I am not so sure "Strangers in the Night" is your theme song. Try, "Taking a Chance on Love."

If all is still well—let us hope—I'd forget the attitude and the jokes and get to a marital counselor or divorce lawyer, get to an AA meeting, get to a rehab; I'd cut it out.

#46.

Calling It a "Disease" Is Just Politically Correct Liberal Crap, Right?

Q. My name is Mona, thirty-two, and just divorced from my second husband, a no-good drunk . . . as was my first. You know what's wrong with men in America? All this talk about alcoholism or drug addiction being a "disease"—which is just some more lefty, liberal, New Age babble put out by people like you. Why can't they Just Say No?

Even AA says they have a character defect. They're morally weak and deficient in willpower, right?

A. Mona, take an alcoholic or drug addict without a penny in his pocket. Deposit him, friendless and alone, in a blue-nose town (like the old-time Philadelphia that W. C. Fields used to bemoan). Dump him there at 6 A.M. Sunday morning, broke and hung over, the bars and liquor stores closed. He'll find a way to get high before noon.

That's willpower.

Willpower is short-term, a kind of sprint emotion. It will carry you into a burning building to rescue your dog, but booze and drugs have stamina, they're in it for the long run. They never get old, they never get tired, they don't get stale or discouraged. They wait, and one day, the addict's willpower flags.

Bingo! Hooked again.

The other thing I don't like about the supposed magic of *willpower:* It wastes your life. Are you thinking about maybe going to the ballgame, next Saturday night's nifty date, paying for your kid's college education, going skiing or moving to Key West? No, you're sweating bullets, so obsessed with resisting dope and booze you can't think of anything else. How much fun is that?

So much for Just Say No, and willpower too.

In 1956, the American Medical Association officially said alcoholism met three standard criteria for being declared a disease: (1) it had an identifiable set of symptoms; (2) it followed a predictable and malign progression if not treated; and (3) it did respond to treatment. What this meant was that the insurance industry—not markedly a bastion of lefty, liberal New Age babble—agreed to pay for treatment, just as if you came down with diabetes or cancer.

I will again address the question of AA and "character defects" in Q. #48 but on the whole, Mona, I do like the idea of calling alcoholism and drug addiction a disease. It ameliorates shame and/or guilt, two ideas which never helped anyone get sober. But I myself prefer the term *addiction.* You didn't catch your habit by kissing the bartender.

Addiction is a disease and you do it to yourself. The good news is recovery is possible, and, once again, it's up to you. But, Mona, you asked me a question. Let me ask one of you.

You married two drunks in a row. Do you think it is in the stars or something in your unexamined anger that leads me to believe, odds on, you're going to try for three?

#47.

"One Minute We're Fine, the Next at Each Other's Throat!"

Q. Whenever someone goes off the rails in their job or marriage, especially when there's liquor or dope mixed in, well-meaning Nervous Nellies get up on your show and talk about "professional help." I get tired of this psychobabble. Looking outside themselves for help is where they went wrong in the first place. It used to be in a bottle of liquor or pills, or a pipeful of dope. Now it's in some "doctor of social work."

Bill, these are weak people who need to (1), shape up and stop drinking, and (2), now that they have their full, unliquored-up brain available to them maybe for the first time in their lives, show some moral backbone and figure out for themselves what's wrong. The answer is never "out there" but in yourself. Until they do figure that out, psychotherapy will never work, and if they do, they don't need it.

A. "One of the oldest injunctions to the human race," said Marjorie Ward, a former Clinical Associate at UC Irvine School of Medicine, who now practices psychotherapy in the town where I live, "comes from the ancient Greeks, 'Know thyself.' And so I agree with your caller that the answer to most human relational problems lie within ourselves. But I find that when mood-altering chemicals are involved, the people using them often want to ignore, or can't see the part they play in the quarreling, name calling, and physical abuse that often follows. We're all so conditioned to think of alcohol as a 'relaxer,' to associate it with good times, that it's hard to see it as part of the problem. What goes wrong is a mystery, and so it's easy to blame the other. In good psychotherapy the role of client as questioner and the therapist as source of all knowledge is frequently reversed. The client has the answers but is unable or unwilling to recognize it."

"So the therapist's job," I said, "is to identify to them the stimulus that causes their own bewildering behavior?"

"As long as mystification remains, the client is defended against recognizing how much s/he is contributing to the problem, and the destructive situation seems unsolvable."

"You're saying the answers must come from the client?"

"My job is to help the client see the power that comes from assuming responsibility for change."

"Changes are difficult."

"And will occur only if the client *chooses* to make them."

"Give me an example."

She did, and here it is as she wrote it down for me.

CLIENT (slim, auburn-haired, middle-aged Mrs. S.): I was on disability, living with my son in Monterey when Tom and I met. He is retired, a recent widower. We met at a dance, which we both like. He wanted to sell his house, but had just let the yard go. I used my insurance money to buy plants and the new landscaping helped with the sale. When we married, we moved up here and I thought everything would be fine—new house, new friends. It's been a year and a half now, but if things don't change between us, I don't know what I will do. I feel helpless and scared. Everything seems fine between us, and then all at once, we're at each other's throats. Look at this (pulls up her sleeve to reveal bruises like finger and thumbprints on her upper arm). He called me a bitch and shook me till I was dizzy.

MW (Marjorie Ward): This kind of behavior isn't acceptable. I can see why you feel frightened and helpless. How did this happen?

CLIENT: We'd been working in the yard, which we both enjoyed. We came in and showered. Fresh clothes feel really good. I got a glass of wine, gave him his first beer, and started to make supper. While the spaghetti sauce was simmering, I made a salad. He was watching TV: first the news, then *Law & Order*.

I said, "It must be pretty nice to sit around until somebody gives you dinner." I was teasing, but really meant it too. His answer was, "If dinner was ready sooner, I wouldn't be sitting around, I'd be eating." Well, that made me pretty mad. He's so selfish, he never thinks of anybody but himself, and I told him so. He jumped up and shouted that I was always nagging at him and he'd show me who was boss. I told him he was lucky to have a young wife to help him in his garden and cook his meals. There were plenty of men that envied him. I wouldn't have any trouble finding somebody else to live with. That was when he reached out and began to shake me. It was awful. He just wants me to wait on him and keep my mouth shut. Then everything is fine. (Begins to cry) I can't do that. I'm a person too. Sometimes I think there is nothing to do but leave him. But I don't want to. What can I do?

MW (handling client a tissue): You could leave him, of course, but let's see what other options you have. You say you were working happily together in the garden. Fine, but both later changed in attitude while you were preparing dinner. He was resting and you were working, but you were still sharing one activity.

CLIENT: What is that?

MW: You were both drinking.

CLIENT: I only had a couple of glasses of wine and he had two or three beers. Neither was drunk. How could that make a difference?

MW: Alcohol affects the cortex of the brain, reducing normal self-control, and impairing our judgment. We speak impulsively, without regard for the effect on others. What were you feeling when you told D. that dinner was nearly ready? Were you really just teasing when you said it must be pretty nice to be waited upon?

CLIENT: I guess I was irritated and wanted him to know it was unfair for us both to work all afternoon and then I have to fix dinner while he rests. But that was no reason for him to holler and grab me.

MW: Right. But your story just changed from one glass of wine, one glass of beer, to several of each. Beer affects judgment just as much as does wine. So D.'s behavior can be partially attributed to his drinking. I think that is important for you to be aware of. How is communication between you when neither has been drinking?

CLIENT: Pretty good, except when I want to spend money. Then he gets all excited. Says I'm a spendthrift, that I'll put him in the poorhouse. And I don't really know how much money he has. I have only Social Security and that isn't enough to live on. I don't want to be walking on eggs all the time, trying to watch my words while he gets to go on acting like he always does (cries again).

MW: Life often seems too much to bear. The amazing thing is we mostly do. Human beings cannot remain at the bottom of a pit too long. So let's figure your way out together. What can you change?

CLIENT: Well, I can cut back on my drinking.

MW: Are you willing and able to do that?

CLIENT: Yes, I think so.

MW: Will you be willing to use a support system to help you?

CLIENT: You mean AA? Oh, I don't think I'm that bad. I've cut down before. But even if I did, that doesn't affect the way D. behaves.

MW: If D. finds you're not drinking right along with him, we can't be sure how he will react, but we can be sure there will be some change. Second, you yourself will be seeing things differently, not making decisions through an alcohol filter. Can you lessen your resentment toward him by changing some household routines? When he wants you to help in the yard, maybe say you'll be out as soon as you have the spaghetti sauce made.

CLIENT: Play a role?

MW: The hard part of making changes is you're doing things differently, you don't feel yourself. But the wonderful thing is, you can decide to change. You've made it this far. I feel confident you can deal with this. When you need help, it's available. Can you encourage your husband to be a partner in this? Would he come with you to see me and work on these changes?

CLIENT: I don't know if he would agree there's something wrong with himself.

MW: I believe there is more to your differences than the drinking. His abuse of you is not a negotiable item. You must make that clear to him. You also seem to have two different worldviews, different values about money and how to spend it. You are still exploring one another's capacities. If you can do that nonjudgmentally, and you still want to live together, you can make that not only feasible, but happy. When people say, as you did, "Everything seems fine between us, and then all at once, we're at each other's throats," that sounds like alcohol is at work. Changes need to occur and it will be a lot easier if you can work them out soberly and together.

CLIENT: I'll talk to him. And I'll cut back on my own drinking. Maybe we can make this better. Maybe I won't have to leave him.

An Afterword with Marjorie Ward.

"These two people are dealing with many stressful situations. I'm still uncertain how much the alcohol is to blame, but obviously it liberates them to vent various forms of anger, at aging with its accompanying aches and pains; for disappointment that in their new marriage, they disagree on so much."

I said I'd noted how Mrs. S. wove the potentially explosive fact of their drinking into her story as if it were just another textural detail of everyday life: They met at a dance, they work in the yard, shower and change clothes, she gives him a beer, he watches *Law & Order*, she has a glass of wine, makes a salad . . .

"Just the merest hint she's drinking wine right there with him, glass for glass. Later, she tells us she's cut back on alcohol before. This means she'd been drinking enough to worry about. Temperate people don't cut back. They don't have to. Marjorie, my bet is they're both drinking more than she's ready to let you know."

"Or perhaps to let herself know. There'll need to be a lot more work before things really improve. If they see it might mean giving up their alcohol dependence, they might give up working with me instead."

"Alcohol," I said. "Proving once again that it's cunning, baffling, and powerful?"

Marjorie laughed and said yes.

#48.

Disease or Character Defect?

Q. I went to my first AA meeting but left when they began talking about character defects. That sounds very moralistic and Victorian to me, an outmoded idea. I'm ChiChi, nineteen years old, and I sing with a band. If AA really believes alcoholism is a disease, do they mean you catch it because you're bad?

A. Once again I turned for help to John A. MacDougal, the United Methodist Minister who is also Manager of Spiritual Guidance at Hazelden. "Addiction is a disease that feeds on our character defects," he says. "A chronic disease that, while not subject to cure and characterized by relapse, can be managed with a program of recovery.

"Just 'not drinking' and 'not drugging' aren't much fun. Recovery isn't a matter of quitting. Most of us have, many times, only to pick up and use again when in turmoil.

"Recovery consists of developing a spiritual way of life that gives us resilience. If we have our character defects reduced or removed by a higher power and by working the program, then we replace our drinks and drugs with a way of life that is genuinely more satisfying."

I said to John that judging by myself, the great character defects of most addicts are selfishness and grandiosity. "Add irritability and impatience," he said, "and I'll agree. If in our relationships with a higher power, with others and ourselves we are selfish, grandiose, and irritable, conflict and inner turmoil result. Then we drink and drug to relieve the mess we have created."

"John, give me an example of a character defect at work, and how it interplays with addiction."

"The husband comes home wanting a drink. He then picks a fight with his wife so that he can storm out and go to a bar. His character defects have been mobilized to keep his addiction going. Addiction isn't caused by character defects, but giving our character defects free rein keeps us sick."

#49.

"Her Sponsor Says Okay, Mine Says No"

Q. My name is Hank, my wife is Tina, both in our early thirties, married almost two years, and the drug of choice for us both used to be cocaine. We met at an NA meeting, but did not get serious until we'd both been clean and sober for a year. We both recently celebrated our third drug-free birthday.

I'm in sales, Tina's work is in advertising. A lot of business in each field is done over lunch and dinner, and that often means meeting customers in a bar. My wife's sponsor is cool with that. She says as long as it is in the line of business, it is okay for Tina to meet her clients anywhere they like. Since liquor was never my temptation, I thought my sponsor would feel the same, but he says alcohol is a drug and he doesn't want me anywhere liquor is sold.

Bill, do I have to change my job? My sponsor is a great guy, fourteen years' sobriety, Tina thinks hers is great too. Which sponsor is right?

A. Both.

Ever see a stage magician work? The words and the pretty assistant, the movement of Mandrake's hands, all keep your attention . . . the real trick is happening somewhere else. I think the same goes for sponsors and sobriety.

For reasons given in Q. #31, you may want to ask someone else about how far to follow a sponsor's advice. But if you do want my opinion, here it is.

Every sponsor in the world is the world's greatest authority on only one thing: how he got sober himself. So I am not convinced a sponsor's words and sometimes subjectively crackpot ideas are the dynamo that makes the relationship work. Going through the Steps together, the advice and conversation keep your attention. The trick is happening somewhere else: in your emotional connection to someone you like and admire and whose qualities of sobriety you want to emulate. That you and Tina both have such a connection is evident from your own words, and the three years' record of sobriety. That's why I say both sponsors are right.

As for the rest, let me again quote Larry Bouchard. "In working with addicts for over twenty years," he says, "I've come to think recovery is not an exact science. It's 80 percent art, 10 percent science, and the rest, guts and hope." Somewhere in that 90 percent of art, guts, and hope, there's room for debate and discussion with your sponsor. But, remember, the emotional connection comes first.

#50.

A Wife's Denial

Q. Recently, we bought a big new house, the kind I have always dreamed of. I'm Marsha, forty-two. My husband says we can afford it. He makes good money selling but is addicted to cocaine. He says it is his best business tool. Before he makes a cold call, he does a line off his thumbnail. It gives him the kind of enthusiasm and self-confidence he needs to make the sale. He says without cocaine, he wouldn't be able to maintain sales high enough for us to afford the house. I love my husband, but have very little experience with drugs; I barely drink myself. Can I believe him? What can I do to help him?

A. The doctors call addiction "a progressive disease." Like a snowball on a hill, it speeds up, getting bigger and bigger with time. Where one line used to do the job, it now takes two, three, or ten. "With my customers," says my friend, Downtown Jack B., a recovered (twelve years) cocaine dealer himself, "immediate gratification wasn't fast enough. They were always shooting for a quicker, bigger high . . . more, more, more . . ." I suspect, Marsha, sooner or later that will be your husband's story too, and you will then have to make some difficult choices. First, a word about the odds.

Downtown Jack persuaded me to volunteer as a facilitator at Scripps McDonald, for which I am forever in his debt. One of my jobs was to do the orientation lecture. New patients got the speech that had been made to me years before when I went through rehab myself.

"Out of every ten of us in this room today," I would begin, "one or two will be dead within five years. Suicide, a blown liver . . . maybe an auto accident or overdose. Five out of six of the ten will have gone back to drinking and/or doping. The insurance companies keep statistics on these things, and they know. Only two or three will still be clean and sober."

There would be an outcry. "Don't tell us news like that," said one woman. "I've never been a lucky gambler. I hate those odds."

I told her that recovery from addiction has nothing to do with luck or odds. "We have a disease," I said, "but not the kind where the doctor cuts out your appendix, and you're cured. This is a hospital, but with your disease, we do not cure you. You are the doctor. You make the odds, you cure yourself. What we do here is teach you how to maximize your chances of being among the two or three out of ten who stay sober. That's not luck. That's your choice."

I'm grateful to you, Marsha, for the reminder that chemical intoxicants distort the minds of sober people too. What I hear in your question is a kind of denial that matches your husband's. He does not want to know his addiction will get worse and worse. You're buying his rationalizations because you don't want to know it either. Hard not to, since you seem to be dependent on him for information on what drugs do. What I would suggest is a course of self-education.

You can get informative literature, free, at any Al-Anon meeting, a step toward the kind of independence from your husband I think you will need. Some info on co-dependency is in order too (See Q. #53).

Your husband may or may not recover. In Al-Anon, you'll meet people whose marriages have gone either way, people who will share their experience, strength, and hope with you. How far you want to go with your husband is up to you, but Al-Anon and some knowledge of co-dependency will help you make an informed choice.

Values enter too: When I spoke to Marianne Peck, a noted family therapist in Modesto, California, about the dilemma Marsha faced, Marianne suggested she ask herself—How much is a big house worth?

#51.

"I'll Die If I Don't Have a Drink Soon As I Leave the Meeting!"

Q. Bill, my name is Liz, I'm twenty-nine and listening to your show on my car radio, driving to Albertson's. I've been sober eleven days, but it's been hard time. I'm shaking and about to jump out of my skin. I need a drink. I don't want to, my husband will leave me and I'll lose my kids. Because when there's booze, sooner or later, there's another man.

I know it's wrong but I'm obsessed with the idea of two drinks, the first fast to kill the shakes, the second, long and slow, maybe a cigarette. (I've been trying to quit those too.) After that, I don't care.

Don't tell me about lung cancer or one day at a time. I can't wait that long. Can you say anything that will keep me from buying two fifths of Jack Black when I get to the supermarket, a carton of Luckies, soda and ice, and then locking myself into a motel room for a week?

A. Liz, can you hold out ten minutes?

I first heard it near the end of an AA meeting on Lexington Avenue, in New York City: The chair closed with the conventional announcement: "Anyone with a burning desire to say one last word?"

A young woman, maybe eighteen or nineteen, got up. Shaking, trembling, white-faced, and close to tears, she said this meeting was her last hope. "I can't hold out. I'll die if I don't have a drink," she said. "As soon as this meeting ends, I'm going to get drunk."

"Can you take it one day at a time?" said the guy in the chair (an old-timer called Bud). "These anxious desires to drink often leave us as suddenly as they come. If you take that first drink, you become someone else. You won't care, and you won't stop with one."

"I'm going to drink as soon as I walk out the door."

"Can you hold out an hour?"

"If I had a gun, I'd shoot myself right now."

"Ten minutes?"

"I'll try."

"Someone please go out to the corner deli," said Bud, "and buy a quart of milk and a jar of honey. Anyone here have a wrist alarm?"

He turned back to the girl (whom I will call Jane). "You did one smart thing," he said, bringing her up front to sit with him. "You didn't try to John Wayne it out alone, you asked for help."

Most people left. A few stayed, gathered around Bud and Jane. Some guy who had a wrist alarm watch took it off. Bud set it for ten minutes and put it on the table. He poured a glass of milk, spiked it with a generous dollop of honey, took a sip himself, and encouraged Jane to drink the rest. I remember seeing one woman holding the girl's hand, a guy in the back closed his eyes—maybe he was praying. Mostly we watched the minute hand move on the clock.

The alarm went off.

"Still want a drink?"

"More than ever."

"Can you hold out another ten minutes?"

"I'll try."

Bud reset the alarm, poured another glass of milk and honey. "There's a lot of sugar in booze," he told Jane. "It ever occur to you to have a Snicker's or Hershey bar with your beer or gin?" he said. "Of course not. You were getting the sugar you needed from your alcohol. After a while, your system gets used to it, wants a lot of sugar in the bloodstream. Booze will kill the shakes, sure," he said. "But when I went through rehab, they told me maybe it isn't alcohol you're shaking for, but for a sugar rush. That's the idea behind the milk and honey."

After a while, Jane's hands stopped shaking. She was smiling, covered with a light sheen of sweat. Another half hour, she'd drunk the quart of milk and finished the honey. The motherly woman who had been holding her hand said she'd take Jane home in a taxi.

The episode echoed behavior of my own after I got out of Chit Chat, and was living with my wife once more in our house in London. Every morning, I'd lie like the drunk I was, and tell her I was going out for a walk. I'd go around the corner, buy a newspaper, and three or four half-pound Cadbury with Nuts chocolate bars, stop off at a Lyons, order tea, read the newspaper for an hour or two, and eat all the chocolate. A pound, maybe two or even three pounds of candy a day.

Part of the thrill was old behavior, a drunk's sneakiness in satisfying his desires. But a lot of it was just that I craved chocolate.

"I gained fifty pounds before I kicked that habit."

I was telling this story to the woman—let's call her Jane Two—who had called me at the radio station on her car phone. We were sitting in a booth at Denny's where I had asked her to meet me. And she was drinking a black-and-white ice cream soda.

"All well and good," she said. "I can see you're sober, but how did the story end for Jane?" she said. "Did she drink the next day?"

"All I know, she did not drink that night. Or at least, that part of that night when I could see her. I was in New York City on a brief visit, and never went to that meeting again. But that's all any of us ever have—one day at a time . . . maybe only ten minutes at a time."

Jane Two's straw made a sucking sound. She finished the ice cream soda and laughed ruefully as we stood up to walk to her car.

She told me I had been right about one thing. "The soda and maybe the little time that passed while we talked, Bill, they killed the urge to drink and have a cigarette all right," she said. "But do I have to put on fifty pounds?"

"You know how they say in AA that we were willing to go to any lengths to get sober? That's what it took for me. When, later, I had some solid sobriety behind me, I went on a diet, lost the weight, and nowadays, no longer crave chocolate."

"If that's what I have to do every time I get the urge to drink or smoke," said Jane Two, "I'll get so fat my husband will leave me anyway."

She got in her car and turned the key.

"Yes," I said, "but nobody ever got arrested for fat driving."

I never saw her again.

#52.

Am I an Alcoholic? (An Unscientific Test)

Q. Hey, Bill, I'm calling from a pay phone in a bar. I'm going to have an early lunch, and thought I'd have a drink first. You know what? I'm on my second. That make me an alcoholic?

A. Did you finish the drink and order another before you stood up to phone me?

Q. No, it's waiting for me on the bar.

A. You have nothing to worry about.

#53.

Keep Booze in the House?

Q. Bill, I heard your show on the Internet, and was very interested because my husband is in the same rehab that you went to. He is coming home next week. I visited last Sunday, and asked him right out. Should I throw out all the liquor that we usually keep in the house?

I like a glass of wine, maybe a drink before dinner, but I am deathly afraid that just the sight of it might lead him right back to his own drinking again. I told him I'd gladly give up my own occasional drinking if he thought it represented any danger to him. He told me that he didn't believe in what he called *artificial conditions*. He said I was trying to baby him. "Tina," he said, "there are bars on every corner. I have to get used to living in the real world, and not make our house a place to hide from my addiction."

Bill, all this sounds fine, but is it just an excuse for having booze in the house? I am terrified of ever seeing him take one single drink again. Specifically, would I be wise not to listen to him, to have the house alcohol-free when he comes home? I know that in the end, his recovery is up to him, to choose it or not, but at the beginning at least, when his recovery is still new and fragile, what do you think I should do? Or is all this worry about him just what I hear more and more these days called "co-dependent behavior"? (How I hate that term. Where does love end and co-dependency begin?)

A. In my own case, when I came home from rehab, I did not ask my (then) wife to get rid of the booze in the house. It did not matter to me if she had a drink or not. I knew I did not want to. And in fact, at the six-month point, when I did have the one awful relapse that I write about elsewhere in these pages, it was not at my house, but at a New Year's Eve party somewhere else.

Nevertheless, I think this idea too important to give you merely my own opinion. Paul Ehrlich, director of the Addiction Studies Program at John F. Kennedy University in Orinda, California, was a guest on my show one day, and I was so impressed by his cool clarity when it came to discussing co-dependency that when I got this question, I called him when I got off the air.

I told him about a couple I knew. Betty wanted to go to a baseball game; Harry wanted to go bowling. They went to a movie instead, which was neither one's first choice because it was more important for them to avoid conflict than to express what either truly wanted.

"Which, after a while," Paul said, "begins to breed that silent, nagging resentment in both against their marriage."

"And each blames the other," I said. "On their silver anniversary, people say, *Wow, twenty-five years married and still going strong!* Sure. Maybe the marriage is going strong, but both people are dead—numbed to bear the angry boredom and resentment they feel from being unable to break out and speak to each other truthfully."

I offered a definition of co-dependency that I liked. "Co-dependence means worrying about someone else to the point of your own denigration. As the old joke says, when the co-dependent drowns, it's someone else's life that flashes before his eyes."

Paul laughed and added the definition he uses in his practice: *Co-dependence is a pattern of painful dependence on compulsive behaviors and on approval from others, in an attempt to find safety, self-worth, and identity.*

"However, what I'd like to stress," he said emphatically, "is that recovery is possible."

I said let me see if I understand that. "Take a mother with her baby, constantly monitoring the child's state. Too hot, too cold, does the kid want to go to the park, need his nose wiped, his coat buttoned, etc. If the kid has a runny nose and a temperature she'll pass up the most glamorous dinner party of the year to watch over him. He is her life, and if she were drowning, she would hand him into the lifeboat first. All this may seem a one-way street but no one would call her co-dependent. Why?"

"Because," said Paul, "it's developmentally appropriate for a mother to care for an infant that way. Co-dependence tends to 'infantilize' the adolescent or adult alcoholic or addict in ways that are not helpful and in fact tends to prolong the problem and make it worse.

"Let's go back to the definition I put forward earlier," he went on. "The core of this is the focus on a *'painful dependence on compulsive behaviors and on approval from others.'* Let's also remember that men can be co-dependent as well. When Mom or Dad is taking care of the baby in a healthy and balanced manner, there is no painful compulsion. They're not doing it for the approval of others but out of a true mothering or parenting spirit, and to fulfill a deep biological need in themselves. One, they love doing it, and two—in the main, it makes them feel great too. They feel amply repaid. The healthy parent encourages the child to learn to walk without Mom or Dad. The co-dependent sees that as abandonment, a frightening betrayal."

Paul went on: "In a wholesome adult relationship, it works the same way. Whenever you do something for another because you want to do it, you feel amply repaid."

"You don't resent doing it or feel frightened," I said. "You don't nag the other, 'See how much I am sacrificing for you.'"

"I see you've had some experience with co-dependency yourself," Paul said dryly, and went on:

"Once we understand this, we can turn to Tina's question about keeping liquor in the house. First, I'd like to agree with her when she says she hates the term 'co-dependent.' I dislike it immensely as well. It seems to pathologize the very best in human nature; the true altruistic desire to help and care for one another. This is especially true for women who have been acculturated as caretakers, to mother and to nurture; not to mention the powerfully deep biological drive to have and raise families. But healthy love is spontaneous and free. It is never controlling, demanding repayment, or denigrating to the other in an attempt to find self-worth."

I asked why is there always control and rigidity in co-dependency?

"One possible explanation may be that any spontaneous action on the part of the beloved rouses fears the next might be to leave. The constant nagging kills initiative and works to instill anxiety in the other. Another common belief is, 'Whatever I do will most likely be wrong. Therefore I better do nothing, but wait for clues from my partner.' And thus there is the unending effort to avoid conflict."

"So we have all these controlling, rigid forms of behavior," I said, "that come to us disguised as love?"

"Whenever the one professing to love you says, 'I'm criticizing you for your own good, you'll be happier if you do what I say, etc.'"—the words may come disguised as love, 'taking care of you,' even supposedly 'nurturing you,' but somehow you don't feel better for it. They tend to have the opposite effect."

Paul went on: "Love between adults is a balance, a give-and-take that has to be constantly navigated, and there are no hard and fast rules. It differs for each couple.

"Lack of balance arises when you pay so much attention to your partner's need that you ignore your own and forget to take care of yourself. Ironically, this can cause trouble for both. The other feels guilty about your sacrifice and resents any implication that it buys you the high moral ground. You feel the partnership is one-sided, and may come to resent your partner. And love suffers.

"To my mind," Paul continued, "the key point in Tina's question comes when she says she is 'terrified' of ever seeing her husband take a single drink again. She has to learn to recognize and deal with her own fear. Once again, it is a matter of navigation and negotiation. The question of should they keep liquor in the house or not cannot be answered when she is in this emotional and panicky state.

"For instance, if they both agree on a particular approach, there is no difficulty. But when she asks would she be wise not to listen to him, to have the house alcohol-free when he comes home—the question carries overtones of she 'knows best.' She is attempting to control the environment and/or his behavior. You get the sense she is going to watch him like a hawk."

"Breeding resentment in him?"

"She is powerless over his alcoholism. That's one of the first things she must learn. In my practice, I would advise someone like Tina to take a good long hard look at her own fears . . . perhaps with professional help. Internalized, they keep her from using good judgment. Externalized, they spill over and become behaviors and attitudes which create the opposite of what she hopes for most. Al-Anon too is very useful in helping someone get the balance right."

Paul went on: "The point here is that addiction is a family disease and everyone in the family has to make parallel efforts to overcome it. Her fears must not control him any more than his drinking can be allowed to control her."

"And should they keep liquor in the house?"

"There is no magic, one-size-fits-all answer. The first step in their sober, new, non–co-dependent life and in how they handle their marriage might very well be a discussion of that mutual problem."

Driving home from the radio station last Saturday after my show, I heard *Tristan and Isolde* broadcast from the Met. The beautiful music, the romance of the story were overwhelming. But thinking of what I had learned from Paul Ehrlich about the mysteries of love versus co-dependency, led me to wonder:

When someone says I love you, I cannot live without you, does that sound like one adult to another, or a frightened baby to his mother?

#54.

How Does Addiction Arrest Emotional Development?

Q. I went to my first AA meeting the other night, and afterwards, some guys invited me to go with them for coffee and. They all had long-term sobriety, and so I was glad to go.

I began telling them about the trouble I was having with my girlfriend. They told me whatever the incident we were fighting about, the real problem was that I had stopped growing when I began to drink and dope. "How old were you when you first started to fry your brains?" someone asked. I said I had used pot and beer all during high school.

"So, emotionally, you're still about fifteen, sixteen years old," they said to me. "That's why you have trouble with girls."

Bill, I'm thirty-two now, and hear all sorts of slogans and mottoes at AA meetings. No one ever explains them. So I was afraid to ask these guys what they meant.

A. You hear it often—that you stop "growing" when you begin using booze and dope in a big-time serious way. I never liked that formulation—too New Agey and glib to my ears. I prefer the way Larry Bouchard (a friend whom I often quote in these pages) puts it. "What booze and dope do," says Larry, a clinician with a mental health provider in my county, "is stop you from experiencing your own life. It sounds like that's what happened to your thirty-two-year-old caller.

"When you're using, you do not fully feel the emotional events that are the raw material which we turn into emotional maturity. Setbacks, adversities, and overcoming them too—joy, sadness, grief, birth, death, rejection, fulfillment, whatever—compulsive substance abuse keeps them distant from you, your life goes on as if behind a pane of glass."

Marianne Peck, another friend who is a family therapist in Modesto, California, puts it like this: "When your primary relationship is with intoxicating chemicals, everything else usually falls by the way-side. When your brain is poisoned with alcohol or dope, intellectual growth is stunted and your relationships with others are mostly based on finding pals who are interested in getting high with you. These are *not* often relationships that challenge you to grow, mature, and change."

Talking to Larry and Marianne reminded me of those bewildering years from junior high school years when I was in love with Lillian Gaar and Reba Milton and thought I was outside the common experience of the human race—the only boy alive so freaky he was in love with two girls at the same time.

I was far too shy to mention my feelings and, in fact, as far as Reba and Lilly knew, what brought us together was we were three of the smartest kids in our class, clubbing together because we were so uneasy with experiments that some of our classmates were beginning with cigarettes and what we called "reefers," with beer, whiskey, and (rarely, but not unknown) "all-the-way" sex.

The flag we flew was that we were great pals and on the surface, that's what we were: homework and lunch together, walking home from school as a trio, sometimes going to the movies, all for one and one for all. I hid the despair I felt when they exchanged a glance and withdrew into their secret all-girl world . . . the turbulence a special, private smile from either or both would start in my heart. I was also thrilled, being on the inside, knowing how they really felt about this boy or that as opposed to what they allowed him to think . . . but how to tell them that if I wrote the word *skirt* on one of the ruled pages of my math notebook, a chill would lift the hairs on the back of my arms?

As I reread the words I just wrote, I've begun to laugh. I don't think I fooled them at all. But for whatever reason (girls are born eighteen years older than boys and one of the drags about being a girl must be this waiting for boys to grow up)—for whatever reason, Lillian and Reba went along with me, often letting me in on their own timidities about the opposite sex. Until one day, Lillian said something a little *too* offhandedly about something she'd done with her current boyfriend, the all too fastidiously prissy teacher's pet, Edmund.

—who, it turned out, wasn't all that prissy after all.

"That doesn't fit," I said to her. "That doesn't sound like you."

Lillian and Reba grew silent. "What do you mean?" Lilly said.

"I never thought you were that kind of girl."

The silence grew more profound. We were friends yes, but I was a male first, ultimately as mysterious to them as they to me.

"What kind of girl am I?" Lillian said.

"Yes, what kind of girl do you like?" said Reba.

Silence.

I was a fair athlete in those days, and played first base on the Comets S.A.C. (Social and Athletic Club). "How come you're hanging out so much with those two girls?" some members—those beginning to put more emphasis on the S. than on the A.—would ask. "Getting any? You making out with both?" and I would grow angry. If Lilly, Reba, and I were walking along together and someone said a four-letter word, I would blush. They were my "friends" but they also were "girls," and "nice" ones at that. I could not put those thoughts together. How explain that sometimes I'd have to turn or even suddenly bolt off? How shameful, to be getting erections over Lilly and Reba?

How could I want to—you know—my friends?

Yes, there were passages with other girls, and, yes, I went through the ritual of having to learn it was up to the boy to phone the girl, and steel yourself against the chance she might say no, she did not want to go to the dance with you, she much preferred to go with (for instance) Edmund . . .

Etc.

But when Reba and Lilly asked what kind of girl did I like, I had no answer. I was still puzzling out what it meant to be a girl, to be a boy, and what did I want from girls in general, and one girl (when she would come along) in particular. Or would there always be more than one—as witness my feelings for both Reba and Lillian?

Listening to them on our walks home from school, it seemed that for girls, love and parties, dating, and even the mysterious business of sex, all that was fun and maybe thrilling but, nevertheless, kid stuff. The real business of life was to find some boy, running around fat, dumb, and uselessly happy, and teach him the real business of life was to support a wife and kids, and the sooner everyone was about this grown-up business, the better. As inevitably as spring followed winter, that was what being grown up meant.

Boys who did not yet see that were still *immature.*

Yes?

I'd never paid attention to weddings until my cousin Jack married the summer I turned fifteen. All the women (including my fun-loving mother) treated the bridegroom as a hero, how handsome and happy Jack looked, what a lucky fellow to get such a good wife, etc. And most of the men congratulated him too: The groom was undeniably the one man on whom the spotlight shone most fiercely that day. But what about those few other males (including my bitter father, whom I swore every day not to grow up to resemble), who talked about Jack getting "caught"? They weren't the heroes of the day, oh, no—they were sardonically clustered around the caterer's bar, glad they were *not* walking up the aisle, glad not to be the hero of the day.

Some women in the family condescended to smile down at these outcasts and losers. "You'll be lucky to be next," Aunt Rose said to the most vehement one. "What kind of life is that, to live alone, lonely as a dog? Some girl is going to catch you. Wait and see, she'll make you happy despite yourself."

In the movies, the emblematic act of the hero, *his defining role as winner,* was to beat out the other guy and get the girl. Was I the only one who thought he was the one who'd lost? What Aunt Rose proposed seemed so eminently right, the ordained, natural order of things, so *grown-up—* what was wrong with me, why did I identify, not with Jack, but with the outcasts at the bar and the movie second banana, the one who rode off into the sunset alone? In my ruled math notebook, on the empty page after the one where I had written *skirt,* I wrote *better to have loved and lost.*

I wanted to talk about this to Lilly and Reba but hesitated before their united feminine front. It would reveal me to be still hopelessly a kid. I was afraid they were already leaving me behind. The idea that there might not be any one right answer to my feelings for both Reba and Lilly, nor to many of life's puzzles was underlined our first day in high school after the long summer vacation:

We had parted in June, three kids swearing we'd be friends forever. Here they came in September, wearing lipstick, stockings, heels, and tight skirts, going out with boys in college who owned cars! I was their past, put away with childish things. They were about their future business, which was the soon-to-be grown-up world of marriage and children and they had no time left for me. I woke out of sleep one night that week, rockets of fire in my head: abandonment, loneliness, and something else: whatever went on between boys and girls, everybody lies to kids and I'd have to figure things out for myself.

All those nights spent wondering what Reba meant when she said this, how Lillian felt when she did that, how would they feel about me if I did not do something else—if I'd been drinking or smoking dope, none of that speculation and introspection would have happened. Arrested development.

I'd just have poured another beer, lit another joint, let the whole thing go. I don't think I'd be a writer today.

PS. These many years later, I puzzled still over the dilemma first posed to me by Lillian and Reba, the subtle disconnect of gender: The boy looks into his heart and thinks, She must be like me, in it for the thrill of sex alone. The girl looks into her heart and thinks, He must be like me. He wouldn't invite me to bed unless he too weren't at least a little bit in love?

Tangential orbits that touch at but one point.

Yes, I have seen over and over that in time most men, even those who most resist marriage, are crazy about their kids when they come along. But isn't it a learned pleasure? A recent illustration came to me from Canada.

Occasionally I devote a radio show to kicking nicotine. The government up there doesn't kid around, going directly to the psychological heart of what each gender thinks most important. There are two (empty) packs of Craven Milds on my desk as I write, each delivering the no-smoking message not only in words but also emotionally, in high-impact pictures.

One pack shows a pregnant woman. "Cigarettes Hurt Babies," the headline says. The other warns men of what can happen to them. The illustration is a limp cigarette.

#55.

The Geographical Cure

Q. I'm Sue, thirty-two, divorced, my husband was awarded the kids, and I just broke up with some guy about his crack habit. I dropped out of high school because of pot and too many boys, and never grew out of those habits. One day last week when I was broke, I told myself I was not going to go to some bar and find some new guy to buy it for me. Before the night was over, I was drunk in bed with someone who, by morning's light, I could not stand.

I decided to try AA and at my first meeting, I said I was addicted to alcohol, drugs, sex, and stupidity in general, and was thinking of packing up and moving to Alaska—start all over again as a virgin—before I lost *all* my looks, which I told them I was realistic enough to know were my only remaining asset.

You see, Bill, I was being honest, but they only laughed at me and said the "geographical cure" never worked. But new friends, new associations and surroundings, maybe a new job and a new life, away from alcohol and pills, away from everything that reminds me of past failures—what's wrong with running away from a failed past and building a better future?

A. Wherever you run, Sue, you take yourself with you.

#56.

"Why Can't I Drink? I'm Addicted to Pot, Not Beer!"

Q. Beer and alcohol never meant much to me. Pot and crack, a little meth were my thing. I'm going to graduate from rehab next week. They tell me not to have even one beer when I got out. But I'm addicted to drugs and dope, not alcohol. Aren't they being overly puritanical? What's wrong with me having a glass of wine at dinner, a cold beer on a hot day?

Another thing I have in mind is getting back into shape. I'm PT, thirty-four years old, a welder by trade. I told my counselor that I was going to join a gym, quit smoking too. He said that 86ing dope was hard enough—not to try to quit cigarettes at the same time. "Sobriety at first is going to feel like deprivation. Wait until you've got a good solid stretch of time behind you before you try to deprive yourself of nicotine too," he said.

Bill, the day I get out of rehab is the first day of the rest of my life. Why not start clean of cigarettes too?

A. PT, here's my take: There's something of a dance going on here. The taste of beer may be very nice on a hot day, but so is the taste of ice-cold lemonade. The kick in beer is that like all alcohol, it works to lower inhibitions. It "loosens you up." And from there, it's an easy step to thinking just one puff on a joint won't hurt. "At Sundown M. Ranch," says Executive Director Scott Munson, "our experience is that this seductive idea, that you can 'separate' mood-altering chemicals is one of the most common paths back to relapse."

Dr. Joe Troncale is Medical Director at Caron. I asked him too about PT's notion that since alcohol had never been his drug of choice, why couldn't he have that famous one cold beer on a hot day?

"The danger here," said Dr. Joe, "is how easy it is for the addictive personality to substitute one chemical for another, alcohol for cocaine or meth."

PT, the day you graduate from rehab next week is the first day of your *sober* life. Beer, gin, pot, meth, cocaine, speed—drugs are drugs are drugs and we both know how alluring are the siren songs of chemical pleasures. Just being around any of them, whether they were your drug of choice or not—that just reminds us of the "good times" we once had, and revives our cravings.

"For an addict," says Brian Halstead, eighteen years sober and a Program Director at Caron, "the problem is not specifically with pot or booze or meth, with nicotine or gambling. The problem is thinking that some chemical substance is an answer to the stress and turmoil of life. Slam the door on them all once and forever, and don't think about any of them again."

Which brings me back, PT, to your problem with cigarettes. My difficulty here is I never had to give them up.

If you picture a drunk, it's some guy in a bar, drink in one hand, cigarette in the other. I never smoked so I was easy to spot—the guy with a drink in both hands. So I turned once more to Dr. Joe Troncale for a more authoritative opinion. I said I'd long heard that smoking is perhaps the most difficult addiction to break. Should PT wait until he has a "good, solid stretch" of sober time before he thinks of quitting?

"The first good reason to give up smoking," said Dr. Joe, "is we have clear evidence that implicates cigarette use and crack cocaine relapse. There are also many recent studies that show it isn't any more difficult to stop all addictive substance use at once (including tobacco) than one at a time. The wisdom of not trying is a myth."

#57.

"You Wouldn't Be So Hot to Take My Inventory If You Were Happy with Your Own!"

Q. Call me Old-timer because at a meeting last week, I took my thirty-fourth birthday bronze medallion—thirty-four years sober. Some members were a little put out, and said I should take only a thirty-two-year chip. That was because back on my second AA anniversary, I had a jolt of bourbon, decided I didn't like it, and never drank again. But I didn't get drunk on that two-ounce shot of Old Crow back then and so by my reckoning, I've been sober thirty-four years and entitled to a chip that says so.

Bill, what I've learned in my years in AA is that people who are so hot to take somebody else's inventory—*you're doing this wrong, you're not right about that Step*—they are the ones most in trouble with their own program. I tell them you wouldn't be so hot to check my inventory if you were happy with your own. They want to look outward, at somebody else, not to face the turmoil and anxiety within.

A. When I spoke to Dr. Susan Gordon, the Caron Foundation's meticulously careful Research Director, I asked her if she agreed with Oldtimer that he is entitled to a thirty-four-year chip.

"It all depends on how you define success," she said. "AA cannot be faulted for its strict definition—absolutely no alcohol! That's a definition that has helped countless people. But, another definition for success is based on the idea that alcoholism is a chronic disease.

"If alcoholism is indeed a chronic disease, we need to start looking at it the same way we view other chronic diseases, like asthma or diabetes. Just like alcoholics, people with diabetes or asthma periodically go through bouts of reoccurrence—they get short of breath or their blood sugars go up. But we don't view them as 'failures' because they have become symptomatic (even if the reason is because they spent time around that dog they were allergic to, or because they took that extra piece of cake). Instead, we praise them and consider it a 'success' when they go to their health care provider for more treatment.

"So, another definition for 'success' for an alcoholic is the ability to stick with the program and to quickly return to it following a slip. 'Failure' would occur if the drink leads you to give up trying and you abandon the program entirely. This man slipped, but did not abandon his program. He's a success! Although AA would give him a thirty-two-year chip for maintaining complete sobriety, I would give him a thirty-four-year chip for staying connected to his program, despite a slip. But, either way—thirty-two or thirty-four years, this man is really a success!"

Old-timer reminds me of what often happens in alcoholic co-dependency: one nagging partner determined ever to gaze outward, at the other, and to correct the faults of that other so as not to see their own . . . with a payoff bonus of feeling superior at the same time.

My reading goes along with Dr. Gordon's. Sober that long? Who has the right to tell the guy he's running his program wrong? Not me—an opinion that goes against AA's best thinking. Which brings me to another place where AA's conventional wisdom and I disagree: the Eleventh Tradition of anonymity, which most people treat as an item of morals: Thou Shalt Not Utter Thy Name on Radio.

(See Q. #58, which follows.)

#58.

The Eleventh Tradition: Breaking Anonymity

Q. Call me Slow Learner. From time to time, you tell us in your radio show that you are in Alcoholics Anonymous, and I've also heard that you are writing a book, which, I presume, will also carry your full name. However, the Eleventh AA Tradition warns us to remain anonymous on the level of press and radio. Who the hell do you think you are, puffing yourself up like this, full name and all? Aren't you harming the AA traditions, and thus millions of members?

One of the things I often hear at AA meetings is how self-inflation—grandiosity is the word—led someone back to drinking and doping. I'm in recovery myself, and know that it was my own best thinking—my own swollen ego, in other words—that led me into addiction. My sponsor says my only chance of staying sober is to live up to the exact letter of the 12 Steps. Do you think you are smarter than the experience of millions of members over the past seventy or eighty years?

A. The Eleventh Tradition begins by saying AA works through attraction rather promotion and that members must always "maintain personal anonymity on the level of press, radio, and films."

Fair enough, but written at a time when the President of the United States still wore a frock coat and silk hat to his inauguration, *ladies* wore white gloves when they went out into the street and when Clark Gable said, "Damn" in *Gone with the Wind*, it was a sensation.

To give you further feeling for that now vanished time, pick up an AA pamphlet called *Problems Other than Alcohol*. It was written in the early days of the movement by no other than co-founder Bill W. himself. It's free, and you can find it at any AA meeting to this day.

He begins by saying he sees no way of accepting nonalcoholic addicts into the AA fellowship . . . that experience mandates there can be no exceptions. ". . . No nonalcoholic, whatever his affliction, can be converted into an alcoholic AA member." Today, drug addicts are accepted routinely and without question at any AA meeting; and drug courts, which are set up to deal with narcotics cases only, demand that clients attend so many meetings a week, AA or NA, either will do.

Further evidence that the Eleventh Tradition describes a world very different from our own is that *television is not even mentioned*.

Slow Learner feels his sobriety depends on treating the 12 Traditions as unchangeable and eternal, to be followed to the exact letter. There is no greater expert on his sobriety than he himself. So I have no quarrel, or even comment, on his chosen path. But as with other *religious* writings, there are some—I count myself one—who would like to give the words a more contemporary reading.

If AA literalists wish to act to the letter of the tradition, I would ask: since TV is not specifically mentioned, is it okay to go on David Letterman and give your full name? If they say No, the Eleventh Tradition has to be reinterpreted to keep up with the times—

Well, then, isn't that what I'm doing?

My objection to the traditions is that they are treated not as human invention, with all the possibility of change and/or error that implies, but as a God-given matter of faith. Don't ask questions, just do it. Anything else is wrong. But my feeling is that morals are merely the encapsulated wisdom of a previous generation.

When I was little, my mother had a firm rule. Don't play with matches. Why, Mom? Because, she said, fixing my father's dinner, because I say so. For reasons I was too young to understand at the time, and she was in too much of a hurry to explain, she was protecting me against myself. *Wet matches, safety matches, flammable matches*—she could not be sure I knew the difference and so the blanket rule was right. If I played with any kind of match, it did not matter—it was an article of faith and morals—I was a bad boy.

Then I grew up and made my own rules about matches.

In previous generations, before reliable contraception, when an unmarried woman could not support herself and a child, illegitimacy was an unmitigated disaster. There was hardly a moral injunction more universal in those days than no sex before marriage, and in old-timey movies on AMC, boys and girls move through their courtship dances by unspoken rules we are amazed at today. Screenwriters were always thinking up "madcap" antics to show that while the heroines were going to keep their knees together until all I do's had been duly said, they were not grim little prudes but a lot of fun.

And so the young Kate Hepburn would dare to go to church *not* wearing gloves, Loretta Young would ride downhill on her kid brother's sled while playing the trombone, and when good-girl Bette Davis wore bad-girl red to the White Cotillion, they called her Jezebel and only the dastardly George Brent would take her to the ball.

Don't do it, especially if you're female, was the rule. It's wicked even to be alone in a room with a man, what will the neighbors say.

(The double standard shows what the rule was really about.)

But once the Pill divorced sex from procreation and women became economically powerful, sexual morals *changed*, and stood revealed not as God-given but merely society's rules of thumb, changing with the times, disposed of when no longer pragmatically useful.

The marriage of virgins is almost unknown today and for tax, pension, alimony, or other reasons some people never bother to marry, no odium attached at all.

This is not to say there is no wisdom in the Eleventh AA Tradition. For instance, if I got publicly drunk tomorrow, people might say, Fat lot of good AA did him. His own hubris—puffing himself up, as Slow Learner puts it—brought him down. Devastating for me. But I do not flatter myself that I am so significant a figure that AA would not survive.

On my radio show, as in this book, I never give the full name of anyone in a 12 Step program unless they specifically ask me to. Many, proud of their sobriety, do. "If I told people my name when I was falling down drunk and disgusting," one woman said to me, "why be ashamed to give my full name now that I'm sober?" If I choose to give my own full name, identifying myself as a member of AA, it is because my experience is anonymity can defeat its own well-intentioned purpose of "carrying the message."

When I was living in Florida I went to a cocktail party given by a distant cousin, new to town. I asked for iced tea, talked to one or two people, stayed a half hour or so, and left. Never thought of it again. Five years later, after an AA meeting, the secretary came up to me. "You don't know me," she said, "but I was at that cocktail party in Key West where you said you were in AA and asked for iced tea. You were the first adult I ever met who did not drink. If I thought of AA at all, it was as of some shabby organization, people ashamed of who they were, hiding behind no-name initials and locked doors. Winos, skid-row bums, or you had to be some kind of religious maniac, and if I went to a meeting, they'd make me sing hymns. Not for me.

"But there you were, at a cocktail party, amused and amusing, clean and sober, telling a joke or two without a drink or even seeming to miss it! The people I was running with, I did not think that was possible. The memory that you said you were in AA and didn't care who heard it—that stayed with me. Then one day, near the end of my rope, I thought, Ellie, why not try AA yourself? Bill, you never said a word to me, but memory of you at that party changed my life."

And while I'm at it, here's another contrary opinion:

I cannot remember a meeting that did not ritually start with readings from the AA canon, complete with references to "God," without whose help, I was assured, I could never get sober. If I took these injunctions literally, I'd have to take a hike since the language of faith does not speak to me. And, yet, especially in recent years, I'd often be among the two or three in the room with the longest sobriety.

If I choose to take these references to a Higher Power as formalisms, to be interpreted in the light of my own experience—and if that interpretation kept me clean and sober all these years—who is to say I should not do the same with the Eleventh Tradition?

My Own Demur: I am not so certain of the above as my own words make me sound.

Recovery After Addiction, and How to Stay That Way

The Rev. Alon White is Chaplain for the General Theological Seminary in New York. When she was a guest on my show, I admired her wit and the intellectual clarity of her belief. I presumed on a relationship born of several additional off-the-air telephone conversations to send her the above Q&A, asking her to play my spiritual advisor.

"Not being a member of a 12 Step program," she said when I phoned, "I can't speak from that point of view. But, Bill, you do know there's a difference between telling people at a private cocktail party you're a member of AA, and saying it on the air. Would you," she raised the moral issue of my grandiosity and self-inflation from a new point of view, "would you have gone through all the work of writing the book if it were going to be published without your name?"

I hesitated.

She heard it.

"Think about that one second's doubt," she said. "It's the part of you that knows the Eleventh Tradition argument has weight." I thanked her and hung up. I've thought about it now for a day and a night.

The hypothetical point I was finessing even to myself was this: If I should begin to drink again, and if some unknown person who was hypothetically thinking about joining AA would hear of it, hypothetically that someone might say, AA didn't do much for him, I won't join.

Adding up to two *ifs*, one *might*, and three *hypotheticals* on top of someone unknown (even if I put them in myself to underline the point). Not an inexorable chain of logic compelling me to choose this course of conduct or that, but enough of a moral quandary to take me back to my old schooldays and Kant's categorical imperative—his famous restatement of the Golden Rule in logical form.

"Act," is the way the maestro put it, "as if the principle on which your action is based were to become by your will a universal law of nature." He called this *categorical* and *imperative* because he saw it as unqualified, and a command. So what if, like me, every member of AA dropped their anonymity? Most divorce lawyers would be out of business, perhaps some surgeons would be a little less rich, more patients would be alive, and there'd be a lot less shame in the world. If gays can come out of the closet, why can't we? The day of Mark Twain, of Currer, Ellis, and Acton Bell is long over. I'm a professional writer. I sign my work.

#59.

My Father Can't Sleep Without a Drink

Q. I'm Virginia, seventeen years old. My father is just home from rehab, and as part of his new life, he sat down with my mother, my sister, and me, and did what he called "making amends." Which meant, among other things, straightening out all the lies he told us while he was drinking.

He began with things that made him drink so much. Fear that he would not sleep was very high on his list. As the day wore on, he'd get into a kind of panic about insomnia, and would drink faster and faster, so the problem never really came up. "I would pass out instead," he told us, and whenever he woke up in the night, scary thoughts would chase themselves around in his mind to the point where he would pretend to my mother that he had to go to the bathroom, where he kept a pint of Gordon's vodka hidden in the toilet water tank.

He says that while he no longer keeps vodka in the toilet, he still dreads the night. They told him before he left rehab that it would take some time before healthy new sleeping habits set in, and that nobody ever died from lack of sleep, but he says everything looks grim and black at three in the morning, and if he ever takes a drink again, that's when it will be.

Bill, how can I help my father? I know pills are totally out of the question, and please don't give me any old wives' notions like a glass of warm milk.

A. I know your father's song, Virginia, I've sung it myself (see Q. #73). He and I could do a duet.

Here's the drunk/doper's unending circle: As problems pile up due to his addiction, his answer is to hide from them with his drug of choice. He wakes the next day, the rent one more day overdue, the boss one more day fed up with him, his wife one more day not speaking to him—he himself one more day sunk in hopelessness and self-disgust. He can't stand himself or his life, and reaches for the bottle or the pipe.

He wakes up tomorrow, does it again, and the next day, it's worse.

Toward the end of my pathological drinking, I no longer slept with my wife. She was so hurt, angry, and fed up, she didn't want to be near me. Fine. I could take a bottle to bed, dosing myself with gin every time a fearful thought entered my head. I didn't really sleep those last two years in London before flying the Atlantic in a blackout. My nights were a succession of drunken mini pass-outs until the dawn.

Like your father, I spoke to my rehab counselors when my twenty-eight days were up, telling them about my fears of not sleeping, and the anxious night thoughts that insomnia brought.

Everybody suffers from these anxieties, they told me. Fears become exaggerated at 4 A.M. because you feel helpless to do anything about them. Virginia, your father has to learn to live with them too.

I would also tell any insomniac that sobriety is an action program. Don't just lie there and stew. Read a book, go down to the kitchen and bake a cake. Form your own support group: Ask at your next AA or NA meeting if there are other, similar middle-of-the-nighters who would not mind getting a 4 A.M. phone call for a talk. When I lived in Key West, I would go to a dawn "Attitude Adjustment" meeting. There are many such early meetings, especially in big cities.

Second, you now have your full brain available to you, unfogged by booze or dope. Use it during the day to meet these anxieties in a realistic way, and get rid of them. Action, once again.

The third is an idiosyncratic idea of my own. Watching TV at any time leaves me feeling angry and bored. At night when I can't sleep, it irritates me so much I grow more wide awake. Reading a book means the light is on. My solution was to buy myself a Gründig Yacht Boy portable shortwave radio.

I listen to it with the plug in my ear so I don't disturb anyone else. All is quiet and dark, my head already on the pillow and I fall asleep with some soft radio voice droning me to sleep, a modern lullaby.

And when I wake in the middle of the night, instead of my own fears chasing themselves around and around in my brain, there's this soft-voiced BBC announcer telling me about a ground nut scheme in East Africa, or a detailed weather forecast for East Anglia. ZZZzzz . . . I'm back asleep in ten minutes.

If reception is bad, or the BBC is off the air, I tune to one of the local

AM sports talk stations. (Wherever you are, there's always one.) These shows are so numbing and mindlessly devoid of emotional content that once again, five, ten minutes, and it's double ZZZzzz. In fact, I've been doing this so long it's become a conditioned reflex. As soon as I put the earplug in and turn on the sound, most nights, that's the signal.

I fall asleep.

#60.

Is There an "Addictive Personality"?

Q. When Noel and I met and went out, I said how about a drink? He said fine, and led me to a table. He explained that he was sober five years, but was still nervous about standing at a bar. He did not mind if I had a drink, he said, as long as it was okay with me if he did not. A little quirky, I thought, but we took it from there, and now we are to be married.

I'm Trish, twenty-six; Noel is thirty-four. Addiction is new to me. He's tried to explain it, and I've read up too, but it's still a mystery. Is there an "addictive personality"? Before we exchange our "I do's," is there something more for me to know about addiction, and what it might do to our future together?

I want a family. Noel says he does too. At an Al-Anon meeting, one of the old-timers told me that if someone is sober five years, the rule of thumb is they are a pretty safe bet to stay that way. Is that right?

A. You know how scientists sometimes do experiments on a computer, in a wind tunnel or lab to model what happens in full-scale disasters? Let me tell you about a new little toy addiction of my own, how it began, how it progressed, and how I could see my own addictive personality become reborn and start to take over my life.

Bev and I rarely eat dessert and don't keep cookies or candy in the house, but last year, starting with pies for Thanksgiving and a lot of cakes, nuts, and treats stored up in December for the Christmas party we have every year, the house was awash for two, almost three months in chocolate bars, Hershey Kisses, Reese's peanut butter cups, chocolate chip cookies, and on and on.

Infected with the Christmas spirit, and telling each other we'd burn it off skiing, we ate so much candy we had to buy more for the party. And then friends brought us more. As everyone knows, neither Christmas candies nor gift chocolate contain calories. By January 6, when we took down the tree, Beverly said, "I'm going on a diet," and when I got on a scale, it showed I'd gained six pounds.

Annoying—because when you don't drink, keeping the weight off is usually not hard. Okay, I told myself, there's no more candy in the house. A new year. Start now. Cut it out. On January 7, I missed my daily chocolate fix. I told Bev I wanted a newspaper and drove into town. The lying had begun. I bought a paper all right but a Hershey bar too, the first in years. This won't hurt, I told myself, driving home with the paper, as long as you don't buy another tomorrow.

My usual feeling about newspapers is this: I don't like them. Filled with stories of fires, murders, rapes, and assaults, terrible things you can do nothing about, they leave me feeling impotent and depressed. So I rarely buy one, and get my news from the BBC on my shortwave radio. On January 8, I drove into town, bought a paper, and another Hershey too, telling myself it was okay because I would control this burgeoning chocolate habit with an iron rule: Never buy another Hershey bar, I told myself, except when you buy a paper, and that would work because I didn't buy them very often.

I bought a paper every day that week, and by the tenth, I was buying two Hersheys—one to eat in town, and a second to sneak past Beverly for when I was alone at my computer. Like the chicken pox virus left over from childhood, that lay in wait for my immune system to hit a low point and suddenly came back last March as full-blown shingles, the chocolate addiction from long ago when I lived in London (see Q. #51) had bided its time too—giving me false confidence by allowing me to eat a Hershey bar now and then. But when I did it every day for two months, the chocolate addiction came roaring back.

I can see now a lot was going on. Two that I will mention:

One, a certain sly satisfaction in putting one over on Beverly.

Two, a certain shame that I was putting one over on Beverly.

In other words, I was already treating her like a controlling co-dependent. (Which says more about me than her, since she knew nothing of any of this.) I said to myself, this chocolate habit is turning into an addiction. It's progressive, speeding up. Avoid the occasion for temptation, just don't go into town to buy another newspaper.

And I didn't.

"What's happened?" said Beverly. "No newspaper today?"

I told her the weather was so lousy that I did not feel like driving in. What was really going on: If I wasn't going to buy a Hershey bar, what was the use of going into town? Who needed a dumb newspaper? This so clearly paralleled the drunk who will not go somewhere unless he is sure a drink will be waiting that I had to laugh at myself.

Okay, I thought. Self-knowledge is the first step to recovery. Days went by, no Hersheys. Then I found half a stale chocolate cookie at the back of a kitchen cabinet and held it in my hand. You know the feeling when you start a diet? Allow yourself one extra piece of buttered toast and immediately you say, well, I blew it for today. I might as well have some of that coffee cake too. I'll start fresh tomorrow. I ate that stale half cookie, got in the car, drove in, got a paper, ate one Hershey bar while reading the sports section in the car, ate a second driving home, with a third to sneak when I was alone at my computer.

Addiction had narrowed the world. My chocolate fix, or lack thereof, was all I could think about. Forget telling Beverly the truth, forget friends, the Super Bowl, and the imminence of spring. Forget love, baseball season approaching, reading books, taking walks—even skiing was beginning to pale. If there was not going to be any chocolate action, why bother? I sat glumly watching television, eating chocolate and wishing I had a fourth bar to get over feeling ashamed about eating the third. Speeding up again. This could not go on.

I went to an AA meeting and said I was powerless over chocolate and did not know how to stop. Nobody laughed. Driving home from the meeting, I stopped at a little all-night deli and bought two Hershey bars. I ate one as I drove and, mad at myself, threw the other out the car window and got mad at myself for doing *that*. As my friend (and editor) Bob Gleason says, "Most of us are harder on ourselves than any enemy ever could be." I did not sleep well that night.

Next AA meeting, I told my chocolate story again. Nobody

laughed. I didn't stop at the all-night deli driving home. Meanwhile, Bev and I had arranged to spend five days in San Francisco. Jazz at Pearls, and busy with friends, away from my usual haunts, the idea of buying chocolate never came to mind. Habit had not yet shaded over to full addiction, not yet reached the point where, as Caron's Doug Tieman puts it, it destroys "the capacity to have an intimate lasting relationship with yourself, with another human being . . . with anything but the disease itself."

When we got home, I said to myself, Bill, you have five days' chocolate sobriety running. Don't blow it. I told that story to my AA meeting that night. They all applauded. Driving home after the meeting, I stopped in the parking lot in front of the all-night deli.

Who would know? I sat ten minutes, but did not go in. What was wrong, what vacuum was I trying to fill with chocolate? The answer was immediate. I'd been working on a new novel, gotten discouraged and used "the Christmas Season" as reason to pack it in, telling myself I'd go back to it again with fresh eyes in January. I had not.

Still sitting in front of the deli, I told myself, Bill, this is cowardice and sloth. The sweetness of life that's slipping by like time itself is the feeling of writing well. That's what you want, not chocolate. I went back to work, setting out afresh not only on the novel, but on this book too, both at the same time, and haven't had a Hershey since.

In fact, whenever I feel the old yen come over me, I run a quick moral inventory. What crappy thing have I done, what crappy little feeling do I want a bit of chocolate to help me forget? Didn't ride the exercise bike today? Let a shoddy bit of novel plotting slip by uncorrected? Got mad at myself for any/all of the above, and barked at Beverly instead? Bill, do a chocolate version of Steps 8, 9, and 10—amends to Beverly first, then list on a piece of paper all the other stuff you need to fix, and then *fix it*, instead of fat-headedly dreaming how can you get more candy.

And the urge to sneak another Hershey is gone.

Every time I drive into town now and don't buy a chocolate bar, it gets easier not to. The temptation sometimes floats up again, but now I have a record, so many continuous days of chocolate sobriety—I don't want to lose that. Sitting down at the computer just now, I realized I hadn't thought about buying a chocolate bar for I don't know how long—in fact, until I began writing this. Am I cured of chocoholism? No. But I have not had one today and I've rediscovered the prime rule of habit formation: Never allow the first exception to occur.

P.S., Trish, about that five-year rule of thumb: I've known people to go out drinking and doping again even after ten, twenty years' sobriety, so you never know and one day at a time is the rule. But isn't life about making decisions without knowing all the facts? If Noel has been five years sober, there are no guarantees, but in my experience, that's a pretty good bet. Good luck to you both, and Noel, if, like me, you have an addictive personality, don't allow that first exception ever to occur.

#61. Am I an Enabler?

Q. I'm a twenty-nine-year-old mother of two, Penny. My father died an alcoholic, and left my mother very bitter. She didn't want me to marry Jim. She said he was an alcoholic too. The truth is, Jim is under heavy pressure at his job. Maybe he does drink more than I realized, and maybe more than ever after the birth of our second child.

I told my mother that sometimes, no matter how much a man may love his children, there's a little bit of resentment too because they feel they're losing the wife's attention. And maybe he's right. But when I try to pay more attention to Jim these days, my mother says I'm just enabling him to drink all the more. After Jim's second DUI, she said if Jim died an alcoholic, and leaves me a young widow, it will be my fault.

A. Penny, if I had a blame-layer like your mom for a wife, as a friend of mine used to say about his lousy job, "death would be a promotion." But that does not say she's entirely wrong.

When I went through facilitator training at the Scripps McDonald rehab in San Diego, we were given a list of a dozen or so enabling behaviors. I kept notes. I'll go through them, and you keep your own score. Remember, this is not about Jim, but about you.

1. Denial

"I know Jim's had two DUIs, but that does not mean he's an addict/alcoholic." Is that your song? I notice you never directly use the word alcoholic in describing him.

Another form of denial: Do you expect Jim to be rational about his drinking, to be able to control it?

And a third: Do you take the blame on yourself?

Fourth: Do you drink or use with Jim, hoping to slow him up?

2. Justifying

Making excuses for the addict. Jim is under pressure at his job, etc. Minimizing comes in too: It's not so bad, things will get better when . . .

3. Bottling It Up

By now, you must often be pretty mad at Jim. You never say it.

4. Keeping the Peace

Penny, do you believe lack of conflict makes a good marriage?

5. Protecting

Addiction turns our best instincts against us. Trying to help the man you love from the reality and results of his use/drinking just prolongs the addiction.

6. Avoiding

Taking tranqs to feel better, maybe overeating, gambling, occasionally drinking too much yourself. . . . Another form of avoidance is taking over the responsibilities of the addict to avoid him getting fired, etc.

7. Blaming, Criticizing, Lecturing

What this Terrific Trio does is help you avoid pain, and feel superior to the addict. Says Larry Bouchard, "The gain for some enablers in treating the addict like a child is so strong that they never face their problem directly. Enduring enters here too," he went on, even religion. "The theme song here is, This Too Shall Pass . . . he'll stop in God's time, not mine . . ."

8. Controlling

Everybody's favorite. "We just won't go to the office party this year."

Penny, how'd you score?

A last word of advice. Go to an Al-Anon meeting, and talk over your answers with people who've had more experience in how someone else's addiction makes enablers lie too, to themselves first of all.

#62.

Can the New Drugs Help?

Q. I'm Pauline, and was listening to you last week while driving my car. You had a Professor Noble on, who seems to have done a lot of work on molecular brain chemistry. I was distracted by traffic but if I heard him correctly, he said there were two kinds of addiction: One is genetic, and another which he called "environmental" . . . drinking because of stress, etc.

He said that there are new drugs being developed right now which will radically change the way that genetically prone addicts will be treated in the near future . . . though they will have less affect on the "environmental" addicts.

Bill, I remember reading that cocaine was once advanced as the "cure" for opium and heroin addiction. I am sure Professor Noble is aware of this too. Please tell me a little about his credentials, and ask him to enlarge upon his remarks. If he is correct, this is the best news about addiction I ever heard.

A. I share your enthusiasm, and also your caution. If I had heard these remarks from anyone else, I would have taken them with a truckload of salt. But Ernest P. Noble is very eminent—both a Ph.D. and an M.D., Pike Professor of Alcohol Studies at UCLA and also Director, Alcohol Research Center at the UCLA Neuropsychiatric Institute. I phoned him with the above question, and he was kind enough to talk to me about the two kinds of addiction, and the effect new drugs will have on them.

Here is Dr. Noble:

"Our research shows that there are two different forms of addiction. The first, which I would call *environmental,* is the kind with which we are familiar. People begin drinking or drugging because of stress. A bad job or marriage, etc. The use becomes habitual, and eventually, addictive. Clinical evidence, however, shows that when the stressful situation is alleviated, use of alcohol or drugs is diminished."

"How about people who have an auto accident," I said, "and suffer severe pain. Or the thousands, millions who suffer from bad backs for no reason except that we no longer walk on four legs. Their lives may be otherwise serene and happy, but they often become addicted to painkillers anyway, don't they?"

"Environmental, once again," Dr. Noble said.

He went on that the second kind of addiction is molecular. "These people are born with a mutation in the reward and pleasure centers of the brain. They have too few D2 dopamine receptors, which means they suffer a deficiency in feelings of everyday satisfaction with life."

"The phrase I like is that the genetic type of alcoholic was born two drinks behind."

"Exactly," Dr. Noble said. "I have also heard them called, 'The great army of the unenjoyed.' This mutation is found not only in alcoholics, but in cocaine and speed users, gamblers, sky-divers . . . people who look for their pleasures and rewards in places most of us would never go."

I mentioned that there is terrific new growth on TV of what is called extreme sports. "People diving off a mountain on a pair of skis, incline skating on a high wire without a net, stuff like that. Do you think their explosive popularity means more and more people are being born with this D2 dopamine receptor deficiency?"

"I think it more likely," Dr. Noble said, "that the increased stress in our lives makes these people take extreme measures to find their satisfactions."

While NA, AA, and rehabs have some success with the environmental kind of addict, he went on, the genetic kind not only suffer more severe forms of addiction, but are also harder to treat by conventional methods. "Luckily, there is a whole new area of brain chemistry coming along, drugs like bromocriptine, which go to the heart of this problem."

I said that mention of the word "chemistry" rang the same alarm in me as it had in my caller, Pauline. "Wasn't cocaine first touted as a 'cure' for morphine addiction?"

"Yes," said Dr. Noble, "but it was soon abandoned when patients became cocaine addicts. Bromocriptine, on the other hand, which has some side effects, and the newer D2 dopamine agonists coming along right now, are not addictive. They are pharmaceuticals, like insulin, that correct a deficiency in the body's mechanism. When the patient takes them, he does not get high . . . he merely comes up to the level of life enjoyment that the rest of us were born with."

"And like insulin," I said, "the patient will have to take these new drugs regularly for the rest of his life?"

"Yes, but any diabetes sufferer will tell you that is a small price. And if taking a daily pill will end your enthrallment to addiction, that's not a high price either."

Too good to be true?

Dr. Keith Humphreys is Assistant Professor of Psychiatry at Stanford University School of Medicine, and has been a fluent and funny guest on the radio show. I called him about the above interview and asked it again: Too good to be true?

"There are some exciting things happening in the science of medication development," he said, "but no pill can change the reality that all addiction involves motivation, behavior, and environment. For example, Naltrexone is a medication that can stop the positive effects of certain drugs cold, but only about one in six street addicts will take it because they like the positive effects of drugs."

"And so if you walk into a bar and say, 'Listen, everybody, I have a pill here that will stop alcohol from making you feel good'—?"

"Don't expect a big line to form, yelling, 'Hey, give me that pill right now!' "

Keith went on: "Medications don't hop into your mouth each day. You have to *decide* to keep taking them day after day, and that takes motivation, support, and good, everyday reasons in your environment that weighs out as better to be clean than on drugs."

Keith finished: "Too good to be true? No. But motivation, the human element, still enters the equation, the final intangible."

#63.

Three-Time Loser

Q. Bill, if you could see me, my arms are covered with jailhouse tattoos, and that's what you can call me, Jailhouse. I'm one of those people who are allergic to alcohol. As soon as I take a drink, I break out in handcuffs. I've been a hard-core heroin user since I was sixteen. Thirty-two now, and spent more time in jail than I like to think. Busted for strong-arm twice, so you don't have a more serious listener than me.

I go to NA and AA meetings three or four times a week because I'm scared to death. While I am not addicted to alcohol, I know that if I take even one beer, it will lead to whiskey and inevitably back to heroin. And the only way I can support a big-time smack habit like mine is go back to crime. But next time I get busted and convicted, here in California it's three times and out—it will be for life. I think going to meetings helps, but when the craving is on me, I need more than just some wise counsel and talk. You had a show on a whole new generation of drugs coming along that are supposed to end addiction once and for all . . . kill addiction flat. Do you believe that's true? Where can I learn more about them?

A. This was a tough one, and I called for help once again on Dr. Keith Humphreys, Assistant Professor of Psychiatry at Stanford. "Motivation is all-important," he said, "and Jailhouse seems to have plenty, both from inside (i.e., his own goals in life) and outside—the threat of life imprisonment. He would be wise to seek treatment in a good methadone maintenance clinic. It will help his craving, and he will also get good counseling and other support services."

"I wouldn't want to disparage the efforts of professionals involved in methadone programs," said Blair Pettis, formerly Executive Director at

Oasis Treatment Center, Anaheim, California, "but in our experience, their success is extremely limited. Methadone users often continue to use heroin on top of their methadone regimen. That's when we see them—they come in for detox, and an ugly, lingering, agonizing, gnawing, itching withdrawal it is. And while I speak not from empirical medical data, my observational experience is that methadone seems to significantly impair cognitive brain function."

This kind of negative feeling about methadone floated through almost every conversation I had with people in the field. Therefore I asked Dr. Joe Troncale, Medical Director at Caron, if there weren't other ways to reduce heroin craving.

"There are newer, long-acting opiate medications (like LAAM)," he said, "that stay in the body longer than methadone, and are more convenient: dosing three times a week, for instance, instead of methadone's five to seven. There is also Naltrexone, which 'sits' on the same spots in the brain that opiates normally use, and helps weaken the craving for heroin and other opiates."

Sharon Hartman, a relapse prevention specialist at Caron, agreed that methadone can help. "If you use it to treat a population with a criminal history," she says, "research shows a decrease in the kind of behavior that got them jailed. The bad news is people get dependent on methadone, and are then not highly motivated to get clean. That's selling yourself short—life's too interesting to go through forever blurred by drugs."

In my conversations with Dr. Susan Gordon, Caron's Research Director, I've always found her opinions backed by specific facts. And so faced with this ambivalent *Yes but* attitude toward methadone by so many people in the field, I turned to her for a last word. She began by saying there is a lot of data on methadone because it's been used now for more than thirty years in the treatment of heroin addiction.

"Although it's an opioid, like heroin, it operates very differently from heroin in the brain. Methadone's effects last about twenty-four hours and do not produce the quick "rush" that a person gets from the much shorter-acting heroin. Since methadone can be a highly addictive substance, it is strictly controlled and only dispensed at licensed clinics. The best methadone treatment occurs at clinics where addicts receive attention for their other bio-psycho-social needs.

"Research on the long-term effects of methadone maintenance has found it to be medically safe with very few side effects. Does this mean that methadone is the treatment of first choice for heroin addiction? Let me ask the question differently. If you suffered from diabetes would you want to control the disease through diet and exercise or would you want to become dependent upon injections of insulin? Most of us would want to try the drug-free method first. But what if your diabetes could not be controlled by diet and exercise—would you try insulin? If your heroin addiction is so severe that you cannot maintain abstinence through a drug-free program alone, then I would suggest that you look into adding a medication management program, such as methadone, or as Dr. Joe says above, the newer, long-acting opiate medications like LAAM, or Naltrexone."

#64.

"My Brother's Wife Is Drinking . . ."

Q. I've been sober now for almost eight months, and all my family is proud of me. Last night, my brother called to say his wife is hitting the gin pretty hard. He's found Marylou drunk when he comes home from work, drunk in front of their two kids. He wants me to talk to her. I've been thinking about this. What can I say to her? My own wife is afraid for me to go. She says she doesn't want me to be tempted to drink right along with my sister-in-law.

A. When you were tiny, all you had to do was think I'm hungry, and a breast was shoved into your mouth. Your mother knew you were cold before you did. A blanket appeared as if by magic. You didn't even have to state your wishes, they were granted. As I said in an earlier discussion on self-inflated grandiosity, the doctors call this stage of life *infantile omnipotence.*

One of the seductions of intoxicants is they rearouse these seductive and dangerously unconscious memories of early life.

Drunks think they can do anything.

In my experience, the newly sober go through a stage of omnipotence too—overconfidence in the powers of one's own sobriety. One of AA's teachings is that we are powerless not only over our own drinking, but other people's too. When you were drinking, was there anything anyone could say that would make you want to stop? What makes you think your sister-in-law would be different?

When I got out of rehab, I had experiences not unlike your own. People would come up to me, often at a cocktail party. "I've been watching you," they'd say. "All you have in your glass is a slice of lemon, ice, and soda, but you seem to be having a pretty good time." They would wave their own martini glass in the air. "I know I've been drinking too much, and, in fact, my wife thinks I should stop. Could you teach me how?"

I would tell them to phone me the next day.

"We'll talk about it then, when we won't be interrupted."

They never called.

Shakespeare said it, readiness is all.

And no matter what they said with one or two martinis under their belt, they were not ready; maybe never would be. And there was nothing I could do about that. This is not to say that talking to someone, offering to take them to an AA meeting, for instance, never works. Never is a long time. But in my experience, it rarely does.

The downside to talking to your sister-in-law before she is ready is this: If you prematurely make what AA names a Twelfth Step call on her, the odds are overwhelming that she won't stop. Instead, she will from then on see you as another one of the guilt-layers, worriers, preachers, and well-intentioned squares—people to avoid. If she ever does really want to stop, the logic of booze is this: She'll still avoid you because you're living in her head as her guilty conscience.

A safe rule is: If someone won't call you themselves, don't waste your breath. Wait till they're ready and *know* they need your help. Then you arrive fresh on the scene, moral authority intact, a sober person who has been there himself, and no past nagging baggage getting in the way.

Step 1: Ask your brother to have Marylou call you herself. If she won't and you nevertheless decide to go talk to your brother's wife anyway, read Step 2.

Step 2: Your wife is right about one thing. As newly sober as you are, don't ever make a Twelfth Step call alone. Take someone with you—your sponsor, preferably a female, someone you know in AA—someone with a long history of sobriety.

Drunks are as dangerously seductive as the stuff they drink.

#65.

How Can One Cold Beer on a Hot Day Hurt?

Q. I hear you talk a lot about rehabs and AA, but that's not the only way to get sober. I'm Strom, thirty-seven years old. Bill, I hit bottom when I got fired and my wife walked out. I had one last big Niagara of a drunk, and blacked out—woke up with two nails driven through my eyes and no memory of what I had done. I poured out every drop in the house and I didn't need AA's help to decide never to buy another drop.

That was fourteen months ago, and I was flat broke. I'll say this for sobriety. You have what I've heard you call a thirty-six-hour day—no morning hangover, the evening isn't spent in a bar. There isn't anything to do but work. I'm a software programming consultant. So I'm not hurting for money. I'm not going to go back to drinking, and I won't touch dope. But Bill, these long August days, a thought's begun to tickle me from the back of my brain. Wouldn't just one glass of ice-cold beer taste good on a hot afternoon? I can just see the beading on the side of the glass, I just can't get the picture out of my mind.

A. Just one beer? You're putting me on, right? Let me tell you about the day I learned about drinking and sex.

When I was brand-new in the army, eighteen, virginal, and never in a bar in my life, I got a seventy-two-hour pass from basic training and went into town—Jacksonville, Florida—with John K., a fellow private, from Canton, Ohio. He had some errands to do first; we'd meet two hours later. What to do early mid-afternoon and alone in a strange town? What do Hemingway heroes do? I decided to have a drink.

A dozen stools stood yawning and empty at the long Green Cockatoo bar when I walked in. I sat down at one end, hoping to appear confident to the bartender. A young woman came in, and of all the stools waiting—gulp!—she decided to sit beside me. She wore a long full skirt, hands deeply thrust into patch pockets in front. She swiveled around, parting her hands: The skirt was slit to the waist and it parted too. She wore no underwear, the Delta of Venus was shaved, she was tattooed: a bright red cherry with a single green leaf.

"Still got yours, soldier?" she said, and I fled.

Still secretly smarting an hour later with the ignominy of realizing how little I knew of the world, I met John K. He took me into a hotel bar and explained the laws of grown-up drinking. "If we have less than three, that's a waste of money." Another mystery. Since drinking was wasteful to begin with, weren't three more wasteful than one? Wouldn't none be thriftiest of all?

I copied his cross-legged stance at the bar and listened carefully as he ordered "Park & Tilford Reserve," by full brand name. *How knowing,* I thought, how sophisticated and grown-up, what a world metropolis must be Canton, Ohio—if only I'd grown up there myself!

After one drink I relaxed, after the second told him about high society in the Cockatoo bar, and after the third was laughing at myself right along with him. What terrific stuff was this Park & Tilford Reserve! It took me a long time to learn P&T was as cheap and nasty a whiskey as could be, but I did learn that memorable day that commercial sex was not for me and why three drinks were better than one.

Since that time, I don't think I ever set out to have "one drink" in my life. And, Strom, if you've progressed to blackout drinking, no longer do you. What does one drink mean to people like us?

A cold beer on a hot day! How many times have I heard someone extolling that supposedly innocent idea. But when I hear those words, what I suspect I hear talking is not the person but the cunning, baffling, and powerful voice of his addiction. *One cold beer, and stop with that?* If you were a member of AA—I gather you are not—just to utter those words would get you laughed out of the meeting. That's one of the difficulties of trying to sober up alone.

AA offers the accumulated wisdom of the millions of drunks who have gone before you. Doing it alone, you have to find out by yourself what works, what does not. It can be done, but the odds are against you. It's lonely and it's slow, like reinventing the wheel.

PS. I'll tell you what tastes better than a cold glass of beer on a hot afternoon. Iced tea and two Oreos, or have the cookies with a glass of milk over ice. And then take yourself to an AA meeting. Your present state of mind—you're alone, you're in bad company.

#66.

How Can One Cold Beer on a Hot Day Hurt? (Part II)

(Author's Note: I want to stay with this topic because when I first came into AA, most drinkers fell afoul of the hard stuff. Bourbon, gin, and vodka were the money end of the industry. But in recent years, I've seen more and more newcomers with beer habits. A counselor at a rehab told me he felt this was because hard liquor could not advertise on TV, while beer gets to put on these terrifically seductive *Life of gusto* commercials that attract young people. Since I used to be in the advertising business myself, this suggests to me that the beer people are going to be putting out more products, more variations on the beer idea, so they can be marketed through TV. The Q. below is a case in point.)

Q. I once heard you say on the radio that beer never interested you—that even in your worst drinking days, you don't think you ever finished a whole glass of beer no matter how hot the day. Well, I'm Toro, one of those people who used to truly love the taste of beer. With the help of AA, I've been sober, on and off, for three years now. I like it all right, and I never want to go back to those days when I used to go to bed drunk more often than not.

But now there are these new beers, advertised as nonalcoholic. All the taste, none of the alcohol. Since you never liked beer, I suppose you're going to warn me against them.

A. I know AA old-timers who would say that "on and off" sober sounds very like "on and off" drunk, but to my ear, the intention, at least, is there, so congratulations, Toro—you're further along toward continuous sobriety than you think.

I suspect it's your own conscience and common sense that's giving you warning. But the addicted half of you still wants to get mad that you can't drink, and so instead of looking a little more deeply within, you project out—and find Blue Nose Bill to blame. He hates beer, so of course he's going to say no, don't touch any of that new, nonalcoholic stuff.

Unstated corollary: Therefore, I don't have to listen to him?

Old-time addicts call their use of booze and dope their *habit*. Sobriety is a habit too, and the first rule of habit formation is Never Let an Exception Occur. Entertaining fantasies of finding the perfect beer, one that will never get you drunk, still allows the old thinking to go on. I can almost hear your addiction, laying up there in the dark at the back of your head, devising plots and slippery rationalizations, saying, Beer is wonderful; you didn't really need to stop. How can one of these new nonalcoholic beers hurt?

That keeps the door permanently ajar, keeps the new habit of never even thinking about that first drink from becoming more deeply embedded, a permanent part of your life. Before we go on, let's have another look at that ambiguous statement—that you've been sober, "on and off," for three years.

Ever go on a diet? You eat just one cookie—and mop. You've blown the diet for the day. The door is ajar. You tell yourself, I'll eat whatever I want today and start fresh tomorrow.

And tomorrow never comes.

PS. With nobody here but you and me, let's run a quick self-diagnostic test to see if you're falling back into those other alcoholic habits: denial and lying.

You knew that no matter what these beers say in their advertising, the label says they contain about a half percent alcohol, right?

If you knew that, why ask the rest?

#67.

Too Gay for AA?

Q. I'm an illustrator, Denny, recently moved to this part of the world when rents in the Bay Area became too steep for me. I've been sober now for eight years, and as I've often heard you say, I believe my continued sobriety depends on group morale, the lift of solidarity I get from AA.

But I am gay, with a gay sensibility. I prefer ballet to baseball, opera to bowling, and when I go to an AA meeting here in the Mother Lode, I get discouraged. What do I have in common with four truck drivers, an out-of-work bank teller, a beautician whose own hair is a tacky, improbable blue-black, a ranchhand, and a bunch of Valium-happy housewives? I just can't identify with these people or their stories.

Nor they with me: In this fundamentalist part of the world, it is forever 1952. If going to a meeting makes me feel more isolated than ever, what is the use of AA?

I know this sounds elitist, but what is wrong with elitism? Bill, if you needed a brain operation, would you want the surgeon to be the next guy on some democratically chosen and ethnically balanced list? Maybe I can't find a gay meeting in this part of the world, but I am thinking of starting a men's group. What do you think?

A. When I lived on Southard Street in Key West, maybe a quarter of Old Town, including the then mayor, was gay. Half my friends were gay, I owned a little cottage that I rented to a gay couple, and the only rule I followed was gay parties were fun but leave early. "To be young and gay and living in Key West right now," I remember a friend saying, "is more fun than I ever thought the world could hold." He was a waiter at the elegantly sunlit and pink La Ti Da, where you could rent poolside rooms for an afternoon, lunch before and a swim after. I sometimes think I was the only person who ever arrived in Key West sober, lived there a dozen years, and left without ever having had a drink.

I was living there still in the early eighties when AIDS came along and the fun came to an end. Denny, I know your song.

I also know there are gay AA meetings, rape survivors meetings,

Cocaine Anonymous, and all the rest. None of which needs permission or blessing from me, and which a lot of people find helpful. That being said, my own belief is any special, exclusionary group tends to feed the malevolent and hard-to-put-behind-us idea that we are in some way unique or special—a dangerous and expensive illusion we fueled in the bad old days with booze, pills, speed, crack, and name-your-own accelerant.

Nevertheless I called a long-term sober friend and read him your question. Quentin R. is gay, a distinguished actor whom I first knew back in New York, when he was just getting started. "My experience," he told me on the phone, "is the kind of snobbery I hear in this question is very often based on fear that the other people will not like you first. The magnificent democracy of the AA program is the best way I know to overcome that. It was only when I pitched in at meetings to empty ashtrays (people still smoked then), made coffee, organized a home group, did whatever was needed—when people see that you are capable of giving love to them, they will come to love you. AA taught me that people can disagree and still be friends, and still work together for the good of the group.

"The *official* roles we play in life, truck driver, housewife, rocket scientist, do not define us. My advice is get involved with the program, not just go to meetings. You'll grow as a human being once you are free from the snobberies that isolate and entomb us."

#68.

"You Against Women's AA Groups Too?"

Q. I heard you say you felt special AA groups are not a good idea. Some male prejudice at work here? My name is Chocolat, twenty-six years old, and sober six months, fourteen days. If women want to have their own meetings, who are you to stop them?

A. Revolutions are started by passionate people—who else would do all that marching? And so when feminism hit the deck running, Gloria and the Ms. All-Girl Revolutionary Band proclaimed women the equal to men in every way. I would ask: equal before the law, sure—but the same in biological drive? Leave it to a man to ask that question.

Everyone knows that any such notion of limiting feminine sexuality was due to the Paternalistic Ascendancy's desire to control and diminish what used to be dismissed as "The Second Sex."

Never again. I Am Woman. Ta-daaaAA!

Thus the one-night stand became a feminist political statement, lesbian explorations were seen by many straight women as a bit of radical chic, and Hugh Hefner from his Harem Tower in the Bunny Mansion wrote reams of Playboy Philosophy saying how wonderful it was that women had at last divorced emotion from getting laid.

Reading a new generation of women writers, I can see that while women still want equal pay for equal work, etc., most are no longer interested in freedom to have immediate sex with men who do not care a rap about them after the moon has detumescenced and gone.

A nifty *New Yorker* cartoon showed a couple under a palm tree. "Beth, you don't understand," the guy passionately declares. "I love you, I adore you, I want to spend the rest of my vacation with you!"

As a friend recently remarked, "Anatole France once said the law in its equal majesty granted rich and poor alike freedom to sleep under the bridges of Paris in winter. I don't care for the freedom to find my own cab Monday morning and ride home alone, knowing the telephone call from that guy will never come."

I remember a Central Park West dinner party in the seventies, the women dressed down and drab in accordance with advanced thinking of the time: reactionary to play to testosterone-sodden male desires, unsisterly to try to look more beautiful one than the other. (Let me add a personal note; it did not matter what they wore. These were dazzling New York women, beautiful beyond bearing. The evening reminded me of Marie Antoinette's thé dansants at the Petit Trianon—how amusing to come dressed as poor people and peasants.)

A distinguished anthropologist took exception, arguing this showed the (then new) feminism rooted more in gender politics than genetic dynamics. "Why are women generally smaller than men?" he asked. "Because evolution's Grand Strategy was to hook feminine size up with something in the male genome that sees gender reinforcement (which the male needs more than the female) in protecting smaller people.

That pairing of needs produced families with the greatest number of surviving children, thus contributing most to the next generation's gene pool, world without end." The new and rising statistics of men abandoning families, he went on, showed something radically amiss.

"The cliché 'women want everything from one man and men want one thing from every woman' reflects evolution's Stone Age indifference to individual happiness as opposed to continuation of the species. One boon of civilization was to socialize men into realizing there are more sophisticated satisfactions. But it's a learned idea. If you deride a man's need to feel strong and protective toward women and children by pejoratively calling him *paternalistic* . . . if you construct an economic system in which they don't really need him . . . don't be surprised if he takes a hike back to those earlier, Stone Age pleasures. Yes, a lot of bullying, role-playing, chauvinism—and unhappiness too—goes along with it, but you can't unhook one from the other without causing profound psychic imbalance in evolution's basic male/female bargain."

In the same way, the anthropologist went on, male reaction to the beauty of women was not "subject to theory, will, or what Carol Gilligan wanted most for Christmas." It too was in the DNA, once again selected for by evolution for continuation of the human race.

"It's fine for women to say they've evolved and can look beyond mere physical attraction," said another man (perhaps it was me), "and choose a mate who's emotionally available, reliable, and all the other virtues preached by the New School of Social Research . . . so why do men still get hung up on a pretty face, which is mere Paleolithic packaging? But erections never lie. Poor, dumb things, they know only one trick. They point at what they want, and if you point them at something else, they lose heart and go away."

Betty Friedan glowered and both men were thereupon snubbed for the rest of the evening, but a recent MIT computer-imaging study of the male brain (reported in *Neuron*, alas twenty-five years too late), scientifically quantifies their argument.

According to the Associated Press, coauthors Dan Ariely and Hans Breiter found that "Seeing a beautiful women triggers a pleasure response in a man's brain similar to what a hungry person gets from eating a meal or an addict gets from a (cocaine) fix . . . (it affects) a man's brain at a very primal level, not on some higher, more intellectual plane . . . (these) findings counter arguments that (female) beauty is nothing more than the product of society's values. 'This is hard-core circuitry,' Breiter said, ' . . . not a conditioned response.' "

James Thurber was onto something when he did his famous *New Yorker* cartoon series, "The War Between the Men and the Women," rueful recognition that each gender wants something the other is not prepared to cede without struggle. Police blotters do not list many female flashers or Peeping Thomasinas—*Playgirl*'s circulation is only a fraction of *Playboy*'s. Women find male hands sexually freighted and turning the idea around, spend tons on unguents to make their own more seductive. But do men feel the same and cop quick fantasy glances at women's fingers? Don't make me laugh.

Women have a right to any sexual behavior they choose but I believe the feminist notion—that the genders may differ in plumbing but their sexual psychology is the same—is so damaging and contrary to evolutionary dynamics—and, I must admit, caused so much duplicity and harm in my own life—that perhaps I've dwelt too long on what may be old news to most people reading these sentences.

I've never yet met a woman who went in for sexual predation and bragging, but I've known many who wanted a private, sympathetic place to discuss their wounds, skirmishes, and forays in Thurber's war. The short answer to your question, then, Chocolat, is: Women need— you need—no permission or validation from me, but since you ask my opinion, yes, for reason of all the gender asymmetries named above, my belief is women's AA meetings are a good idea.

#69.

Are We Ever "Cured"?

Q. I've been sober three and a half years, and there's always a thought at the back of my mind, maybe it would be okay if I had just one drink. I know that is silly, and I never do. But does there ever come a time when you would no more think of taking a drink than eating a barbed wire sandwich? You can call me Max, and I'm thirty-six years old.

A. One summer an old friend of mine in Florida had a heart attack. I drove from California to see him. When I came in, his wife shook her head. I stayed two days and left thinking this had been a last visit. In this mood, I drove into Louisiana, and found a motel for the night.

I like dried fruits for breakfast and asked at a nearby supermarket where they kept dates and figs. "We get figs in at Christmas," said the clerk, "but what's a date?" I was far from any civilization I understood.

In fact, in a boozer's paradise.

One thousand miles away from anyone who knew me, or how to find me. Emotionally upset at the imminent death of a lifelong friend, staying alone in an anonymous motel. No place I had to be for the next four or five days, and two gold credit cards in my pocket.

But was I looking for gin at the supermarket? No, I was asking the clerk where I might find figs and dates. What I think remarkable is that I didn't have to say to myself, Keep away from booze and dope. That night in Louisiana, it came to me that I had turned a significant corner. I didn't have to "Just say no." I'd been sober so long that no other course of conduct came to mind.

As I sit writing this paragraph, Beverly is in San Francisco and a quart of Tanqueray is in the booze closet upstairs (she likes an occasional martini). That gin is of no more interest to me than a quart of boiled shoe soup. Does this mean I've beaten addiction? Am I "cured"? No. Just as I am certain that if I took one step off a roof, gravity would hurl me to the ground, so am I equally certain that if I took just one drink I would fall back into the worst of my addiction again. What these years of sobriety have done is free me from the desire to take that first drink. Max, it just never enters my mind.

#70.

Does Antabuse Work?

Q. My daughter just got her second ticket for speeding while drunk. She won't tell me what's wrong, why she's drinking like this. She flatly refuses to go to AA. I tried tough love, and told her as long as she lives in my house, this can't go on. She says if I'll get off her back, she'll take Antabuse. "Dad," she said, "you can give me the pill yourself every morning. So you know the liquor cabinet is locked for the day."

Bill, this sounds too good to be true. Does Antabuse work? Or is she just setting me up for another disappointment?

A. The history of AA is one of trial and error, rule of thumb, what works, what does not. And so what may have begun as accident, merely a felicitous manner of speech, stayed on because it worked: One of the little things that strike me as important is the day you come into AA is called your birthday. You've been born again. Your other birthday is not as significant. It is merely your "belly-button birthday." At your first, second, and so on AA anniversaries, you are declared one, two, or whatever years old. The slogans, the mottoes, the cryptic utterances of the old-timers, all work to make the newcomer feel as if s/he is indeed a babe, just born into a new world.

Trying to figure out what they mean, the bewildered newcomer begins to take in the values and ethos of the people around him. *Stick with the winners. One day at a time. Let Go and Let God.*

What do they mean? Their very simplemindedness is a puzzle. Why do these people, sober for so many years, think these seemingly trite mottoes are so freighted with importance and meaning? And why are they all smiling?

Why do they take such pleasure in telling jokes about how dumb and nutty they used to be when drinking and using? *These people know something I do not.* Slowly, slowly, the newcomer comes to realize these slogans and sayings are like those Japanese toy paper pellets that come tightly rolled up into what look like drab little gray rocks or pebbles. Put them in water and they unfold, blossoming into beautifully imaginative, many-colored flowers.

In time, the slogans and AA mottoes thus unfold in the newcomer's unconscious . . . indeed, become his conscience: He has introjected the wisdom of sobriety and made it his own. Recovery, I feel, is this process just described: taking the controls back from booze and dope and putting them inside, where they belong: introjecting them back into your heart and brain. From that conventional point of view, Antabuse would be contraindicated.

And so you may imagine my surprise when, in talking to someone I admire and respect, she told me "contrary to the widely held belief in the alcoholic trade, Antabuse can be a good idea, if properly used."

Dr. L. is a famous writer, educator, and psychologist, an alcoholic herself. "I've been sober over twenty years," she said, "but at Christmas, or if I'm going to travel on a plane or maybe attend a large, out-of-town convention, times like that, the old yearning can suddenly pop up again. That's when I take Antabuse in front."

"You don't live on it 365 days a year?"

"I use it only a few days at a time, when I know my own personal stress is going to be at the max."

She went on: "The trouble with taking Antabuse as your prime sobriety strategy," she said, "is that it places the controls outside yourself, and in a chemical at that. Not a good idea for an alcohol or drug abuser. We've all heard stories about bipolar patients who 'forget' to take their lithium. In the same way, any day a patient on Antabuse wants to get high . . . meeting a new boyfriend or an old lover, for instance . . . all she has to do is skip the pill that day. With Antabuse, you have to make the decision every day to stay sober, 365 decisions a year. Lots of chances for a slip. When AA really works, it teaches you to close that door forever, and never think about it again."

"But you've been sober all these years, on the board at eminent hospitals. You haven't learned it yourself?"

She smiled ruefully. "Alcohol is cunning, baffling, and powerful, Bill. No, I haven't learned it yet."

I said that I'd heard of people on Antabuse who drank anyway. "You ever do that?"

She said no. "Those are sad, torn people who still want to drink, and so you have one half of their brain at war with the other. They can end up in the hospital, bleeding from the stomach. I am not like that. I never want to touch a drop ever again. I wish I didn't think I need to take Antabuse. Maybe I've come to the point where I don't. But I'd rather be safe than sorry."

Dr. Keith Humphreys, Assistant Professor of Psychiatry at Stanford University School of Medicine, was a recent guest on my program. He said there had been a famous study in which some patients were given high-dose Antabuse (disulfiram), others low-dose Antabuse, and the rest no dose at all (i.e., a placebo pill).

"The key fact," Keith said, "is those patients who regularly took their medication were more likely to abstain from drinking no matter which of the doses they were on. So, those alcoholics who regularly take Antabuse, and so for whom it seems to work, they may just be people who are the most motivated to stop drinking in the first place."

"The patient's desire to stop is more important than the physical effects of the medication?"

"Yes."

Which led me to ask if he had any advice for the father whose question prompted this discussion.

"Taking Antabuse," said Keith, "doesn't control behavior or craving. It doesn't make drinking alcohol impossible, and it doesn't affect drug use at all. It just causes a physically unpleasant reaction (for instance, nausea) to alcohol consumption. If someone really wants to use drugs and alcohol, they will do so, which is another way of saying that no pill can help us out of the frustrating, maddening human reality that we can't control other people's behavior."

I said my own take was the daughter didn't sound as if she really wanted to quit drinking, that if I were the father I'd watch she didn't secretly fill the Antabuse bottle with aspirin or maybe hide the real pill under her tongue, and later spit it out.

"But she'd mostly be fooling herself," I said to Keith, "wouldn't she?"

"You're an alcoholic, Bill. What do you think?"

#71.

Overwhelming Feelings

Q. I'm Josie, thirty-two, and have always been very emotional. My feelings sometimes threaten to overwhelm my brain. As a teenager, I was an obsessive reader, and used books to keep what I used to call "bad thoughts" from driving me crazy. When I got older and learned about Valium and gin, I'd do that to feel better. My husband hated me walking around "like a zombie," as he put it, and so I went to a rehab.

I'm three months out now, and sober, but still feel crazy at times. I love my husband, and don't want to go back to pills and alcohol as a way of coping with my runaway emotions. How can I deal with all these feelings? They scare me.

A. "As Freud once wrote, the quickest way to get rid of your feelings is to feel them," says Lynn Telford-Sahl, Certified Addiction Counselor and author of *The Greatest Change of All—A Spiritual Novel*. A friend of mine, and frequent guest on the radio show, I'd turned to her for help with Josie's question. "In my practice," she went on, "I see again and again Freud was right. Here are some specific things you can do.

"First, people who become addicted often grew up in families where there was chaos, anger, depression, numbness of feeling, or inappropriate, out-of-control emotions. Some react by shutting down, becoming underemotional. Others—Josie sounds like one—become high-strung and wrung out by their feelings. Either way, learning exactly how you do feel is the key to self-control and serenity. In my practice, I give clients a writing exercise that I learned from Stephen Bavelok, author of *Nurturing Parenting for Parents and Children*.

Here it is. Are you:

Mad—feeling unimportant and/or unrecognized?
Sad—experiencing loss or the end of a relationship?
Scared—your well-being or safety is threatened?
Glad—all or most of your needs are being met?

"I ask clients to go down the list, paying attention to the unmet need, and to write the feeling down with a number from 1 to 10. The final exercise is to write a letter I learned about from *The Never Diet Again Solution* by Lauel Mellin. It explains why you feel that way.

"Dear—(addressee can be yourself or someone else, to your therapist or even a place or thing. The important point is to get it out of your head, and expressed on a piece of paper).

Anger: (I feel angry that . . . I can't stand it that . . . How could you . . .)

Sadness: (I feel disappointed that . . . sad that . . . unhappy that . . .)

Fear: (I fear that . . . I am afraid that . . . I feel scared that . . .)

Guilt: (I feel sorry that . . . I regret that . . . I feel guilty that . . .)

Acceptance: (I understand that . . . I care that . . . I accept that . . .)

What I need from you is . . . (or) What I need from myself is . . .

Lynn goes on: "These burning, unmet needs can often lead to resentment, as dangerous an emotion for someone in recovery as being locked in a distillery overnight. Living in touch with your feelings and knowing how to express them takes practice. But let me add a note of caution: If you're having intense feelings and feel suicidal, don't try to tough them out on your own. You need professional help."

Lynn looked at me and said I seemed disappointed. I said I felt the problems of people like Josie weren't so easily tractable. "For instance," I said, "don't 12 Step programs promise to get you past these sticky human snarl-ups?"

Lynn smiled. "No program can fix something you don't know you're doing. So far, we've left out the idea of *defenses*—strategies worked out as a kid to cope with overwhelming forces: cruel or addicted parents, bad temper, divorce, rejection . . . Defenses are knee-jerk automatisms, outside your conscious volition. They were the best you could do then, but for an adult they cost too much. They add up to a rigid, Johnny One-Note life. Make yourself another list:

When I met (name) today, I felt nervous and did this:

1. Told yourself (name) was too boring to know. *Is that what you were afraid (name) was thinking of you?*
2. Suspect (name) was lying. *You're probably a liar yourself, and project that onto others.*
3. Was afraid (name) wouldn't like me so drank too much to get my nerve up. *Of course you made an ass of yourself.*

4. Quit before I was fired. "I don't need (name) or (job)." *Rejection anxiety too great to stand. There are soldiers in war so afraid they rush toward the bullets.*

5. Was critical, negative, and sarcastic. *People who fear their feelings are going to be hurt often rush to be the one who hurts first.*

"These kind of maneuvers—sometimes called *paradoxical intentions*—have an expensive payoff," said Lynn. "They ease anxiety, yes, but also kill intimacy and friendship, leaving you ashamed and isolated. The mechanisms are so hidden you don't know they're at work. That's why it's important to write it all down. Every time you have a jangly encounter, reread the list. A pattern will begin to emerge. Admit to yourself there's something wrong. Then do something about it.

"If your pattern is to avoid feelings of abandonment by abandoning the other first, hang in there and see if something new doesn't happen. Instead of quickdraw sarcasm, say something accepting and warm and see if the other doesn't respond the same way. Action, *changing yourself,* ending the shameful passivity of victimhood—that's how you build self-respect. Watch out for people who use the word 'empowerment.' They're trying to sell you something. Beware of ads that say 'take control of your life' by buying this product or that. You don't achieve inner self-worth and self-esteem by paying too much for L'Oréal shampoo."

I had dinner that night with Larry Bouchard and had him read the above. "But what about people like Josie?" I said. "Maybe they're sober at last, maybe they've done the pencil-and-paper exercises Lynn suggests—but still feel AA's 'promise' has not come true. What can they do about feeling stuck, their lives not 'happy, joyous, and free'?"

"Therapy can help."

"Why is that always the answer? What about someone who says, 'I don't need help. I can read a book and do it by myself?' "

Larry smiled. "You can read Euclid and teach yourself geometry, but a live teacher can get you there a lot faster. Same with emotional snarls. A trained professional can get you through them before a lot more damage is done. If you've lost years to your addiction, why not maximize the rest of the time you have left? But remember—"

"Yes?"

"Only when the student is ready will a teacher appear."

#72.

Saving My Brother: Twelfth Step Call

Q. My older brother and I used to drink together, and while I stopped four months ago, he's still out there. I'm Hanford, thirty-four, and Ted is thirty-eight. His wife called last night.

Ted and I were always so close. Could I do something to help? I phoned my sponsor who said I was as powerless over my brother's drinking as over my own. "Your brother's first loyalty is not to you, to his children, or his wife. It's to whatever he's drinking. That's his Higher Power. When he wants to stop, he'll call you himself. Until then, you're wasting your breath."

A. In the years I've been sober, I've been to cocktail parties often enough. "How do you do it?" people often ask, perhaps already half-tipsy themselves, some even suspiciously sniffing my glass. "Everybody else is drinking. You really satisfied with iced tea?"

I tell them I've had my share.

They go on. "You know, lately I've been drinking too much. I envy you, not missing it. Could we have a talk, tell me how you do it?"

I tell them to call me tomorrow. They never do.

Hanford, on the whole, your sponsor is right. Until someone really wants to hear your message, making a Twelfth Step call (as it's known in AA circles) is wasting your breath. It may even be counterproductive: You become just another do-gooder, another nagging voice back there in their conscience. In my experience, if/when they ever do decide to look for help, problems of ego will then enter too. *All he's going to tell me is I told you so.*

You are someone to avoid.

But as with any other rule, there are times to break it.

Going through rehab, you're on your own twenty-eight-day cycle. People come in every day, others go home. At Caron, I became friendly with Jed, ironically an M.D. who'd had a practice dealing with alcoholics.

"I hated being a doctor," he told me. "But my father and four older brothers were all M.D.s. I got pushed into it, it was a family tradition." In the end, like his father and two brothers, he'd succumbed himself, and was there at Caron—his cycle three days ahead of mine.

Time in rehab is very intense. Before the first week was out, Jed and I knew each other's taste in politics and people, in books, food, and love. The same ideas about professional sports (overrated) and favorite movies (how few, how few). We'd be friends for life. When he left at the end of his twenty-eight days, he hugged me good-bye.

"See you in three days," I said.

He left.

When I got back to New York, I called. Jed was a bachelor and lived in a residential hotel. He did not return my call. I phoned twice more that day, the next day, and the next day too. Zip. By that time, I had gotten to know Dr. LeClair Bissell a bit better than when I woke up in Roosevelt Hospital to find her at my bedside. She'd invited me to come see her when I got out of rehab, and I had.

I've already described how she got through my grandiose denial and other baloney, persuaded me to go into a rehab (a word until then unknown in my vocabulary) within—my guess is two minutes flat. I have not yet said she was already a famed and preeminent figure in the alcohol recovery industry, a noted writer and lecturer, chief of alcoholic services at Roosevelt, one of New York's finest hospitals. My great good luck was she'd read one of my *Village Voice* pieces and liked it enough to come see me when my name popped up on her daily intake list. Sometimes I wonder what would have happened if she had not. ("Coincidence," one of my religious friends likes to say to me, "is the name God uses when She wants to remain anonymous.")

Dr. Bissell knew Jed too. I called her and told her about him not returning my calls. I was new to all this, I said, but already knew that addiction turns your best instincts upside down. "Would it do any harm to try to see him?"

"Bill," she said, "three days without calling you back? We both know what Jed's doing. Drunks will break your heart. Most likely you'll be wasting your time, but if you feel strongly enough, go try." I didn't phone, just went to Jed's hotel, went up, and rang the bell. He opened the door. I will not tell you how the room smelled, nor how he looked.

"Bill," he said, "thank God you've come."

He put on his coat. We went for a walk across the street in Central Park. That's all it took. No lectures from me, no alibis from him. We were beyond all that. He was back in touch with the sobriety, the changes and values he had learned in his twenty-eight days at Chit Chat.

"How long were you sober when you left?"

"Maybe an hour."

Going back to the same old solitary, unrewarding life, he got off at the first bus stop and bought a bottle. The last time I saw Jed he'd switched medical specialties to one he loved, found someone to share his life, and been sober over ten years.

Which brings me back, Hanford, to where we began.

Should you go have a talk with your brother, Ted? Is there a right or wrong answer? Larry Bouchard, who I've quoted so often in this book, says recovery is more art and hope than science.

"If it were my brother," he says, "I'd take a chance on hope. But if you do, don't go alone. Take an old-timer with you."

And, Hanford, maybe you better read Q. #36 on intervention, and learn from my mistakes. There's a right and wrong way to do anything. Goodwill and earnestness of desire are not enough.

#73.

Drinking and Insomnia

Q. I heard you talk about Dr. Bissell on your show, and how, at the peak of your drinking, she won your confidence within two minutes. I'm studying to be a licensed drug and alcohol counselor. How did she do it?

A. She asked me about sleep.

"Do you fear the fall of night, that you'd be awake all night?" she said, just about the first words we ever exchanged. "Do you wake up, and say you have to pee, and go take a drink instead? One of the reasons you feel so dragged out is you don't really sleep. Your nights are a series of little pass-outs and then the withdrawal wakes you again."

How did she know, I asked myself, the more I feared being unable to sleep the faster I drank? Enough gin, the problem never came up: I'd just pass out instead. *She's been there herself,* I thought. Listen to whatever she says. One of the wisest decisions I ever made.

We later figured there must have been nights when she and I were both in the White Horse on Hudson Street, but did not know each other then. My own boozing continued with the disastrous results described. LeClair Bissell went to med school.

"In those days, the doctors who ran medical establishments were all men," she told me, "and if I wanted them to respect me, I couldn't present myself as a psychiatrist, which they considered 'a soft option.' I studied as an internist, which even they had to respect. *Then* I studied the psychology of addiction." She was the first woman to become head of alcohol services at Roosevelt Hospital, which is where we met.

Dr. Bissell had a patient she helped get off the sauce. Grateful for his sobriety, Brinkley Smithers donated ten million dollars, and Dr. Bissell bought (Manhattan real estate was cheap back then) the old Billy Rose mansion on New York's East Side and started the city's first rehab.

While I'm talking about one of the most admirable people I ever met, here's a little story she told me herself. In 1946, when LeClair was an adolescent, her father, a general who'd been in charge of the 10th Air Force (CBI) but now stationed in England, wanted his daughter to attend the Very Grand parties to which his diplomatic corps rank automatically gave him and his family entrée.

"Bill," she said to me, "that was the last thing I wanted. I was a shy kid and an outsider. I'd be there on sufferance, on a pass. I hated going to those parties. I very quickly found a drink helped, and two were better." She smiled at the memory of herself. "But you know all those people that my father wanted me to impress back then? I know them now. They're my patients."

#74.

The Drunk's Progress: A New Identity

Q. I heard you talk about the way a doctor caught your attention when you were drinking. She realized you were using alcohol to medicate yourself to sleep. But that's a long way from deciding to stop drinking for good. Can you name a moment when you turned the corner? When you knew you'd be sober for the rest of your life?

A. There is no such corner, and to this day I don't know that I will be sober for the rest of my life. I have my hopes, and I'm not planning on having a drink today, but no matter how many years you've been off it, you're never more than the lift of a glass away from a drink. But I do remember a moment when my identity changed, and I became someone else: someone who *wanted* never again to drink.

Earlier in these pages, I wrote about flying the Atlantic in a blackout, and entering a rehab. Now I was at maybe the two-week mark of my twenty-eight-day stay at Caron. Along with lectures, group therapy sessions, AA meetings, and the rest, they put you to work there, and on that day I'd drawn doing the kitchen and dining room floors.

So there I was down at one end of the dining room, with my bucket and mop, mentally contrasting it with other work I had most recently been doing: a writer for Helen Gurley Brown on *Cosmopolitan*.

I know circles in which it is fashionable to dismiss *Cosmo*, so let me immediately confess I am *parti pris*. When in 1959 I wrote in the *Village Voice*, "the equality of women makes the lives of men more interesting too," I was moved to the idea by my reading, one long, rainy Fire Island afternoon, of Helen's *Sex and the Single Girl*, and it is my belief that historically she is a more important figure than, for instance, Gloria Steinem—having done more to let air, grace, and light into the lives of young American women than ever did Ms. Steinem and *Ms.* magazine too.

Despite me living in London, Helen carried me on the masthead as "Contributing Editor." I was at the time one of their two or three highest paid writers but so little proud of myself or what I was doing with my life that, no matter how the editors back in New York rewrote the stuff I sent in, I never bothered to read it. Send me the check, have another drink, and forget it.

So—at the other end of the Caron dining room that day, Jerry Shulman, the head counselor, and a group of his colleagues had come in, most of them in recovery themselves, joking and having a cup of coffee, oblivious of my bucket of soapy water, my mop, and me. By this time, I'd come to know those guys a bit, knew their stories, and admired them for what they were doing with their lives. You know what I've written about the magnetism of group morale (the 9/11 addendum to Q. #20, and even more directly in #26). Well, on this occasion, I was the loner, and they were the group.

So there I was, scrubbing floors on hands and knees. There they were, getting out their clipboards, experienced and expert, banded together, having a good time doing work they valued and for all I know, what they were going to do on their next day off. They'd been where I was, but never would be there again. A startling moment.

My identification shifted.

I wanted to be like them.

Up to then I'd thought the cool, hip people were the ones standing at the bar, having a drink and thinking about having another to start the evening ahead. People who didn't drink were jerks . . . the unlaid squares you never bothered to know. In that moment of epiphany, I saw that the people at the bar, who drank like me, *they* were the jerks. Who else but a dummy would end up like this, glad to scrub floors because it kept him away from booze?

I do not think it an accident that in time I became a facilitator at Scripps McDonald, began this alcohol counseling radio job at no pay, nor that I am writing this book. All of it is what I want to do, my chosen work—work that makes me feel I am in spirit at least a member of Jerry Shulman's admirable gang who will sit forever, if I am lucky, in unending session at the coffee table at the back of my mind.

#75.

Prozac and Alcoholic Relapse

Q. My name is Winnie, thirty-nine years old and the mother of two girls and a boy. My husband, Lowell, was four years sober when our third child was born. While I was in the hospital, he began to drink again. After six months, I told him either he quit or I would take the kids and leave him. Our doctor said Lowell was depressed, and that he was self-medicating with alcohol. They gave him a prescription for Prozac instead, and told him he would not have to drink.

Things were not great for the first month, but I thought, okay, give the Prozac time to work. And then Lowell tried to commit suicide by swallowing a quart of vodka and a lot of bootleg pills. They saved him by pumping his stomach. Bill, in all the years he was drinking, Lowell never tried to commit suicide before. Now the doctor wants to put him on Prozac again. I don't know what to do.

A. "In my work," says Larry Bouchard, to whom I turned once more for help, "a story like this isn't rare. As a clinician, I don't prescribe medication. An M.D. does that, and the usual minimum course for Prozac is ninety days. That's how long it can take to adjust the patient's seratonin, a neurotransmitter that regulates pain-pleasure response. Most patients begin to react favorably after about two weeks. But it can take longer. My guess about this guy Lowell is he was one of those. By day thirty or thirty-five without a drink, he's got this gnawing hole in his gut. Bill, you know how addicts are—"

"A slug of vodka, he'll feel better right now?"

"Without ever having met 'Lowell,' " Larry went on, "let me guess. He sounds like a classic, 'see-Mom-I've-been-good' kind of guy who needs attention and approval. When he had to share it with one more newborn, he became depressed: anger turned against the self."

"So he's got this hole in his stomach," I said, "that he knows a drink will fix. Like a good boy, he figures: I'll keep taking the Prozac just like the doctor said, but I'll help it along with a quiet little drink?"

"Right," said Larry. "We've often talked about the synergistic effect of adding alcohol to other mood-altering chemicals like Prozac: They multiply each other. Before long, Lowell's inner drama becomes external: drunk driving accidents, bar fights, getting fired from his job. In this instance, he tries to kill himself."

"And if Lowell were your patient?" I asked Larry. "Would you advise him to go back on Prozac?"

"Bill, he was never 'on' Prozac. He was taking orders from his doctor, an expert who was treating his depression and anxiety as requested. We don't even know if Lowell told his doctor the whole story—alcoholics seldom do. Notice that his wife, Winnie, never mentions that he was 'working a program' during the four years she tells us he was sober, no mention of AA, the 12 Steps, or a sponsor, none of that.

"She says they put him on Prozac 'instead.' My hunch is she played a big part in getting the doctor to prescribe it, and she must have talked it up to Lowell too. To him, the attention was gratifying—rescue by the mother he's always looked for. And then, after a month it finally became obvious that both Prozac and Earth Mother were just two more illusions to add to a lifetime of disappointments. Once again, he felt abandoned, just as he'd been by Mother #1."

"Boom, here comes depression, that old anger turned violently against himself—the suicide attempt?"

"Most genuine suicide attempts," said Larry, "are aimed at someone—the ultimate control fit."

"I'll show you, I'll hurt me, and you'll be sorry!"

"Bill, dual diagnosis treatment works 'if you work it.' The doctor prescribes appropriate psychotropic medication and informs the patient in writing of the expected side effects. The patient in turn gives the doc a signed, informed consent agreeing to the treatment, and then follows instructions—not self-medicating by quitting or doubling the dose or slipping a bit by adding alcohol.

"Ideally, after ninety days, the patient will be 'clear.' That means, stable neurotransmitter levels, no alcohol or other mood-altering drugs in the system. Now the doctor and the psychotherapist can truly assess the patient's symptoms of depression/anxiety without the clouding effects of drug abuse."

"The patient is still on Prozac?"

"We are now in a period of maintenance and observation. The dosage of Prozac (or other appropriate medication) is adjusted depending on the patient's progress as reported by the therapist: sleep, appetite, energy levels, mood swings, social adaptations, libido, etc."

Larry went on: "Important in this period—a biggie—is progress along spiritual lines: AA, NA, some church or 12 Step program. Eventually, perhaps in a year or so, no psychotropics at all. But, Bill, there are so many unfair horror stories about drugs like Prozac I'd like to summarize our talk—not why they don't work—but why patients and even doctors won't let them. I said Go, and here's Larry's list:

1. **Inadequate dosing.** The drug is new to the doctor, or he's afraid of side effects. He underprescribes. "In other words," says Larry, "fear and/or stupidity at work. The drug isn't given a full chance."
2. **Unreported substance abuse.** "The patient just nods, sure, sure, when the doctor tells him he has to cut out dope and booze while on antidepressants. Secretly, he never does. All hell breaks loose."
3. **Poor compliance.** Patients forget to take the pill one day and doubles up the next . . . etc. "Some sadly underinsured people can't afford it," says Larry. "They cut the pill in half, or take it two days out of three . . . some take pills their friends are on because they're cheaper."
4. **Side effects.** The big troublemaker here, says Larry, is low sexual libido. "Instead of talking it over with the doctor, who can prescribe something like Klonopin to clear that up, they stop taking the drug, but lie to the doctor and say the Prozac is just not working."
5. **Dropping out too soon.** We are trained to want fast, fast, *fast* relief. AA calls this quitting five minutes before the miracle happens. The patient just stops taking his medication.
6. **Dropping out too soon.** This time it's the doctor who becomes anxious for results, and switches medications midstream. "This happens most often," says Larry, "when the patient—like all addicts, given to impatience, melodrama, and self-inflation— becomes bored describing the old, weary list of depression symptoms: tired, lack of sleep, etc. He comes in with a new list: heart palpitations, panic attacks, red-meat stuff like that. The

doctor retargets his medication plan, and let's say, gives the patient Xanax for anxiety. Hell breaks loose once again."

"Let's finish," I said to Larry, "with a big question. I've heard a lot of cocktail party chat about the horrors of Prozac going wrong. In your clinical practice, have you full faith in Prozac and its variations?"

"When correctly prescribed, and correctly taken, I have seen them work too well, too often, to doubt it."

#76.

My Last Drink

Q. I went to my first AA meeting the other night. Reluctantly, I had to admit. My girlfriend and I were quarreling over what had happened a few nights before when I'd had too much to drink. Or, anyway, she was mad and I was apologizing. She said would I go to an AA meeting, she'd go with me (it was an open meeting).

It was a speaker's meeting, and the guy up there said he never wanted to forget his last drink—the one that landed him in jail, and eventually brought him into AA. He said keeping the memory green was one of the best ways he knew never to do it again. This struck home to me. One of the reasons Rosie and I have these bitter fights is she wants to remind me of what I do while drinking, but I want to forget it as soon and thoroughly as possible.

Listening to the speaker, I thought about the way I had been acting the night Rosie and I had this last fight. It was not a happy reminiscence, and made me realize I've been drinking more than I've allowed myself to know. It showed me what a jerk I've been. So I'm going to go back to AA, but, Bill, I've been listening to you for about a month now. I'd like to hear your story. Tell us about your last drink.

A. How dangerously booze and dope glamorize themselves in memory, how seductive the idea of "just one drink"—elevation of mood, music made sweeter, romance in the air, and life itself planing on top of the wave . . .

Oh, yes?

I've often heard it said that women forget or gloss over the intense pain of childbirth. If they did not, they would not go through it again. Remembered instead is the joy of giving birth.

That's human nature: The bad stuff is forgotten.

This works against us in recovery. How beckoning and easy it is to remember only those good, early times when booze and dope were still fun. Remembering the last drink, the last pill or line, with none of the gory details glossed over, buys you strong insurance against the seduction of falling in love with booze and dope all over again.

If ever I should be tempted to take "just one drink" again, this is how I remember to what it will lead . . .

I came to in one of the seedy little hotels around Paddington Station, 4 A.M., drunk, alone, and getting drunker. I told myself I was drinking because I needed a drink. I told myself I wanted to get so high not even dogs could hear me. I told myself jokes about the drunk who goes into the Magic Liquor Shoppe. The daily special is the Unending Bottle of Gin; no matter how much you drink, it never goes dry. The drunk asks how much for a case. I was drinking to punish myself for being a drunk.

Somewhere else in London I had a comfortable house and a wife who had not yet stopped loving me. I was here because I wanted to drink, to drink my fill, drink without someone crying in the next room, begging me to stop. Hung on the back of the door was my black raincoat. Dear God, I hope there's some left in the inside pocket. I staggered but got there in two tries.

The raincoat pocket held a pint of gin. The bottle rattled against the glass when I tried to pour. I choked some down from the neck, hating every drop—the first fast to kill the shakes, the second slow, hoping this time it would stay down. Oh, you want another, you dumb bastard? Here's a double big jolt, and I hope you choke on it. Makes you want to throw up? Here comes another, bigger than the first, how do you like that? I hope you throw up, I hope it burns, I hope you die, I hope it runs out of your eyes, miserable drunk bastard!

Remember, I said to myself, when drinking used to be fun?

I finished the gin and said that was my last drink. I didn't know how I was going to do it, but swore to myself, this is my last day drunk.

When the shops opened, I went out to buy more.

Two weeks before and six months out of a rehab, I'd celebrated my new sobriety with a glass of wine on New Year's Eve. See, I told my then wife, AA is wrong. I don't feel the overwhelming desire they warn about, to keep on drinking. I corked the bottle and we went to bed. The next day I drank two bottles of gin, beginning of the worst two weeks of my life.

Addiction is like cancer, lying hidden and ravenous at the back of the heart, wanting only to burgeon and grow, not caring that with the death of the host body, it will die itself. I could not stop. I've written this elsewhere, but the memory is so strong, let me repeat it here.

Wandering around London in that black raincoat, a pint of gin in each pocket, huddling in every red telephone kiosk to lift the bottle to my lips. I hope I don't drink this, I would say to myself and drink it. I hope I don't buy another, I'd say, and buy two. This is my last day, I'm going to stop, I would say to myself, and did not know how.

Check back into the rehab from which I'd graduated six months ago? Sure, but Caron was back in Pennsylvania, three thousand miles away. Call my sponsor? I did not have one in England. An AA meeting? Those days, there wasn't one anywhere in London before 6 P.M. I could not wait that long.

I had to stop before I bought more gin.

I phoned two doctors who ran private, AA-oriented live-in rehab clinics just outside London. Sorry, no room for three weeks. Today, I said to myself, I'm going to stop today—drank some more and did not know where to go. I came at last to a railway station.

Was it indeed Paddington? I am not sure. There were some people at a little booth, Salvation Army, Traveler's Aid, the Good Samaritans? I don't know. "Help me," I said, "I can't stop drinking."

They did not say, do you have money or insurance? They did not say, Who are you? You sound like a foreigner, scram. They said, "Sit down right here."

Say what you will about British "socialized medicine." Don't say it to me. Within thirty minutes, I was in an ambulance. When we got to the hospital—it was Friday afternoon—they said it was too late to talk to the admitting psychiatrist. That would be Monday. I said fine. That was the good side of what the British call the National Health.

The downside was the hospital seemed a little run-down, not enough doctors and at that moment, not really room for me. They gave me what they had. There was a long hallway lined with cots. They assigned me one, handed me pajamas and a bathrobe without a belt. "Feeling a bit rocky, are we?" said my neighbor from the next cot. No, I told him. "I feel safe."

He was waiting to see the admitting psychiatrist too, and over the weekend, we spent a lot of time walking that corridor in our pajamas and flapping, beltless robes.

He was a learned fellow, and gave me long lectures on Shakespeare's art. By Sunday afternoon I was so impressed, I said to him, You must have spent years learning all this stuff. "My dear fellow," he said, "Why not? I'm immortal!" and I realized where I was: I had committed myself to the loony bin.

That did not matter. Here's how it was. From the moment the door closed behind me, the obsession with booze dropped like turning off the light. Monday morning, I shook hands with Shakespeare, and went home. The desire to drink gone, never to come back.

I can offer no explanations, and know this is not how it happens to most people, at least not to the ones I hear talk at 12 Step meetings. But that's how it happened to me, that was my last drink.

#77.

Rewin Her Trust?

Q. One day on your show, I heard you recommend going to a rehab as the best bet to get out of an addiction. I took your advice, and don't regret it. I've been here only three weeks, but already feel my life has changed. That little pink cloud people talk about? I'm on it. Only one thing wrong.

Last Sunday, my wife came to visit. I'd hoped she would be happy to find me in such a clean and sober state. She said to me, Jack, I'm afraid to let myself hope. You're fine today. How do I know you won't be back on tequila and crystal a week after you're out of here? A year after you're out of here? How can I trust you? she said.

I've had a bad temper all my life, and one of the things I'm working on is to control it, but here she was shooting me down! I told her I was beginning a new life. She could choose to be part of it or not. Maybe I was hasty. What do you think?

A. I believe one of the striking differences between the sexes is how big a role *trust* plays in women's lives. Ask one guy what he thinks of another, he'll say Oh, he's a good guy (or not). The word trust almost never comes up.

But now Sally and Louise meet. You ask one her reaction to the other. "I don't trust her," is apt to be almost the first thing you hear.

Evolution cares nothing for human happiness, only about what works (meaning, breeds successfully) and what does not. In the millennia of generations in which evolution has worked on us, those women whose nature it was to find people they could trust to stick with them through pregnancy were the very ones who bred most successfully and had the most kids. The women who did not have these genes left fewer generations behind. This may not be fashionable to say but I believe the new genome studies will find the genes for this trust-or-not trust aspect of feminine psychology deeply embedded on the X chromosome.

Jack, your wife put up with you all the years you were an addicted pain in the ass. Which I would guess means she still loves you. But when she says can't trust you, it's a big statement. Listen very closely.

If she's suspicious, who lied to her again and again over the years, who put that suspicion there, who broke her heart? If she is afraid to hope—it is not your job to feel put upon and lose your temper. Your job is to ease her fear. You know you're different because you are inside, privy to all your thoughts. But even you don't know yourself yet. The sad fact is that she's right to doubt you. Rehabs all over the country graduate people like you every day, and they leave floating on your pink cloud. Most of them fail.

If she is afraid to hope, that does not justify you unleashing another of your favorite drugs, rage. Kiss her instead, tell her you understand her fears. Give time a chance to show her she can trust you again, on her timetable, not yours.

That being said, let me add it did not happen that way with me.

One of the last things my wife said to me was, Bill, I never know when I will wake up to find you drunk again. She could never trust me again, and now we are divorced. Just because you are sober, that does not guarantee a happy ending. I can only say no matter what your problem, there is one thing you can rely on.

Going back to booze and dope will make it worse.

#78.

AA Is Boring

Q. I find AA's Big Book too boring to read.

A. Me too. I rarely read it again after my first ten years sober.

#79.

My Son-In-Law Is Boring When Sober

Q. I sometimes think I like Edward, my son-in-law, more than I do my daughter. She and I never got along; she's very serious about life, and so is he before he has a drink or two to loosen him up. I used to love when Eddie and Felicity would come for Christmas. We'd have champagne, some eggnog too, and get in a party mood. I'm a widow, Louella, fifty-two years old, and of course—Don't I know it!—past my first, youthful good looks but Edward would wink and take the glass from my hand and put on some music. "Lulu," he would say with a smile, "how about a dance?"

I never saw him drunk, but my daughter says his doctor told him to quit drinking, and he's joined AA. She just phoned and warned me that if they come here for the holidays, I'm not to offer him as much as a glass of beer. We had a quarrel about that. I don't believe Eddie is an alcoholic, and even if he is, how can one little drink in a family atmosphere harm him?

A. In the adolescent male (I'm not sure it ever changes), desire begins in the eye and immediately rushes to the testosterone with the speed of light, totally bypassing the heart and the brain. The seductions of alcohol to an addict are so cunning, baffling, and powerful that to ask Edward to stop after one glass of wine or beer is like putting that adolescent boy in bed with an enticing naked woman, and later asking him why he succumbed.

"It's the first drink that gets you drunk," says AA.

Louella, Eddie seems to know what he is doing. Do you? If your daughter and son-in-law don't come this Christmas, ask yourself if the competitive dance you seem to be doing with Felicity might not be the reason why. In the meantime, going to an Al-Anon meeting would help you know what she is going through, and if you like Eddie as much as you say, you'd understand him better too.

#80.

Drink Like a Gent Again?

Q. I'm Nolly, twenty-three, and been in AA a year. My cousin recently came for a visit. He laughed at me and said he'd found a program which teaches you to drink again like a gent. He'd tried AA, but said he got turned off because the 12 Steps are too reliant on religion and that stuff. He used to be a terrible alcoholic but he had one beer during the visit, didn't ask for another, and never got out of line. How can I learn to drink like that again?

A. Nolly, now that your cousin isn't here, let's talk to each other straight. You've been in AA long enough to answer: What do you think the chances are your cousin will still be drinking just one beer six months from now? Even more important, what is one beer to people like you and me? Is one beer worth the risk? I never set out to drink one beer in my life, and suspect neither did you. If I am ever going to blow my sobriety, I'd lay in a ton of gin, a mountain of ice, lock the door for a month, and that would be that. They'd find my will on my desk, signed. I know I would never come out.

Let me tell you about these programs that promise you can drink again: They fail miserably. "Did you see the newspaper reports not too long ago," says Sharon Hartman, a Program Director at Caron, "where the head of one of these organizations was busted for driving under the influence, and is facing manslaughter charges? They are not out-and-out charlatans, because, obviously, they believe in their ideas themselves. But that just makes them the more dangerous."

Sharon goes on: "If I were counseling Nolly, I'd say to him, What concerns me here is you don't sound as if you yet have a real grasp that alcoholism is an illness, a permanent one. Drinking is not a moral issue. If you are romanticizing being able to drink, I would suggest you stop and take stock. I understand just because you are sober, life is not necessarily all roses. Your dog gets run over, the IRS comes after you for a mistake in your return, your company merges and you get fired. All that being given, is your life better now than a year ago when you hit bottom hard enough to try AA? If your answer is even a lukewarm *yes*, then ask yourself, Is it worth the risk to find out if you can 'drink like a gent' again?"

#81.

God in a Bottle?

Q. I'm Judy T. On your show last week, I heard you say that some priest once told you that alcoholism was a "left-handed attempt at religious experience." Coming from you, this is a laugh. You as good as tell us you are an agnostic, or atheist, with no belief in God at all, and then you lay this crap on us.

Isn't the truth simply that you were a drunk, and that this kind of talk is an attempt to dress up that fact, give it some kind of cosmic rationale or importance?

A. I needed no rationalization or justification when I was drinking. I drank because it was Monday or because it was not . . . because I felt good or felt bad . . . with a crowd of drinkers, or because I was alone. People used to say, Why do *you* drink so much, Bill? Are you shy? Does a drink loosen you up, make you feel you're more interesting? Judy, I used to tell them, I drink to make you more interesting.

The desire for transcendence, for exaltation, escape from doing the laundry, going to work, TV at night, and waking up to find it's Monday again—the *dailiness* of life—runs deep in human nature. Paleontologists and anthropologists tell us that every culture ever studied, no matter how primitive, always had two constants, fire and intoxicants: beer . . . wine . . . mushrooms . . . cocaine . . . loco weed . . . *something.* The Incas of Peru were a sophisticated civilization. They never discovered the wheel, but they had cocaine. Father Jack, the Jesuit of whom I wrote in Q. #41, once told me rebellion was a reason so many deeply religious Catholics drank. "It is part of their war with God."

If you're interested in the part religious faith plays in sobriety, I suggest you read the above mentioned Q. #41 and also Q. #42: two discussions of a "Higher Power"—one from my point of view, and second, that of Father Bob, once a professor of theology, now a parish priest.

#82.

Help! The Boss's Wife Put Sherry in the Black Bean Soup!

Q. After a rocky start due to my drinking, Felicity agreed to marry me when I took my one-year AA chip. My work picked up too, and my boss invited us to dinner last night. After the first course, the boss's wife asked how did I like the black bean soup. Bill, she'd cooked it with sherry! (Neither she nor my boss know about my drinking.)

Felicity glanced at me, but I kept my cool and the evening ended. But I've been up all night, worried even that little bit of alcohol will set me off. Sobriety has brought me so much I don't want to lose it. I'll listen to your answer off the air.

A. I've been sober a long time, Mr. Off, and there are still nights when I dream I'm at a dinner with some new people. I lift a glass of water, chug it down, and *it's gin.* It scares me so much I immediately come awake, and oh, the feeling of relief it was just a dream.

As my friend, the talented clinician Larry Bouchard often says, the number one reason for relapse is overconfidence, "I've got the booze beat." It led to my own one relapse, and so I know from firsthand experience that the first good thing you have going for you is how scared you are.

As for the rest, it's a matter of temperament. I know AAs who keep liquor in the house for friends, I know others who will not let it in the door. There's a guy I know who keeps what he calls a "just in case" quart of Bottled-in-Bond 100 proof Old Crow at the back of a closet. He's been sober eighteen years, and that's how long the Old Crow has been sitting there, tightly corked, never unsealed.

We all don't have to do it the same way.

Cooking boils off the alcohol, so I know a lot of AAs who would not think twice about eating that soup. A lot of others draw the line more firmly; boiled or not, they would not touch it.

Once again, whatever it takes for you is right for you.

PS. If you want my own rule: It's the decision that counts, not the inadvertent drop or two you may swallow. If a hostess says up front, Bill, do you mind if I use a little crème de menthe to make the ice cream topping, either I say I'd rather they did not, or decide to myself to skip dessert. If they don't ask, and I find later there was some alcohol in the cooking, I don't worry about it.

Either way, neither has yet made me drunk.

#83.

Problems of Self-Esteem
Who Should a Recovering Drunk Marry?

Q. My ex-wife and I would have long, horrible quarrels which would give me an excuse to slam out, put a case of beer in the backseat of my car, fill the tank with gas, do a line of coke, and drive off . . . always to come back in the end sick in mind, heart, body, and spirit.

I'm Barry, forty-two years old, about three weeks out of rehab, and while I've learned it was not she who forced me to get high (I bought the Coors, I bought the coke), I've also had some time to reflect. Say what you will, it must be easier to stay sober in a harmonious marriage than the opposite. Maybe this is a little off your beat, Bill, but I wonder if you've ever thought of the kind of partner best for someone in recovery.

A. I remember an old drinking pal on whom I modeled a fictional character, A. E. Kugelman. "I fell in love with myself at an early age and was rejected," Ira (his real name) once told me. "But one drink, two—the man inside who looks out through my eyes but doesn't like me, he stops criticizing and becomes my friend." Ira's standard hello was, "Have a drink and be someone." He meant someone else, a drunken rest from having to be himself and Barry, if Ira comes to mind right now it is because he had his own answer to your question.

"Bill," Ira said one night, "I'm going to start Ex-Husbands Anonymous—guys for whom one marriage is too much and a hundred not enough. If a member feels the irresistible urge to get married again, he calls 1-800-MARTINI and we come over with gin and music and a bunch of good-looking girls and hold parties day and night until the urge to marry again passes." I used to laugh at his jokes, and they were indeed funny enough. But in those days I did not realize they were heroic efforts to overcome relentless depression and self-dislike.

When I used to read Freud, Jung, Adler, Melanie Klein, and the later adherents like Karen Horney and Erich Fromm, I don't remember *self-esteem*—one of the central ideas of contemporary psychology—getting much attention. The pendulum always swings, and suddenly, these days, I hear people beginning to deride its importance as too "liberal," too *"touchy feely."* Number me not one of those.

I think it was feminism that first emphasized the keystone importance of self-worth, feminist friends in Key West in the early eighties who first brought the notion to my own laggard attention, Erik Erikson who described the idea in language I best understood. Some infants, from birth, see an unfailing beam of smiling approval in their mother's eye, beginning an introjective process long before words. These people grow up to feel the world is indeed a friendly, smiling place. If they meet someone, they think odds are they will be liked. If they go somewhere, most likely they will be welcome. If they try something, probably it will go well. Not always, not perfectly, but on the whole, things will turn out okay.

Erikson called this Basic Trust. Feminists: self-esteem. *I'm OK, You're OK,* wrote Tom Harris, "the mature, non-neurotic personality," said Freud and even L. Ron Hubbard, who invented Dianetic Psychology before he went on to found Scientology, named it, "dianetically clear."

AA (and I) call it seeing the glass half full.

Half-full people don't mind being called optimists, but half-empties resent being called pessimists—they prefer the term *realists.* Odds are the half-full people will be right half the time, the half-empties right half the time. Question: Who has a better life?

Who has a better chance of staying sober?

I live on the road to Yosemite, a town so small we don't have a red light on Main Street but there is one Open All Night deli/café/grocery. Jeeringly, the sign outside used to say, "Yes, We Have No Toilets." The owner died, and his widow took over. The sign now says, "Sorry, We Have No Toilets." The factual information conveyed is the same, but one sign was put up by a bitter man who felt his glass half empty, the other by a woman who thinks it half full, and I often wonder if the signs are like Rorschach blobs into which we can project the jagged outlines of how happy a marriage?

The notion of half full vs. half empty is so overused, the phrases themselves become so trite we gloss over their power. If I were to name a Grand Predictor on will two people get along, I would say more important than race, gender, political affiliation, or religious belief is do they both see the glass half full or half empty?

Half-empties depress, anger, and avoid each other. Most people are not entirely one way or the other, and so we see most couples, neither fully happy with each other, nor fully fed up. The incidence of marriage between half-empties and half-fulls goes a long way toward explaining our divorce statistics and I believe the occasional union of two half-fulls is the fairy-tale promise of happily ever after.

Half-full people don't easily get their feelings hurt and are seldom filled with resentment. You don't have to tiptoe around their sulky moods, their temperament doesn't have to be coddled nor accommodated. Any petty little quarrel or disagreement is settled with a smile or a joke—in fact, there's rarely a quarrel to begin with.

Half-empty people carry an aggrieved air, they suffered an injustice a long time ago, cheated of a birthright they cannot name, which you can't put right because it happened before they met you, but it's your fault anyway because you're not making them feel better.

From my own (admittedly) male perspective, it goes like this: You shave, shower, put on a new suit, special shirt, and brand-new tie, knock on her door, holding flowers, and she says is that dog shit on your shoe? The perfectionism never sleeps, you're forever walking uphill with her in the rain. She has the brakes on and complains you're slow. Those flowers you brought are the wrong color and "I'm Disappointed" is her favorite song.

To continue this little excursion into MCP territory, Barry, I would caution newly recovered people like you against hooking up with someone who carries too big a grievance against men.

Yes, it still is mostly a man's world, and, yes, there's a glass ceiling for women, etc. If these are understood as descriptions of reality, the outside world, fine. Accurate enough. But if the topic comes up again and again in her conversations, riding in on a certain aggrieved, burning heat, it's likely a description of her inner state. If she has a gripe against men, just remember, the first man she thinks of is you.

Women can name parallel problems with half-empty males, the misogynists who rant there are no great female poets, they don't know how to drive, all cats are gray in the dark, and gals should be seen, not heard. But women do not need my advice on avoiding guys like that.

To broaden the discussion, I believe half-emptiness is why many people join causes, march for the whales or against war. The cause may be good or bad, but ideology is not at the unconscious heart of why they joined up. They are looking for a reason for their aggrieved unhappiness, they want to find it *out there*—in the government, the CIA, or the telephone company, the warmongers, the conservatives or the liberals—anywhere outside, *not* in themselves.

Half-empty people are the stand-up comics, their jaundiced eye never missing a human foible, their bitter talent putting it on display. Remember I was telling you about my friend Ira a few pages back? There was a period when we were going around with two stormy sisters, one more difficult than the other. I phoned one day to tell him mine had walked out on me. "Yours left you?" he said. "Don't tell me about success in my own generation."

None of this means half-empty people cannot have charm and wit, intelligence and beauty, honesty and integrity. That just makes them all the more seductive. Team that inner melancholy with good looks and it brings out the motherly instinct in women, the knight-in-armor in a lot of men. *Rescuing:* the doctors call it co-dependency. I call it my naïvely romantic and failed first marriage.

But, Barry, you make me nervous when you indeed begin talking about marriage. You're wounded, hurt, and only three weeks out of rehab. You still don't know whom you'll be when you're more fully into recovery. Remember one of the rules of thumb they no doubt mentioned before you left? Write it down, and read it every day: *No entangling romantic relationships until you are at least one year sober.*

#84.

Problems of Self-Esteem (Part II) Drinking "at" Shame

Q. Your guest last week spoke of "the dysfunctional family"—how it leaves kids with a legacy of shame. My mother and father were hippies; I can remember them putting a feather in my hair in some native American ritual. I hated it. They never married but stayed together till I was fourteen. I was always ashamed of them; they were always stoned out when they came to school (wearing their hippie clothes) on Parents Day.

I swore to myself I would never do alcohol or pot. Call me "Mr. Proud to be Square." When I fell in love, I insisted we get married right away and in church. We were virgins. I'm a model citizen, vote, recycle, pay the mortgage, donate to charity, and have never been arrested, but there does not seem to be a payoff. I live in a state of righteous indignation.

Where's the fun, the joy of life? My wife likes the idea of a glass of wine at dinner, and lately she's persuaded me to join her. I like the way it feels. More, the idea of a drink has begun to beckon . . . the idea is almost obsessive. From something your guest said about shame, it sounded as if she were talking about me. But I am not ashamed of myself. I am ashamed of where I came from. How does this tie in with my desire to get drunk? And with my loathing of the idea at the same time?

A. Mr. Proud, there are few human conditions more burning and intractable than shame and humiliation. I know something of them myself. As I get older, perhaps wiser, I often find myself clenching my fists, or banging the steering wheel. Painful memories come back against my will. *Oh no, oh no, why did I do this, why did I do that? Bill, how shamefully you acted! How can you be such an unforgivable jerk to have said those words to her?*

"Many things came to my mind when I read this question," said Dr. Susan Gordon, Director of Research at Caron, to whom I turned for help. "First, Mr. Proud seems very tied to his parents. If he's ashamed of where he came from, he's also ashamed of himself (despite protestations to the contrary) because much of what and who we are comes from our families—the environment and the genetics.

"I wonder if some of his shame and 'righteous indignation' springs from fear he is really just like his parents. I would suggest that he learn how to positively separate himself from his parents. He will have to acknowledge the ways in which he is similar to them (the good, the bad, the attractive, and the ugly parts). He then needs to positively claim the ways in which he wants to continue to be like them (perhaps in their creativity or refusal to be like everyone else). Then, he needs to take a hard look at the 'dark side'—the ways in which he resembles his parents but which he wants to change—and then find constructive ways to express himself differently from them.

"Finally, he needs to realize that he can like his parents (sometimes) and be like his parents (sometimes) without becoming his parents. I would caution Mr. Proud very strongly against continuing that glass of wine at dinner. From his writing, it does not appear that he enjoys it—the wine is too obsessive to be enjoyable. He may have genetic and environmental vulnerabilities to alcoholism. Although I cannot be certain from his brief description, his parents may have been addicted to marijuana. If so, this could give him a genetic predisposition to addictive behaviors. Also, he may have witnessed his parents 'relaxing' by getting stoned. Social learning is a very powerful method for learning behaviors (for example, children of smokers tend to become smokers). Mr. Proud probably learned that the way to relax is to get stoned . . . or to get drunk. My advice to him is to not act on this learning, but to discover other, nonaddictive methods of relaxation."

To which let me add an idea of my own. One reason your thoughts and ideas are becoming obsessive, Mr. Proud, is you keep them bottled up. Talking to me about them is a good first step. How about this for a second? The only requirement for AA membership is the desire not to drink. For my money, if you "loathe" the idea of getting drunk—that's close enough.

Take in a few meetings and talk about how you feel to the people you meet there. "Righteous indignation" sounds like a cold, unhappy way to live. This is the one life we get. Why not enjoy it?

PS. This topic is too important for just one Q&A. See Q. #85, which follows.

#85.

Problems of Self-Esteem (Part III) Isn't Al-Anon for Losers?

Q. When my husband's drinking turned grim, my mother suggested I go to Al-Anon. My father was a drunk too and she said it helped her. You can call me Cynical, thirty-three years old with one little girl who's five. Since I think it's pertinent here, let me add that I'm usually considered very good-looking.

There's a lot of airy-fairy talk on your show about Al-Anon, but isn't it just a lot of sad, timid, and fat, fat, fat women afraid they'll never find another man, looking for excuses to stay with their lousy husbands? I didn't feel comfortable when I went to one of their meetings and stayed ten minutes. It was my last one too. I'm afraid their loser attitudes might be catching: I don't want to end up like my mother!

A. Cynical wrote me c/o the radio station. When I read the letter to Marianne Peck, a family therapist in Modesto, California, she laughed. "Cynical stayed ten minutes and read all that into women she'd never seen before? Bill, you believe they were all sad, timid, and fat? This is an example of the sheerest projection. Remember the time we were having lunch? A man fell in the bar, you thought he'd slipped! You're so long sober it never occurs to you someone might be drunk. In the same way, liars think everyone else is lying. People with low self-esteem read that into people they meet."

Marianne went on:

Did Cynical's drunk father give her the idea that she was good for nothing but her looks? "At thirty-three, she's afraid it's a diminishing asset; that without them, she'd be worthless? Cynical ought to hang around Al-Anon a bit longer. She might develop a greater sense of self-worth."

Yes?

I've talked before of the importance of self-worth . . . those who have it are most often those who see life's glass half full. At AA meetings, they like to say you can "adjust your attitude," *choose* to see the glass either half full or half empty, but I'm not sure Cynical's bitterness is a matter of choice.

I believe this question so central to sobriety that I hoped my skepticism was ill founded, and turned to Dr. Dave Moore, who used to be Director, Scripps McDonald, the rehab where I was a facilitator for two years. Citing both Cynical and Mr. Proud (Q. #84) I told Dave I meant something more profound than mere change in attitude. "Even in AA, I've seen over and over that people who denigrate their own essential value have a hard time staying sober. They're victims of a relentless perfectionism, afraid to try something important or go out for a better job. They'd never want someone like me.' " I said this frustrating sense of being a failure before you start had to make it tempting to pick up a drink.

"When Charles Dickens wrote *A Christmas Carol*," I went on, "that was his subject: the conversion of bitter and half-empty Mr. Scrooge into a benign, self-accepting, and generous soul. But even Dickens thought it would take supernatural intervention to do the job. If you feel down deep," I went on, "that if people really knew you, they'd find you shameful and crappy—to change that would take a profounder conversion experience than I believe humanly possible."

Dave had no doubt I was wrong.

"Why do so many people at AA meetings say they are 'grateful alcoholics'? *Because otherwise they would never have found their way into a 12 Step program and become what can only be called better people.* When it comes to developing positive self-worth and ending feelings of shame, these programs are extremely powerful. They can radically alter the root personality by indeed providing a therapeutically controlled *conversion experience.*

"In a culture of peer support, people like Cynical and Mr. Proud find they can break out of false pride and consequent isolation, and in absolute certainty that there is a power greater than themselves—one with which they can connect—begin to find forgiveness with all of which they are ashamed. From there, it's a step to realizing you must go on—as Dickens shows us Scrooge did—to create a life of self-reflection, humility, empathy, and community service."

Dave, now on the faculty of the University of Washington, continued: "Second, personal development is only half the equation. Positive social interaction with others is needed, relationships with people who care for us and enjoy being with us. That builds our feelings of self-esteem and self-worth: the very antithesis of shame. And the best place I know to do that is, once again, a 12 Step program."

Yes? Let me confess bias. Given my agnostic queasiness (Q. #41), is it surprising I felt uncomfortable with Dave's "absolute certainty" of a beneficent deity? His life is witness it works for him, but since the notion of a Higher Power is enshrined in the 12 Steps, can they effect change in people of a more skeptical nature? No use taking myself as model—I was born believing better times are always just ahead on the other side of the next hill. Enter two new witnesses:

First, "Nancy," a full professor at a famous East Coast university. I was taken by the serene quality of her sobriety—seriousness combined with what I can only call a Mozartian lightness of spirit. Acerbic, a certain precision and hard edge to her speech—no facile AA sloganeering. So when I learned that her disbelief in a Higher Power echoed mine, I asked her the same question: Can AA's 12 Steps effect a radical change—half empty to half full—even if you have no religious beliefs? Her E-mail reply was on the screen when I finished writing up my talk with Dave Moore.

Nancy: "When I was drinking I did a lot of meaningless research and publication merely to keep my university position. I can see I was competitive, judgmental, bitter, full of pride, arrogance, and continually anxious; I was also lonely with few colleagues or friends. After twenty-four very active years in AA, I feel like a different person, 'radically different,' as you put it, Bill—thanks to the 12 Step program.

"Although some externals are the same—I live in the same modest condominium and teach at the same university—my research on 12 Step and other mutual help groups is enriched by my personal experiences. It brings me kudos in academia but more—I take pride in work that's useful to the community.

"I still think the notion of a Higher Power is an unnecessary term in logic, but while fear and alcohol used to isolate me, in my increasing serenity and sober new trust that the world is basically a benign place, I was able to go around the world by myself in 1999. I could never have done that in the days when I was drinking against my suspicions and fears, which, of course, only made me fearful all the more.

"Students and colleagues seek my counsel, and younger women whom I sponsor call me their role model! Best of all, after two brief and disastrous marriages in my drinking years, I recently celebrated a twenty-year wedding anniversary with the most fascinating man I know!"

Witness #2: After saving Nancy's message onto disk, I drove out to see Mary Walker, who works for tobacco abatement in Alpine County, California. The discussion was about her forthcoming guest shot on my show. We hit it off and I asked how she'd like to be introduced.

"I used to be a dependent frightened mess," she said, "married twice to alcoholics, and always attracting the kind of man who wanted a wimp he could bully. I used to hope that inside I was not really like that. I knew I wanted to live in the mountains, in my own house, and learn to be brave enough to do work I liked—like this tobacco control job—rather than take a horrid, boring, meaningless job whose only payoff was greed and more money. You can introduce me by saying that if I could change enough to do all that, anyone can."

"What was the agency of change?"

"I started by going to Al-Anon because of the alcoholic men I chose to marry, date, and have relationships with. I'm not an alcoholic myself, but I went to AA meetings too. I love them all: Coda, OA, Al-Anon—I learned who I was by following the programs they talk about at 12 Step meetings. I gained courage too. They changed my life."

So there you are. I remain unsure a half-empty nature can be changed into half full, even through profound adherence to a 12 Step program. Dr. Dave Moore and two other honest people say I am wrong. I hope I am. Take your choice.

#86.

Just Because I'm Married to an Addict Does That Make Me a Co-dependent?

Q. I'm Helen, mother of a four-year-old and five months pregnant with our second. If I know my husband was out spending his paycheck on cocaine, how can I not go through his wallet, take what was left, and give him only enough to get to work the rest of the week? If he's shaking and too hung over to go to work, how can I not call his boss and say Tim had to have a wisdom tooth pulled, and might be out tomorrow too? I hide the car keys too—he'll kill someone if I let him drive.

I heard your talk with Paul Ehrlich . . . how co-dependency enables both the addict and the wife to go on without changing their lives for the better. You seem to be saying any woman married to an alcoholic is by virtue of that fact alone a co-dependent. I resent that. If I did not love Tim I would have left him years ago. What definition of co-dependency do you go by?

A. Marianne Peck: "*Co-dependency is a compulsive focus on another person's behavior, problems or feelings: It is the ultimate loss of self, full of guilt, anxiety, resentment, blame, and control. It is most assuredly not love.*"

A licensed marriage and family therapist in practice for twenty years, a friend and often a guest on the radio show, Marianne Peck was trained in the treatment of co-dependency by the famed John Bradshaw. Since co-dependence is so pervasive in addiction, and because Helen's question slanted the idea a little differently from that in my discussion with Paul Ehrlich (Q. #53), I turned to her for help.

I got her at her office, and we spoke in the ten minutes between clients. Talking about Helen, Marianne continued:

"She's caught in the trap in which so many co-dependents find themselves—men as well as women—confusing love with guilt and obligation, anger, caretaking, and her own dependency needs. Self-knowledge and self-care seldom surface. No life or money of her own, no job, and children to raise. It is easy to advise someone like her to just get out, but the practical and emotional issues can be overwhelming. Even if finances can be worked out, this kind of compulsion holds people like sticky, inescapable glue."

"Why?"

"Helen is so preoccupied with Tim's behavior and the ensuing survival issues there is no time at all to understand the complexity of her motivation. She'd say she's acting in response to life being out of control. The paradox is: Something in her likes it. *She needs to be in control, of Tim, of the whole world.*"

"She hides this need behind her martyrdom?"

"Compulsion and denial keep her from ever looking at or feeling the pain inside and how awful she feels about herself. Comparing herself to her barely functioning cocaine addict husband, she looks good."

"Which gives her a small dose of feeling superior, of self-aggrandizement—Earth Mother, etc.—on which to secretly feed?"

"It may even keep her going for a lifetime," Marianne said, "the star in her own drama."

"At what price?"

"Enormous. A huge toll on self-esteem, parenting ability, and even on mental and physical health. I've had clients so anxious they could no longer remember even the simplest routines of daily life. One began carrying around a shopping bag full of notebooks in which she wrote down, in detail, what her schedule was for every moment. The notes included when to have the children brush their teeth, when to go to the store, and what time school was out. She was obsessed about what food she ate and about everyone in the family dressing perfectly and always being clean, no matter what their age. She vacuumed and cleaned every inch of the house well into the early morning hours."

"She was using obsessive behavior to hide her fear from herself?"

"Her marriage was literally falling apart; she was trying magically to hold it together by making everything look okay. Like Helen, my client did everything but deal with the real and painful issues. In families such as these the drinking or doping is rarely seen as the root of the problem. It is excused and overlooked with a vengeance."

"If Helen were your client, what advice would you offer?"

"First, there must be a reason for the co-dependent person to change. Sometimes this can be pretty painful and extreme like illness, losing your job, starting to get drunk yourself, bankruptcy, or even the addicted spouse getting sober."

"And the effect on their kids?"

"If Mom and Dad smoke, children will smoke. If they're addicted, the kids are likely to become addicted too. Most of the time the co-dependent's life has to become unmanageable—hit bottom—before they can focus their attention on their own need to change."

"Any early warning signs?"

"Constant emotional and physical exhaustion usually brought about by doing so much for others, depression and anxiety, sleep problems, or many stress-related health issues (headaches, stomach trouble, back problems). It is a difficult pattern to change especially for someone like Helen, who feels like she is holding up the whole world by herself. The co-dependent needs true support. This is where Al-Anon or CODA can be tremendously helpful in coming to terms with the everyday practical problems as well the personal ones. There is something wonderfully liberating in learning you are not the only one."

I said that one of the great insights of the AA was recognition that cutting out the addiction was only the first step. "Drinking and doping have their own sinister glamour, a hold on the imagination. You can't drop them without putting something heavy-duty in their place."

"That's the next step," said Marianne. "Find a new answer to the need for spiritual connection. This is particularly important because in people like Helen self-will runs riot but calls itself victimization. The answer is to allow the self to be part of something bigger than her need to control Tim's life. Psychotherapy can help Helen work through her own deeper issues. She chose this way of life. If she ends this marriage, greater self-knowledge can help her avoid choosing Tim the Second next time out. Co-dependency cuts us off from the spontaneity of life and from truly loving relationships. Like all serious problems it requires serious solutions and treatment. If the co-dependent is willing to commit her time and effort to the healing process, her reward will be the ability to love herself and others more fully and joyfully than she ever dreamed possible."

"To answer the question Helen asked at the beginning," I said to Marianne, "if you are married to an addict, does that automatically make you a co-dependent?"

Marianne said she had a friend who was a minister and teacher, "married to a full-bore, 18-wheel, practicing alcoholic whom she loved. I admired the spirit in which she stayed with him without losing herself. She did what she could to support and take care of him, but beyond that, she had a full life . . . close friends, travel, and meaningful work. Was it a perfect marriage? No. How many are? But she had herself, a spiritual connection, and also happened to love a man who had serious problems. She stayed with him through choice."

"That makes her a non–co-dependent?" I asked Marianne.

"Bill, do you hear an undertone of, *Well, Helen is like that, but I'm not* in your questions?"

"You think I'm not asking about Helen but myself?"

"Are you?" Marianne said.

I paused in thought.

Marianne said, "You never want to think you were co-dependent yourself, do you? That's how men are," and hung up.

What do you do when you're convinced against your will, when you ask for an opinion and get one you don't like? You ask someone else, right? Along with Marianne Peck, Lynn Telford-Sahl too has been a frequent guest on my show. I phoned her both as another wise therapist, and as a friend.

I began by saying she was the third psychologist I'd talked to about co-dependency. "I just can't put the issue to sleep. The psychological theory sounds fine, and may even be textbook right, but none of it seems to address the way it felt to me on the inside."

"We're talking about your first marriage, right?" said Lynn. "How did it feel on the inside?"

I remembered it well.

We'd been out late. I said time to take her home. She opened the car door and threw herself out. "Lynn, we were going sixty miles an hour. I can remember the moment, I can remember the lawn we sat on, near some rocks, how shaken we were, the moon above, and how beautiful she looked, her eyes filled with tears. It was four o'clock in the morning, we were twenty years old. I said how could she try to jump from a speeding car. She said unhappiness made her reckless. 'Bill, you have to take care of me,' she said . . ."

"And you felt—?" said Lynn.

"As beautiful as she was, and she needed me that much? I could have picked her up and carried her to the moon in my arms."

"Like a tyro gambler winning ten thousand dollars his first day at the track," said Lynn. "And after the poetry was over, how did the marriage go in everyday terms?"

"The more I took care of her, the more she needed it."

"A bottomless well," said Lynn. "Suffocating?"

"She couldn't even go to the grocery alone."

"You bottled up your resentment? Did nothing to change the basic bargain?"

"She was so helpless without me."

"Remember the opening line of your first novel?" said Lynn. " 'I don't know how other guys feel about their wives leaving them,' it said, 'but I helped mine pack.' Was that autobiographical?"

"She met another guy."

"In effect, she got you both out of the mess?"

"Yes."

"She was less paralyzed by co-dependency than you," said Lynn. "Or less addicted to it."

"Addicted? I wasn't drinking—that came much later."

"Gamblers don't necessarily drink either," said Lynn and played back one of my favorite ideas. "Addiction is *behavior that may have begun as fun but now goes on even though it adversely affects your life and happiness, your finances, rela-*

tionships, and health. The thrill is gone, you hate it, swear you're going to stop, but you never do. Bill, you were addicted to co-dependency before you were addicted to alcohol, but with Wife Number One gone, those feelings never got resolved. I suspect that's why you had trouble with Number Two."

"Larry Bouchard said that too—that I haven't yet come to terms with what happened in my second marriage."

"No wonder it ended in disaster," said Lynn, who knows me perhaps too well. "You'll never be entirely whole until you recognize your part in what happened. She may not want to forgive you, but you must forgive her."

"Forgive her!"

"Yes."

"*I suppose you want me to pray for her too?* You're not a priest, you're not even my therapist!"

"You're my friend. Where'd the anger come from?"

Where indeed?

"That's resentment talking," said Lynn, "an ice-cold flame you guard in your heart. Resentment says the game isn't over yet, she hasn't won, there's still time for revenge. Bill, until you forgive her, your resentment keeps you tied—"

She did not have to finish the thought. You can hear it at any AA meeting anywhere in the world: *and resentment will get you drunk.*

Father, mother, husband, wife, sister, brother, lover, friend—we've all come to that moment when we look into the face of a beloved and realize the soul is gone, the addiction itself is looking back at us, grinning through the other's eyes. This was such a moment. Lynn was my mirror. I saw myself in her eyes. Resentment was my addiction and I wouldn't give it up. I'd die first.

#87.

"Why Does Resentment Get You Drunk?"

Q. My wife and I met at Caltech when I was still drinking. I had a copyright on a little software program; Betty had an idea for another.

We went into business together, the money rolled in and we bought a big house in the company name. I'm Jim, thirty-seven, married eight years, and sober now for three.

A few months ago, the IRS claimed that I had not paid full taxes on my original copyright. Our tax lawyer, Arthur, said with penalties and back interest, we could take a $3 million hit—all we have. He suggested we put the house and the entire business in Betty's name. If the IRS sees there's nothing left to collect, Arthur said, maybe he could work out some low-cost compromise. I said okay.

Bill, they used the IRS to set me up!

When I signed everything over, not a penny left in my name, Betty told me she was in love with Arthur, and he presented me with papers for divorce. Meanwhile, the IRS "estopped" my bank account. I can't even hire a good lawyer to fight back!

When I think of that double-crosser living in my house, sleeping with my double-crossing wife in my bed, I feel betrayed. My sponsor told me get over it, resentment will get you drunk. *"How do I do that?"* I said. He told me the AA rule: Pray for the people who have harmed you. I told him I wasn't Jesus Christ.

Bill, you ever felt so grievously injured that resentment and fury burn in your heart day and night? Did you get over it, or did you get drunk?

A. As I began work this morning an E-mail came in saying that my old friend, "Jed" (about whom I wrote in Q. #72), had gone back out drinking and now taken his own life. Who knows what secrets he took with him? I suspect I know some of his unacknowledged angers. Dishonesty even by omission is dangerous stuff. The lesson once more is we are never safe. And so while a question like yours, Jim, was one of the first I ever got when I started my radio show, it is time to say I was dishonest in my answer back then.

I sidestepped, merely falling back onto the official AA word: *Resentment will get you drunk, after overconfidence it is the second most prevalent cause of relapse, etc.* More shameful still, I advised my caller—official AA line again—to forgive, even pray for those who had harmed him if he wanted to stay sober. The fraud comes in here: I believe in none of that myself.

So, yes, your sponsor is right, Jim, and I should say it to you too: You must forgive them. My sponsor said it to me. *But forgive people who cold-bloodedly double-crossed you, pray for those you know are smiling together now in fond memory of how dumb you were, how easily tricked, how impotent, trusting, and helpless?*

How say that to you? I haven't yet been able to do it myself.

When I think of how my own marriage ended, despair fills my heart, anger heats my blood. My face grows red, I begin to shake and want to yell—what a New York cop once called *The Fire* threatens to return, a flame so fierce not all the gin in the world will put it out.

But while I work in radio, I'm an occasional novelist too and know something of fiction's distancing symmetries and elisions. Here's the skeleton of a novel—so far called *Memories*—I've been writing concurrently with the pages you've been reading, to be finished now that this book is done.

Chapter One: He remembered the night they met. He was up for a job in Baltimore. His work, the far end where journalism shaded into showbiz—good news came by phone, bad by E-mail or silence. Well, the phone didn't ring and the phone didn't ring, he'd been in a lousy mood, almost didn't go. Listen, he told himself, trim your fingernails and fall in love. He took a cab at 85th Street across Central Park to Daisy Tempson's cocktail party and when he rang the bell a woman he didn't know opened the door.

You know how someone's looks can hit you first sight? He remembered the quick cut of her cheekbones, the *noli me tangere* of her eyes. "Hi, come in," she said "I'm Irene," and he felt like someone had popped a bottle of champagne. She turned to resume a conversation, he stopped at the bar, lightning flash signals already sent and received.

Chapter Two: He remembered her first words an hour later, leaving Daisy's. He closed the cab door on her side. "That guy you were talking to when I came in," he said, "applying for your dance card or already listed?" She was on her fold phone, making an excuse to someone else.

She put her hand over the speaker. "You know how some good-looking men like to talk about their famous suffocation? What they respond to best is mixed signals, stop and go, both at the same time—green light and red, three parts no to one part yes. I think maybe you're the first I ever met who can stand all yes." She asked what he was like in the morning. "Okay," he said, "if you don't count being operatically stupid about women." "Oh," she said, "then that's all right, of course, if at night, at least, you snore."

She folded the phone away, a stemmed glass she'd carried from Daisy's raised in her hand. "To the three great pleasures of falling in love," she said, leaning back against the cracked leather cushions. The driver stepped on the gas. "A gin martini before, the first cigarette after."

He did not yet know her bravado was bought dear, "Someone to Watch Over Me" her favorite song. The fall of her skirt showed the line of her thigh. She reminded him of legendary racehorses who are fed only on roses and do not know what it is to lose. She took his face in her hands and said, "So this is how you look." She put her hand in his pocket and said, "Am I the worst girl you know?" She kissed him and said, "We're going to live forever. Will you love me that long?"

She had not finished her drink. He took the glass from her hand and did.

Chapter Three: He remembered morning on a Norwegian freighter out of Newport News sailing downhill to Aruba. They were celebrating a double-header, he'd gotten the Baltimore job, and when WASH-TV heard she'd been up in 30 Rock interviewing with NBC, the station put her on the D.C. Nightly News, the Celebrity Interview slot. They were in each other's arms, talking about the contradictions of love.

She was twenty-nine and never been married. She said she had always gone for the Unattainable Man, the smiler with the knife. He said it was safe to fall in love if you knew it could never lead to marriage, wasn't it? She said life often resembles one of those big, neon-lit and shining, busted movie house candy machines where you can't get even what you don't want. He said don't tell me about success in my own generation.

One thing about life, he said: Get married as soon as possible so when you get divorced, you're not too old. "I used to think that the meaning of life was could I get laid before lunch. I became less stupid," he said, proposing marriage, "when I met you."

She was just out of the shower, putting on one of his shirts. She paused, three or four buttons still undone. She said had he ever felt the sweetness of life was there in your mouth but you can't taste it, "like sucking on a Hershey chocolate kiss with the silver wrapping paper still on?

"No, don't kiss me," she said. "Sit down and help me be calm. Let me tell you why I'm afraid of how can I bear to say the word, I'll say it in quotes, 'commitment.' "

She stepped into last night's shoes. "Two days ago at breakfast absentmindedly I put some sugar in my coffee and was overcome with pleasure."

"And?"

"I'd never done it before. All my life there was something in me that loved coffee with sugar, and I never knew it. I was cheating myself. So many other sensations, experiences, moments all around us, waiting for us to discover them. We may never know they exist, don't even know we're missing them. That's unlived time," she told him. "Nothing sadder than unlived time. Tell me why you want to marry me."

"The trick of the Big R—"

"—another fell word—"

"—is figuring how to be together, and separate too. I never could work that out before you. And, also, PS. first things first: You pass the scientific N.A.N.C.Y. Test."

"Which is?"

"Which is that I've always wanted a tall, lanky someone who looks like you, and who, most of the time, would think most of what I do is mostly okay. Not necessarily wonderful, she doesn't have to think I'm perfect, just she's Not Another Nagging Controller, Yes?"

"The glass half full?"

"Half-empty people, you shave, shower, put on a new suit, shirt and special tie, you knock on her door, she says is that dog shit on your shoe. Half-empty, you're forever walking uphill in the rain, she's got the brakes on and complains you're slow. You say, you know where the garden hose is and she says wherever you left it last time. The flowers you brought are the wrong color and 'I'm Disappointed' is her favorite song. It's never that way with you."

She took off the shirt. "And with no one else?"

"With no one else who looks like you," he went on, hoping to say something perfect. "No one else with your spirit," he said. "Until I found you," he said, "life was half empty. I don't want to live without you," he said. "No more unlived time."

"Marriage pays for the honeymoon," she said.

"Not ours," he said.

She squirted perfume into the air and put her face into the mist. He kissed the scent off her eyes and she said okay. They decided the date over orange sherbet and Veuve Clicquot. She hadn't finished hers by the time the bell rang for breakfast. He finished it for her and they went up.

Chapter Four: One of the last things he remembered her saying was her Dr. Fred was reluctant to act as their impartial marital counselor.

His drinking had always been extravagant. She'd started therapy when it turned sordid and baroque. The occasion was a quarrel, he'd stormed out, she thought to cool off, maybe for a drink. He'd flown the Atlantic in a blackout.

They'd been married twelve years.

She'd begun by seeing Dr. Fred twice a week for almost a year, tapered off after a while, but now, though the drinking had long stopped, had begun therapy with the good doctor again.

"Fred says ethically and legally, his first loyalty is to me, but just this once, to help us out . . . He knows me so well," she said.

Dr. Fred said his wife's prime issue—he called her "Reen"—Reen's prime issue was abandonment—her beloved bipolar father shooting himself while she was eating a Mr. Sno-Cone in the car. "Because of Reen's dreadful childhood," said Dr. Fred, "she developed certain compensatory attitudes. Infantile seduction seen one way, cool sangfroid seen another. Behind this wall she puts up—her courage and carriage, the wit, intelligence, and good looks, fire-and-ice at the same time, the high heels she put on in the ship's cabin when you proposed—clinically speaking, a sexy joke in service of a self-distancing parody to hide anxiety—all that is character armor, *surface-y stuff*," the doctor said, "but that's who you think you married."

He went on: "I understand when you proposed, you did not say you loved her? Merely told her you needed someone to validate and affirm you . . . to tell you that you were 'okay.' Is that the term you used at the time? You see, that merely tells us you have emotional needs yourself . . . needs that kept you from ever looking behind your wife's glitter and sophistication. To see what *she* needed. If you had looked, you'd have seen a frightened little girl."

"My wife's afraid of me?"

"Or to trust this marriage."

"I haven't had a drink in eight years."

His wife did not answer.

"You stuck with me though all the drunken stupid times," he said to her. "What happened? What's new?"

He said to Dr. Fred, "Why this talk about leaving me now after all these sober years?"

Dr. Fred said perhaps they were getting a little off the track. "Your wife is struggling with fear that like her father, and everyone else she's ever loved, *you* are going to leave *her*."

"*I* will leave *her*?"

"You did once. For your addiction. It can happen again, maybe for another woman, who knows? That's where we are," said Dr. Fred, his voice kindly, a bit gruff, diffident about giving advice to a man a decade older than he, no fingers pointed, all in this together. "We need to discuss how to put that fear of hers behind us," the doctor said, "forever," and his wife's shoulders did that convulsive inward shudder that tells you how painful it is when women won't allow themselves to cry.

He asked nothing more. He'd traded away the right, sold it for nights at the expensive 94.4-proof bar Mr. Tanqueray keeps on the other side of the moon. He said they'd come through a lot together, he loved her and wanted to be married to her forever.

Dr. Fred leaned in. "Can you convince her?"

"Prove a negative?"

"Convince your wife that you will never abandon her again?"

She was wearing an ankle-length Vicki Thiel green suede coat that

day over a silver motorcycle mini, the suede lavishly trimmed with
green fox at collar and cuffs—a present the previous Christmas.

"I'll never leave you."

She sat huddled in her chair, huddled down and hiding in her coat,
long legs cocked to one side in elegant parallel lines, ankle boots, face
averted as if ashamed of her fears, little white face hiding from his eyes
behind the big green fox collar . . .

"I will never leave you."

She looked up at him at last, tremor in that short upper lip, maybe a
half smile coming through the green fur, afraid to hope—

They'd bought a house soon after they moved in together, an old,
weather-beaten, and extravagantly roomy fixer-upper in a dim and forgotten corner of Bethesda—in those days, a dim and forgotten suburb,
just over the line from the District. "Civilized, and gay, and rotted, and
polite," Scott Fitzgerald wrote of the city where Zelda once spent time
in a madhouse. Baltimore was still "Nickel City" back then—cheaper
than Washington. But that was before dotcom biotech firms began to
cluster in the shadow of the National Institutes of Health in Bethesda
proper, before the new PIA, wanting to distance itself from the CIA in
Langley and the NSA in Fort Meade, began buying local real estate
too. And before a famed brewer, blackballed for scandal in St. Louis,
started a hunt and tennis club down the street—the kind of club, his
wife liked to say, where you sat on a throne in a steam-heated duck
blind and rang a bell. "A waiter brings a martini and a butler hiding in
a nearby tree shoots off a gun and throws a herb-roasted duck out at
your feet." Horsy people from Virginia, the Main Line, and the Caroli-
nas flocked to join, real estate prices zoomed, the three-story Victorian
at 2110 Florence Lane beginning to draw astronomical offers over the
phone, three million and soaring last time out . . .

"I will never leave you," he said. "I'll put our house in your name."

Chapter Five: And he remembered a morning two weeks after he'd
signed the papers. To end their dumb fights about his snoring—his
wife was a light sleeper—as a gesture to show his hope they'd be sleeping together forever—he'd just had his deviated septum surgically
reamed. Oh, yes, there he was about eleven, eleven-thirty that morn-

ing, wearing a blue plastic ice mask—*I'm an alcoholic, doc, no Demerol or vikes, thank you very much*—swallowing aspirin and making two tuna salads with romaine and Bermuda onion on rye, saving scraps for Edna, their cat.

The phone rang.

She said, "Hi, sweetie, you going to be home for the next hour?"

He did not say the cavities behind his face felt as if they were packed with broken glass. He said yes, he was making their lunch and not to be late for their next session with Dr. Fred (who practiced in the District, forty-five minutes away).

Their last meeting had been about forgiving each other, "growing in empathy in a rebirth of healing karma," as Dr. Fred put it, maybe indeed winding up these marital counseling sessions entirely. They were to discuss it again when they met in Dr. Fred's office today at two.

His wife came in at one with a woman he did not know.

His wife said, "This is my lawyer's of counsel associate."

The of counsel associate said, "This is your summons for divorce."

He'd just learned the prime rule for people who fear abandonment. They rush to leave you first. His nose began to bleed.

His wife may have had the hurt, the malign desire, but groping for a paper towel, blood turning it red in his hand, he knew the cunning and the guile belonged to someone else—legal papers long worked out, meetings behind his back, machinery whirling at full speed, the trap now sprung, the kill made, trophy of the other man's cunning and strength, a wedding feast for them both. "Fred," he said to himself and tore the ridiculous blue ice mask from his eyes, "Dr. Fred." He began to gag and throw up. Covered with blood, reeking with vomit, some belief left from childhood wanted to say *this isn't right, it isn't fair,* but his wife wouldn't meet his eye and who would he say it to, the divorce lawyer?

He said it to his wife's back: "You break my heart."

She said, "Have a drink and drown your sorrows."

Chapter Six: He remembered calling a friend in Florida. "Polly, I swore I'd never be like my father, but there I was, red-faced and yelling—"

He'd thrown a toaster through the window.

"Are you drinking?"

"I feel ashamed."

"That you thought she loved you?"

"That I loved her."

"You have your life back," said Polly. "Nothing to be ashamed about that. What's left is not to drink."

"What's left is you're going to say I have to forgive her."

"It would be noble to try."

She said resentment will get you drunk and invited him down for a few days. He said he didn't have plane fare, he was calling collect. She said when he got to the airport, a ticket would be waiting in his name.

Chapter Seven: Walking under the palms facing scrabbly Smathers Beach in Key West, he remembered telling Polly the rest.

When he'd shucked out of his blood-and-vomit stained clothes, told his wife she could keep the cat and walked out of the house that he no longer owned, he had twelve dollars and sixty-seven cents in his pocket and was about to learn anyone dumb, blind, and stupid enough, braggadocio enough to let himself get trapped like this gets what he deserves.

Their joint checking account had been emptied that morning: The ATM machine said tilt. Schwab said their joint investment account was cleaned out, the payroll clerk at the office said his salary had been legally "estopped," all their joint credit cards cancelled, and the Citi Visa he'd had forever, to which he'd added her name so she could sign after they married? Maxed out, please remit at once: His wife had charged a $4,200 double-breasted Armani man's cashmere-and-camel hair coat and $379 pair of English handmade cordovan shoes at Baltimore's most expensive men's store, to be delivered to a room number he knew in the Medical Arts Building in the District, "before," he told Polly, "she came home with her lawyer to serve me the papers for lunch."

"Sign on their terms," Polly said, "or Bleak House—sit hungry in the dark, no gas for the car and the telephone shut off."

He said well, his drinking had put his wife through hell. Polly said so she fell in love with someone else. "Who needs a drunk husband?"

Polly said. "I'd have divorced you myself, but why suddenly now, after eight years sober?"

She took his arm. "Let's say I did something nasty, let's even say you and I had a fight. I might kick you in the balls, you'd punch me in the breast. It would be ugly, the friendship might end, but I would not expect you to pretend to kiss me and plunge a knife in my back.

"Bill, you know the country and western song, 'What Made You Rich Made Me Poor'?" said Polly. "You were tricked into signing your house away." That was malpractice plus fraud, she said, and asked if he had called a lawyer. He said the first three laughed when he asked would they work a divorce on credit and he suspected the one he did find took him on only because she was blowing cocaine.

"And when you called young Dr. Fred—?"

"Young, kindly, gruff Dr. Fred would not take my call."

Polly said was the doctor getting divorced too.

He said that's what he heard from Ms. Cocaine Esq.

"He and Irene planning to marry?"

He said yes.

"And you haven't had a drink?"

He said no.

"Sigmund Freud move into 2110 Florence Lane?"

He said yes.

"You see that picture, she's dancing with Donald Trump?"

"The Hays Adams charity ball."

"How much younger is the good doctor?" Polly said. "She'll be getting a face-lift next. She loved you the way a tiger loves a lamb chop. You knew it and didn't want to face it. That's why you feel ashamed."

Chapter Eight: They were making lunch in the kitchen of Polly's Fleming Street condo. She'd been in the fashion business when young, and even now was still very jazzy and good-looking, always smartly turned out. She looked thin and frail and beneath her long white butcher's apron wore wonderful shades of cream, ivory, and tan. "I ever tell you," she said, "that cancer runs in my family?"

Sally, Polly's lynx-point cat jumped into his arms. "You been to the doctor?" he said, petting the cat.

274

"I keep losing weight."

He'd been chopping garlic for salad, she looked up from stirring lasagna with a wooden spoon. "I've come to the time of life," she said, "when my clothes are braver than me." She suffered dizziness, and had begun to fall. She pulled up a sleeve. Purple splotches on both arms. "Legs and thighs too," she said. "Black-and-blue. The bruises won't heal."

She smiled. "'Don't worry,' " she told him. "I won't lift my skirt."

The lasagna burned. They drove to a waterfront café run by two young AA friends of Polly's—the sound system a wedding present from her. Pink, purple, scarlet, and gold, the sun floated up over green water. Palm trees rustled. Sam the Man Taylor played "Someone to Watch over Me." He said to Polly, "We're here all alone." The unspoken half of the sentence was, and they both knew she was soon going to die.

He asked a question important to people like them.

"You're alone in the world," he said. "Widowed a long time, your children grown, immersed in their own lives and living far away. Now cancer and living in pain. You ever think of taking a drink?"

" 'All neurosis starts with man's attempts to escape life's legitimate sufferings,' " she said, a quotation from Jung—one they both knew. "I cannot escape this one," Polly said. "I have only one thing left. That's my dignity. I'm not going to die drunk." Five weeks later, he got an envelope in the mail. It was a bronze AA medallion. It said XXXIII— sober thirty-three years. Polly was dead.

He punched a hole in her medallion and wears it on his key chain. He thinks of her every time he starts his car, every time he unlocks his door. She left him something he will never forget. Sober thirty-three years. "Maybe you'll get over your resentment," she said last time they spoke, "maybe not. I suspect you'll be fighting anger the rest of your life but one day the divorce will be over. Don't die before you wake once more in the arms of someone you love on board a Norwegian freighter sailing south. Don't take that first drink even if your ass falls off."

The Subject Is Hope

In 1935, Bill Wilson and Dr. Bob Smith created the 12 Step Fellowship that would later be known as Alcoholics Anonymous. It has since helped millions of alcoholics and addicts find recovery, and been termed the most successful grassroots sociological movement of the twentieth century. It may not be the only solution to ending addiction. It has proven to be the most universally successful.

In the mid-1950s, the World Health Organization and the American Medical Association declared that alcoholism was a disease. At about that time, the "Minnesota Model" came along. This treatment modality was based on core belief that addiction is a multifaceted disease affecting the individual medically, psychologically, socially, and spiritually. The first three are more easily understood than the last.

Spiritually, addiction is now seen as a soul sickness, *destroying the capacity to have an intimate lasting relationship with yourself, with another human being, with your god; —with anything but the disease itself.* Research on the biochemical processes of the brain indicate positive implications for recovery among people involved in 12 Step spiritual programs. The most important of these, the federally funded Project MATCH, found that AA attendance predicted high rates of abstinence for participants.

In another rigorous study (1996), Mathew, Georgi, Wilson, and Mathew found that people in recovery from chemical addiction significantly increased their spirituality from the time prior to recovery.

At Caron we believe successful behavioral changes are a product of both character change and spirituality . . . that developing a relationship with your Higher Power is a critical first step in recovery. Coupled with abstinence, spiritual growth restores purpose, enabling the recovering addict to rejoin the human race as a fellow member, rather than a frightened and frightening, numbed liar, loner, user, and exploiter.

Spiritual values, as Bill Manville says in these pages, give meaning to life but your accountant cannot find them in his books—nor are they identical to religious values. I see this every day. People in recovery are the most spiritually centered I know yet many have little or no organized church involvement.

Another valuable aspect of Bill's discussion is the question of what to look for when choosing a treatment center. At Caron, we believe in having a full-time member of the clergy—one well trained in dealing with addiction—on hand to assist patients with the spiritual aspect of their disease. Our chaplain at Caron often replies to questioners about the meaning of spirituality, "You'll know it when you have it, and if you're asking, you probably don't have it yet."

Developing spirituality requires dedication. Like recovery, we see it as a journey. Since scientific research suggests that spirituality increases recovery rates for all chronic illnesses, it's worth the trip. Bill's book is a captivating, honest, informed, and firsthand look at alcoholism, addiction, and recovery. As he says on his radio program, "The subject is hope." We are proud to number him one of our graduates.

—Doug Tieman
CEO, the Caron Foundation

#88.

NEED HELP RIGHT NOW?

You're smoking the end of last night's joint and sucking on a water glass of vodka to face the day . . . maybe your kid's turning blue with bad dope . . . or Dad's doing meth in the garage, threatening to burn the house down . . .

Need help right now?

There are these terrific commercials on radio and TV, written by talented people in New York or LA, about problems like these. They end with an 800 number, but when you call, a tape recording in Rockville, Maryland, tells you to send away for a pamphlet from Pueblo, Colorado.

Thanks a lot.

I'm Bill Manville.

The Caron Foundation saved my life, one of the best rehabs I know. They gave me permission to print their 800 number below. If you phone, a trained, sympathetic, and live human being will answer your questions about alcoholism and addiction 24 hours a day, 7 days a week. Don't know what to do next? Help is just a phone call away.

Call right now. The number works from Canada too.

(800) 678-2332

Index

Index

Index

Index

Index

Index

Index

Index